Epic Fail

The book that got me sent to prison. (And no seriously, that's not just a catchy title)

Lawn Mower

Attributions

Special thanks to:

Open Moji – the open-source emoji and icon project.
License: CC BY-SA 4.0 https://creativecommons.org/licenses/by-sa/4.0/#
Emojidex www.emojidex.com
Canva www.canva.com
Pornhub www.Pornhub.com
Amazon www.amazon.com
The Google www.google.com
Chuck-E-Cheese www.chuckecheese.com
My Space www.myspace.com
The Power Rangers- For saving our world countless times
Mohamed Salah- For being the greatest footballer *ever*
Chuck Norris- For being Chuck Norris
Peter Cullen- For being the voice of Optimus Prime
MP- For answering my relentless questions
SG- For being an epic pain in the ass, and a mediocre editor

And of course, Kitten- For being the greatest thing to *ever* happen to me

There will be no special thanks to The Sister. You're a cunt, and I hate you.

I dedicate this book to the memory of my mother.

And as a reminder to us all that no addict seeking recovery need ever die, without a chance at a new way of life.

I love you and miss you mom.

DON'T SKIP THIS FUCKING PAGE ASSHOLE.

I've put enough heroin in my body to kill countless men.

I've used dirty puddle water and smoked cigarette filters I found on the ground to inject some very questionable substances into my body.

And, surprisingly, I'm in damn good health.

Along this journey, I've lost a lot of people close to me because of drugs and addiction.

Yet, *I'm* still alive and kicking.

So, I pose two questions:

1. How the fuck am I still here?

2. Why the fuck am I still here?

The following pages are my feeble attempt to answer these questions.

Maybe.

Attention:

This book is written
for people who have a
sense of humor,
a deep appreciation for sarcasm,
and who aren't fucking snowflakes.

CONSIDER YOURSELF WARNED.

I'm not a big fan of repeating myself. Well, more specifically, I'm not a big fan of repeating my *words*. Actions, on the other hand, are a different story. But we'll get to that a little later.

Now, even though on the previous page there was *literally* a neon sign with all sorts of warning symbols about the contents of this book, I *still* find it necessary to insert a second disclaimer here.

Why is this?

That's because I've discovered that most people on this planet are fucking hopeless. These people will simply skip over the in-your-face danger sign and continue on their merry fucking way until they suffer some sort of offensive injury. Once that happens, then magically *I'm* the one at fault because no one wanted to heed my warnings. These are the same assholes that need a "CAUTION CONTENTS HOT" warning on the cup of *steaming hot fucking coffee* they just purchased.

So, for the sake of all you helmet-wearing, window-licking, easily offended snowflakes who can't even wipe your own ass or cross the street without proper supervision, this is for you. Because you literally represent everything that's wrong with this world.

This is also for you, L****. But I'll get to you later. You goat-blowing piece of baboon shit.

If you're one of the aforementioned people, please do us *both* a favor and stop reading now. Things are going to get *a lot* worse from here on out before they get better. I promise you that. I've paid for the right to say what I say in here with my blood, sweat, tears, pain, grief, misery, and most importantly, years of my fucking life.

Translation: the contents within are scurrilous.

With that being said, and after not one, but *two separate warnings,* if you decide to continue reading and incur some sort of psychological and/or emotional damage from my words, then it's your own fucking fault. I have ZERO sympathy for you. Go find a therapist, or someone who cares.

And don't worry, L****. Your fifteen minutes of fame will come. You rainbow dildo butt-monkey.

Fuck me. 98% of you won't know what *scurrilous* means.

Well, that is not a Lawn Mower problem. That's a *you* problem. I will, however, do you a solid, and suggest that you keep a dictionary handy while reading this. I might be an asshole, but I'm an asshole with an extensive vocabulary who likes to sound super smart. So don't blame me for your shortcomings.

Now that that's all settled, let's get this shitshow going!!

Oh, and if you don't like anything I have to say in here, well.....

Well, hello there!

I'm Lawn Mower, and I'm here to tell you a story. A nonfictional (that means true) story at that. I'm sorry but this isn't some Walmart, bargain rack, paperback novel. So, if you do happen to purchase your major reading materials at Walmart, you should probably stop reading now. There is no celebrity gossip in here, I *loathe* reality TV, and I tend to use words with more syllables than cat, dog, fish, and Bieber.

For those of you with a reading level above pop-up books and Hooked on Phonics, please continue.

Even though this is a true story, I've taken the liberty of changing the names of everyone involved, including my own. This is mainly because I don't want to get sued for libel. Translation: I didn't want to do any of the legal bullshit involved with getting informed consent from people. Plus, let's be honest here, no one wants a bunch of jerk-offs knowing everything about their personal life.

If you do happen to know who I am or you figure it out along the way, and I wrote something about you in here that you don't like, here's a suggestion: go eat a bag of dicks. There's nothing you can do about it.

Also, if you actually read the warning page then you would have noticed that I didn't change L****'s name, I just starred it out. This is because I wanted to actually print this douche canoe's full name instead of a pseudonym. During the course of my writing, however, I discovered that if I printed someone's name (public figure or not), then I'd have to be able to actually *prove* the things I had said about them. And while I have my suspicions regarding L****'s sexual proclivities, I can't prove that he actually has sex with farm animals, enjoys Cleveland steamers, and masturbates to his parents' sex tapes. So, until I can actually prove that L**** uses horse semen in his coffee instead of creamer, L**** is what we'll have to deal with.

There is one small loop-hole...

If you happen to *infer* who L**** is, well, that's not on me.

So go fuck yourself, L****. You fucking pederast.

Furthermore, if you're a snowflake and decided not to heed my warnings at the beginning of this book, go do us all a favor and kill yourself. I've got a fucked-up story to tell, and I poke fun at it as much as possible. I say offensive shit that I will **not** apologize for. I lived through it. You didn't. I've earned the fucking right.

Now just because I make fun of something in here, it doesn't mean I found it funny at the time. In fact, it's usually just the opposite. Compare it to shitting your pants at the state fair. Right then, it's the worst situation conceivable. You're embarrassed, ashamed, it's hot as fuck, you're covered in your own fecal matter and you smell like two hobos after an hour of anal sex. Not very funny, is it? It's only *after* the experience is over that you can laugh about it with your friends. If you've got the balls to tell them, that is.

Okay. Now that that's out of our way, we've got a few more points to cover before we can move on:

I identify as an asshole. Just like Denis Leary.

I'm best explained like this: imagine Wade Wilson and Tucker Max made some sort of Wilson-Max super sperm in a lab. Then, Jenny Lawson and Amy Winehouse made a Lawson-Winehouse super egg in a lab, and then both super sperm and super egg were carried to term by Harley Quinn; I would be the product of said awesomeness.

I'm a sardonic, sarcastic, wise-ass, know-it-all.

I can be both very mature and *oppressively* immature. Sometimes simultaneously.

I'm a recovering addict.

I'm an ex-con.

And it took me going to prison a couple of times in order for me to get my shit straight. But in my defense, one of those times shouldn't count (I'll explain later).

So in case you're not too quick in the reading prediction department, this a story about life, drugs, prison and change.

Because, prepare yourself for the most clichéd statement ever– prison changed me. And not in the I-went-to-prison-straight-and-came-home-with-a-husband sort of way either. I mean the I-went-to-prison-and-came-home-a-completely-different-and-better-me, sort of way.

Alrighty then. Is everyone still with me?

Swell.

You may now turn to the next page (that would be the page to your right) for the beginning of the story.

HAVE you ever woken up after a night of partying and shenanigans with that feeling of *What. In. The. Ab-so-lute. Fuck?*

There's that splitting headache, your entire body hurts, you've got that god-awful taste in your mouth (which you can't get rid of), and of course the simultaneous questions of

Where the fuck am I? What the fuck did I do last night? And where the fuck are my pants?

Followed by the ever-popular statement: *I'm never drinking again.*

If you don't know what I'm talking about, then you've lived a sad, sad life. For those of you who do know that of which I speak, we all know that those nights can be summed up into one of two categories: A) really *good* or B) really *bad*.

I've personally experienced this type of situation on more than one occasion. The last two of which I actually had to categorize in a new manner: ***epically fucking bad.***

Here's why:

The second-place award goes to a day out drinking with my buddies. We got started sometime around noon that day because I had a particularly difficult morning. Then, around three, Señor Cuervo came out to play. Shortly thereafter, I started time traveling. Time traveling is Mowerspeak for: blacking out.

The next morning, I woke up on the bathroom floor covered in my own vomit and piss. Not the proudest moment of my life. However, it got worse. I had this unidentifiable injury to the back of my head. It was this raw, irritated, itchy feeling on my skin that I couldn't quite place. I scratched at it a couple of times, chalked it up to a night of silly drinking shenanigans, and went about my business.

It wasn't until my girlfriend came over a few hours later that I discovered the source of my injury.

It was a tattoo.

Of a stick figure.

Pushing a stick figure lawn mower.

Right at my hairline.

Did I mention that I'm bald?

Oh, you think I'm joking?

Flip back to the cover of this book. Yes, that's correct, that is an actual picture of my head.

Want to know the best part? It was *my idea to get it done*. Apparently, I had casually mentioned how hysterical it would be to get something like that done and one of my buddies pulled my card, telling me that I didn't have the balls to do something like that. I'm told that I all but ran to the tattoo shop.

That night = epically fucking bad.

The worst part is, I even *paid* for that tat.

But the winner of the epically fucking bad night award came a short time later.

I woke up on a Friday morning to my girlfriend Not Fucking Gwen screaming at me. She was screaming at me because she was *seriously* fucking pissed off at me. And rightfully so (I'll explain later). And instead of me dealing with the situation, I did the mature thing and took off running.

When I woke up the following *evening*, I was experiencing one of those situations on a whole new level. Even though I was awake, I couldn't quite open my eyes, and I felt like I had been gang-raped by a herd of rhinos. I had the worst headache I've ever experienced; there was this horrible, gritty, burnt taste in my mouth and what felt like little pieces of sand covering my teeth. Plus, I could hear this weird, rhythmic, beeping sound. When I tried to move my arms, I found that I couldn't.

I soon discovered why:

My headache: was a migraine.

That taste in my mouth: was charcoal.

I felt like shit: because I was going through opiate withdrawal.

The beeping sound: was a heart monitor.

The monitor: was located next to my bed in the ICU.

And I couldn't move my arms: because I was *handcuffed to the bed.*

There was also a cop in my room who informed me in not so many words that I was in some deep shit and seeing that I was now conscious, a judge would be coming in shortly to arraign me.

When a Judge comes to see ***you***, you can bet your sweet ass that you're in ***DEEP SHIT***.

Which I was.

Like I said, epically fucking bad.

But, before I can get into all the little details, you better strap on your seatbelt. Because once this baby hits 88 miles per hour, you're going to see some serious shit.

* * *

IN CASE you've failed to notice, I don't make the best decisions. I'm pretty sure it's a curse, a birth defect, or hereditary.

If I'm supposed to go left, I go right. Up? I go down. If I'm supposed to bet, I'll check. I've been this way my entire life. I simply wasn't born with good natural instincts or decision-making skills. I place the blame on the large amounts of LSD my mother used to do before I was born.

Tracing it all back, my first *really shitty* decision was to move from upstate New York to Florida. For most people, moving to Florida is a great decision for them. But I'm special, and for me, moving to Florida just got the ball rolling on a whole slew of even shittier decisions.

In my defense, the move to Florida was one of those by-the-seat-of-your-pants decisions. You see, there was someone in town who was extremely interested in talking with me because they felt that I had liberated a large amount of cocaine from them. I will neither confirm nor deny this allegation, however, I will say that it was in my best interest to leave town. Which I did posthaste.

At the time, it seemed like a really good idea.

When I arrived in Florida, I was broke. Having skipped town in the middle of the night, I didn't give myself much time to plan or prepare for anything, so I pretty much fucked myself. My grandparents lived there at the time, and I could only rely on them for so long, so off to work I went. I quickly found a job and was getting myself back on my feet when I decided to start partying.

Drinking mostly.

Then light drugs.

Then heavier drugs

Which led to smoking crack.

Awesome, right?

For those of you who have never taken part in some leisurely crack smoking, I'll tell you what it's like:

On second thought, no I won't. If you want to know what smoking crack is like, go to your local crack dealer, buy some crack, and find out for yourself. You're not going to live out your crack-smoking fantasy vicariously through me.

Smoking crack sporadically led to smoking crack not-so-sporadically.

Which led to smoking crack daily.

Which led to being broke.

Being broke led to having bills. Being broke, having bills AND having a daily crack habit led to an interesting problem. What the fuck do I do now?

In my eyes, there was only one solution:

Forget about my bills, steal money from my employer, and keep the party going.

What?

Did you honestly think that I was going to say: "go to rehab and get help"?

Obviously, you don't know me very well.

It didn't take long for my boss to realize that a significant amount of money was missing. When he started looking into the situation, he quickly discovered why. It wasn't that hard to figure out who was taking the money because I was doing it WHILE ON CAMERA!

Multiple times.

Einstein I am not.

My boss had me arrested and I was introduced to the ridiculous world of the Florida judicial system. Anyone who has ever dealt with the Florida judicial system can attest to what a complete and utter shitshow it truly is.

Since this was my first time being in any real trouble, I was offered a plea bargain of probation, restitution, and withheld adjudication. Withheld adjudication is Legalspeak for: being convicted of a crime, but being able to *legally claim* that you weren't. Pretty sweet, right?

Well, that little bit royally pissed off my ex-boss and he made his opinion known in court. At my sentencing, he told the court:

Ex-boss: "This is a complete outrage! That man stole from me and should be known as a thief and a convicted felon!"

Well, fuck you too guy.

And you know what else? The joke's on you buddy. I stole *way* more from you than you knew about, and now there's fuck-all you can do about it. It's called the statute of limitations.

Asshat.

* * *

I WAS PLACED on probation and was then subjugated to these things called "random drug screens." My PO would occasionally stop by my house with a little plastic cup that I had to go pee-pee in. She did this often enough to worry me.

My crack-smoking days were over.

While on probation, I figured that it was time to get on the right path, for once. I found myself another job *thank you withheld adjudication*, was living with a buddy and slowly getting back on my feet. My probation was going well, my restitution was getting paid and I was being a good boy.

Translation: I was BORED AS FUCK.

Then one day it occurred to me what I needed in my life: a woman.

The way I had it figured, a woman was the solution to all of my problems (stupid, I know).

So, I set out to find her.

I went looking for her in the same place that most other strapping young men went looking for women on the gulf coast of Florida.

On the internet.

Makes sense, right?

Back then, not so much.

Today, this is common practice. You tell a friend that you've met someone online, and they don't blink an eye. If you told someone this back in early 2003, they looked at you like you just said you had anal sex with their grandmother.

* * *

#1 WAS her name and found her I did. Well technically, she found me. But that's irrelevant. We met on an (out-of-date) social media site and quickly hit it off. There was only one small problem:

She was a Brit.

Not a local Brit who lived close by, or even in the continental United States.

She was a Brit who lived smack dab in the middle of England.

A small hiccup in my master plan yes, but where there's a will, there's a way, and we made shit happen.

We started talking online daily, then moved to chatting over the phone. This went on for months until we both fell hopelessly in love with each other, without ever actually *meeting* each other.

Hey, cut me some slack. We were young, naïve, in love, and hip to the online dating movement.

I actually like to think of myself as a pioneer of said movement, thank you very much.

Finally, after nine months of our "dating" – and FYI, do you have any idea how difficult it is to maintain any sort of a relationship with someone in another country with a five-hour time difference? – we decided that we needed to meet. #1 had some holiday time, Britspeak for vacation, and she took the leap across the pond that separated us so we could meet.

Keep in mind that both #1 and I were twenty, about to be twenty-one. I lived pretty much on my own, and she still lived with her parents. Even though she lived at home, her parents didn't seem to be bothered by the fact that their daughter was embarking on a trip to a foreign country, thousands of miles away, to meet some random dude that she met on the internet just a few months prior.

And let us not forget that I was the *only person* that the family knew in this country. And honestly, how much do you truly know about someone you meet online?

I had never put much thought into any of this until years later. I had figured that her parents were just really cool. After living with #1 for several years, I secretly believed that her parents sent her to America with the hope that I *was* a sadistic killer who was going to butcher their daughter into small pieces and feed her remains to the alligators.

Now don't get me wrong here, Buddy and Rose are actually amazing people and excellent parental units. Anyone would be fortunate to have parents like them. Even to this day, we still have a close relationship. I just wish that they had warned me that #1 was an evil, moody, narcissistic sociopath, on top of being a vindictive, relentlessly overbearing, selfish, vicious and vile **_cunt_**, who had to get her way, or you would feel a wrath of epic proportions.

A little forewarning could have saved us *all* quite a few headaches.

Just saying.

#1 ARRIVED JUST a few days prior to my birthday. Our initial meet and greet went off without a hitch, with no awkwardness at all. We were like two long-lost lovers reuniting after months apart, rather than two people meeting for the very first time.

The awkwardness came a few short hours later when we were *really* getting to know each other.

Do I really need to translate that?

We were in a hotel room, having a few drinks and fooling around. #1 was just about to enjoy her first American cock-meat sandwich when I heard her exclaim:

#1: "I'm not touching that!"

Me: "Excuse me?"

#1: "Your willie. I'm not touching it."

Me: "My what?"

She pointed to my penis.

#1: "Your willie! What's wrong with it?!"

Mind you, this is our first time together, we're naked, and I'm hard as a rock, looking between her and my penis thinking, *"What the fuck is this bitch talking about?"* AND *"Oh my fucking God, is something wrong with my dick?!"*

Lawn Mower

Awkward....

Me: "Uhh.... There's nothing wrong with it?"

#1: "There abso-bloody-lutely is. That doesn't look like any bloody willie I've ever seen."

So, I asked the obvious question here:

Me: "And how many *bloody* willies have you seen?" (Not: What exactly is wrong with it?)

#1: "Oh, I don't know how many, but quite a few."

Great, she's a slut.

Me: "What's '*quite a few?*' Ten? Twenty?"

#1: "Oh, no. Way more than that."

Me: "Uh-huh."

Now, I'm less concerned with getting laid, and more concerned with:

A) Something might be seriously wrong with my dick.

B) What the fuck am I going to catch from this chick?

C) Her number is way higher than mine.

Naturally, this is the point where I started to go soft.

Then her eyes started bulging out of her skull while she pointed at my 'willie.'

#1: "See! That! That's not normal. It doesn't look right."

Me: "Look. I don't know what the fuck you're talking about. This is a perfectly healthy, American co......

I'm an idiot.

She's British.

They're weird over there.

They don't circumcise.

After the circumcision revelation came to light, was discussed, and briefly researched, we continued on with our attempt to strengthen foreign relations.

Three weeks later, we were married.

Like I said, good decisions aren't really my thing.

* * *

Lawn Mower

I WISH I could say that my marriage to #1 was great and we were still in fact happily married today. But if that were the case, I wouldn't have anything to write about, would I?

The truth is, my marriage to #1 was absolute shit. I suffered through what I called "The Wrath of #1" for several years until I couldn't take it, her, or life any longer.

My master plan of finding a woman, settling down, and leading a normal life was as fucked-up as a pay-by-the-hour hotel room after a scat party.

So, I went to plan B: self-medicating to ease my pain.

During the execution of plan B, I discovered two things that would drastically alter the course of my life:

Heroin and syringes.

Thanks for that, #1.

Now, before some jerk-off starts saying: "That's not fair, you can't go and blame your wife for the fact that you started getting high and shooting up." I'm going to say two things:

1. Yes, I fucking can.

2. But no, I'm fucking not.

My marriage to #1 was the stone that sank the ship. My love affair with drugs in general had been on-again, off-again since I was a teenager. My swan dive into the abyss of my addiction had already commenced and had been a long time coming; I just needed a little nudge off the precipice.

* * *

THAT NUDGE CAME IN 2008, when life should have been great. I was twenty-seven, married, owned a home, owned two brand new vehicles, was a licensed electrician, and had pretty much everything I could have ever wanted.

Externally, things were great.

Internally, I was miserable. I hated both my wife and my life. I felt broken inside and found that the only thing that could *temporarily* put the pieces back together was the drugs.

This was also around the time when Florida was a giant "pill mill" state. Pain management clinics were a dime a dozen; in some cities, you could find a pain management clinic easier than a dealer on the street. Doctors' offices literally had people lined up around the block waiting to be seen all day, every day. It was crazy.

People would walk into a doctor's office and walk out with five or six different scripts. These people paid cash, came religiously every month, and received everything they asked for and more.

This is why all pharmacies are networked together, and how "Doctor shopping" became a noticeable crime. Thanks for that, Florida!

Doctors were giving out opiates like an abortion clinic gives out mason jars. My using became a bad habit which became increasingly worse after I discovered intravenous drug use.

On that day, my life drastically changed forever.

After that day, Nothing. Else. Mattered.

* * *

FINDING drugs wasn't my issue. It was *paying* for them that I had trouble with. Finding a source of income is how I quickly fell down the rabbit hole into my own personal oblivion. #1 worked for a bank, so taking money out of our account was not an option. I was making decent money doing side work as an electrician, but it simply wasn't enough. Again, I found myself pondering the same question I asked myself before: "*What the fuck do I do now?*"

This time, however, things were a bit more complicated. #1 had *no idea* that I was using drugs. If I had decided to get help, then I would have had to come clean (no pun intended), be honest with her and face her wrath.

FUCK THAT NOISE.

I'd rather jerk off with a cheese grater than deal with *that* fucking abortion.

So that's what I did.

Well, not literally.

But I did ignore the problems piling up and remembered a quote from Gandhi: "A good addict will *always* find a way to get high."

And I was a good addict.

I found not one, but two new sources of income.

The first source: Pawn shops.

Have you ever driven down the road and seen one of those "Cash-4-Gold" signs? Yeah, me too. When I was dope sick and in need of money to get high, the sign was like a homing beacon drawing me to the promised land.

CASH-4-GOLD.

CASH-4-GOLD.

CASH-4-GOLD.

Cash is what I needed.

Gold is what I, well, err.... #1, had.

When the idea came to me, I was as giddy as a pedophile in a playground.

For once, her demanding demeanor was going to reap some benefits (for me). You see, throughout our marriage, I'd spent thousands of dollars on all sorts of jewelry which she wore maybe once. She had boxes upon boxes of the shit that was nothing but an eyesore to me. We had debt up to our eyeballs, yet she just *had* to have this or that. She'd wear it once, seemingly forget about it, and never have a use for it again.

Well, I had a fucking use for it.

CASH-4-GOLD, baby.

Plus, it wasn't like I was *stealing* it. We were married, I had paid for it, and it was a *marital asset.* You can't steal from yourself.

It was perfect.

But perfection can only last so long, just ask Adam. The jewelry was soon gone and I was right back to where I started. Cash-4-Gold was great, when you had gold. I had no more gold, but I did have access to another precious metal: copper.

This is where Cash-4-Copper came into play. My second new source of income.

My plan was simple: steal copper wire from my employer and sell it at scrap yards.

Because what could possibly go wrong stealing from my employer. Right?

When I started on my Cash-4-Copper endeavor, I would strip every inch of insulation off of every piece of wire. This would take hours to do, but completely 'stripped' copper wire was worth almost four times as much as wire with the insulation still on it.

Then I became lazy.

Instead of taking a *small* (and unnoticeable) amount of wire and stripping it, I stopped stripping it altogether and started taking *large* (and very noticeable) amounts of wire to compensate.

Naturally, it didn't take long for someone to catch on. I was going to the scrap yard *daily* with huge garbage cans (notice the plural) full of insulated wire. That much wire doesn't disappear without someone noticing it.

The day they caught on? That was a very bad day.

It started with my morning "get right" shot. Get right is Addictspeak for not going into opiate withdrawals. This shot used up the last of my dope, which normally was a bad thing. This day, however, it didn't matter.

I had a van full of wire. A scrap yard that was already open. And the dope man (aka my heroin dealer) had already called me to let me know that he was ready to go.

Life was good.

Until I walked out the front door and found my boss, we'll call him Bugs Bunny, with two cops, standing next to my work van having a friendly conversation.

Well, technically it wasn't *my* van per say.

It was a *company* van that I was allowed to take home.

Bugs' company.

FUCK.

Bugs and I quickly got into a heated debate about the wire in my, err... *his* van. He was claiming that I stole it.

I feigned shock and disbelief. Then vehemently denied such an allegation.

The premise of *his* claim was that I didn't have permission to have the wire that was in the van.

The premise of *my* claim was that I worked on multiple jobs for Bugs on a daily basis, plus that I was an on-call employee at night, which *required* me to have a van stocked with material at all times. It was impossible to foresee what would be needed, so how could I have *possibly* stolen anything in the van?

This was actually a very logical and (mostly) true argument. I did run many jobs for him, and was always on call. Plus, it made perfect sense. What electrician *doesn't* have a lot of wire in their van?

The only issue was that Bugs and I both knew that I didn't need *any* of the wire that was in the back of the van. At this point I was only trying to do damage control and sprinkle some reasonable doubt in the mix in order to save my ass from getting arrested.

Bugs then countered with this:

Bugs: "You're fired. Officer, this man is in possession of my property, which he does *not* have permission to have, nor did he have permission to take. It is my claim that it is stolen, and I wish to press charges on him."

Cop A: "Sir, please turn around and place your hands behind your back. I'm placing you under arrest for grand theft. You have the right to....."

#1: "WHAT THE FUCK IS GOING ON OUT HERE!?!?!"

Oh, fuck me. I didn't see her come outside.

Bugs: "Your husband's a fucking thief and he's going to jail! That's what's fucking going on out here."

Did I mention that Bugs and #1 *hated* each other?

No?

Well, they did. And his comment only enraged #1.

#1: "My husband is NOT a thief and he is NOT going to jail!"

25

Boy was she in for a surprise.

Right at that moment, a shitstorm developed between Bugs and #1. They were nose to nose screaming at each other, and I actually thought that someone was going to start swinging. So did Cop B. He had to separate them several times and even threatened to arrest them both as well if they didn't cut their shit.

Cop A took this opportunity to inch me towards his car and put me in the back of it while Bugs and my wife were distracted, and I was quite content to comply. Neither of us wanted anything to do with the clusterfuck that was starting to develop in my driveway.

After Cop B defused the situation, he got into the car, looked at me and said:

Cop B: "Man, I don't know what's worse. Going to jail, or dealing with your wife."

Me: "Dealing with my wife. Trust me."

I wasn't looking forward to jail in the slightest, but I knew that being stuck there meant that I didn't have to deal with #1. And that was a very good thing.

* * *

AFTER A FEW HOURS IN JAIL, I started to feel very ill. I was fucked, and I knew it. Withdrawal was starting to set in. The only thing I could do was call my family when I got my phone call and hopefully bullshit one of them into thinking that this was just a huge misunderstanding, and get them to bail me out before I started to get *really* sick. It was my only hope.

Then, of course, I still faced the major problem of #1. But honestly, right then, my mind was a single lane highway. Only one thing mattered. Everything else was secondary.

And then it happened:

Cop: "C'mon let's go."

Me: "Go where? I'm already in jail."

Cop: "Your bail's been posted."

Me: "Who the fuck bailed me out?"

Please don't say my wife, please don't say my wife...

Cop: "Your wife."

Fuck me. I'm a dead man.

Me: "Can't I just stay here?"

Cop: "No."

Me: "Please?"

Cop: "Nope."

Me: "When I turn up dead, my blood's on your hands."

* * *

IT WAS time to face the music. I was about to the feel The Full Wrath of #1, something I'd only heard stories about but had yet to fully experience. I'll be honest with you, I wet myself walking to the car. I thought about running, but I figured she would just run me down, then run over me.

I steadied myself with a deep breath, then opened the door and sat down to face my wife. Once I was seated, I slowly turned to face her, fully expecting to see someone resembling Regan (from The Exorcist) with that full-blown demonic possession face. What I saw, however, was far, far worse.

In #1's eyes, I saw a wrath waiting to be unleashed that even the God from the Old Testament -the ballsy one- would back away from. Her knuckles were ghostly white from the death grip she had on the steering wheel. Her nostrils flared with each breath she took. Her jaw was clenched impossibly tight and I'm fairly certain that I saw smoke billowing from her ears.

Being the mature and responsible adult that I was, I put on my big-boy pants and did exactly what I was supposed to do in a situation like this.

I lied as if my life depended on it.

Because quite frankly, at that moment, it did.

I knew that I had to strike quick and fast, otherwise she would eat me alive.

Me: "Can you fucking believe that Bugs had the audacity to lie like that and have me *arrested* because he's mad at me and let his emotions get in the way of his business?!"

She hesitated. She didn't see that coming.

#1: "What the fuck are you talking about? Of course he had you arrested! You fucking stole from him, you fucking twat!"

Me: "I did nothing of the sort! The only thing I *stole* from him was a job or two."

I could see the confusion setting in. I knew that it was now or never. I had to baffle her with my bullshit or I was a dead man.

Me: "Bugs is pissed off at me because he found out that he lost out on a couple of jobs because they went to me."

A very pregnant pause.

Me: "Where do you think all my side work has been coming from? Contractors. I'm Bugs' best guy and everyone knows it. If he got a big job, he'd send me, right?"

#1: "Right..."

Me: "So a couple of contractors asked me if I'd be interested in doing some side work for them and I said yeah. They get the same quality of work for less money and I get to put more money in *our* pockets. It's a win-win. Except for Bugs. He got screwed over in the deal, but business is business. Bugs just let his feelings get in the way."

#1: "But.....but he said you stole all that wire that was in the van."

Me: "He can *say* whatever the fuck he wants, it still doesn't make it *true*. How the hell can I steal wire from him when he sends me to go do a job, and that's the wire I need for said job? That doesn't even make sense, does it?

#1: "Well, no, not really."

Me: "Exactly. It doesn't. The wire was for jobs that *he* gave me, that I was going to start on Monday. What was I supposed to wire the house with, dental floss?"

The wrath had subsided from her eyes and I could see the wheels spinning.

#1: "So.... You didn't steal the wire...."

It wasn't a question, so I let her run with it.

#1: "And he's mad because he found out that his own employee was taking work from him."

Me: "Exactly."

#1: "So he LIED TO THE FUCKING COPS AND HAD YOU ARRESTED!!!!"

Remember now, #1 already *hated* Bugs.

Me: "Ain't that some childish shit? And I'll bet you *anything* that as soon as I was arrested, Bugs was calling every contractor he knows telling them that I'd just been arrested and that I was a thief."

#1: "THAT BLOODY WANKER!!!"

And that, my friends, is how you save your ass in a pinch. You lie like you're Bernie Madoff and run with it until the wheels come off.

* * *

It's said that the best lies have just a *smidgen* of truth to them. And this lie had just that. A smidgen of truth. Bugs had in fact been losing out on a few jobs due to me. He was just completely fucking clueless to the fact. But #1 didn't know that. All she knew was that I had a lot of side work coming in and I let her come to her own conclusions as to where the work came from.

#1 was absolutely oblivious to my drug use, so in her mind I had no reason to steal from Bugs. Far be it from me to let her think otherwise. Also, I mainly bought the material used on my side work from Bugs, and #1 always wrote the checks when the invoices arrived, so she knew that I generally had a lot of material on hand.

With one crisis averted, I still had another one to deal with. My cash cow was now gone, and once again, I found myself in the same dilemma that I always found myself in: *What the fuck do I do now?*

Getting clean involved a whole lot of bullshit that I was not ready to deal with. If you don't believe me, search YouTube for "Candy (2006) Heroin withdrawal scene" and watch.

Go ahead, I'll wait....

Now, would you want to go through that shit?

Of course you wouldn't.

And neither did I.

Plus, getting clean also involved telling #1 the truth.

FUCK THAT.

The only logical thing I could come up with was to keep finding ways and means to get high. Do you see the insanity in any of this? Good.

* * *

OVER THE COURSE of the next year, I was arrested several times. Pretty much every sixty to ninety days I found myself back in jail on a new (yet similar) charge. Mainly, I kept getting caught for pawning stolen stuff. One would think that I would have learned my lesson after the second or third time, but no, I just kept doing the same shit thinking that I would get away with it that time.

They say that the definition of insanity is doing the same thing over and over again, and expecting different results.

I WAS EVEN QUESTIONED by the cops on crime or two, but there was never enough evidence to charge me with anything. Even when there was a witness who could place me at the scene around the time of a crime. I still don't know how I dodged those bullets, but I'm glad I did.

It didn't take Sherlock Holmes to figure out what was going on. Even #1 eventually figured it out. And that's when I had to come clean with "the truth," which was that I started using drugs *after* Bugs had me arrested.

Even when everything was out in the open, I was still a lying, conniving fuck.

The crazy part was that she wasn't even mad at me. She was completely indifferent to it. I was expecting her to lose her shit over everything and she didn't. Even when she discovered that all of her jewelry was gone and that I had pawned it, she still wasn't mad and I couldn't figure out why.

This goes back to me not being able to see the obvious sometimes. Even when it's right in my face, I still can't see it.

Then I discovered the truth. She was getting fucked six ways from Sunday by *anyone* who would pay her the slightest bit of attention.

Okay, so I probably deserved the infidelity.

But she *definitely* deserved the herpes.

Fucking whore.

And DO NOT give me any shit over the herpes/whore comment either. Because I already know that some donkey-raping cum guzzler is going to take her fucking side, and say how I pushed my wife away and into the arms of another man or some stupid shit like that.

Well, you know what??

Sally Super Snatch went out and got pregnant not once, but twice during this little time period.

And aborted both pregnancies.

Within sixty days of each other.

I think she even got a discount on the second one for being a repeat customer.

I suppose it's my fault that she:

A) Wasn't on birth control.

B) Was allowing the dude(s) to not wear any protection.

C) Thoroughly enjoyed being a cum dumpster.

D) Was a complete fucking whore.

That's what I thought.

GO EAT A BAG OF DICKS.

* * *

FOR THOSE OF you who aren't convinced that #1 is a self-centered cunt and believe that I'm just an asshole who treated her badly, I've got two things for you.

One: Go fuck yourselves.

Two: I'm going to tell you about the time when #1's mother, Rose, came to Florida for Rose's birthday.

Now, to begin with, y'all need to know one fact. #1 is a vegetarian, and she's very anal about it. She's the type of bitch that the staff in restaurants *hate*. The type of customer that will go apeshit on you if she asks for her tea water to be boiled for one minute and it only gets boiled for fifty-nine seconds.

You know the type, right?

Good.

Now, all her life, Rose had always wanted to visit the United States, and go to an American steakhouse to have a "proper" steak.

If you haven't guessed, Rose is *not* a vegetarian.

A few years after we were married, Rose decided that she was going to come over for a visit and celebrate her birthday with us. Both #1 and I thought that it was a great idea. And the only thing that Rose had requested was for us to help her fulfill her dream of going to an American steakhouse.

I told Rose that I'd be more than happy to take her out to dinner for her birthday but, she had to help me deal with #1 first. See, you can't just go somewhere and leave #1 home. That's a **BIG** no-no. You can't be doing something and exclude her. It just doesn't work like that. For example, if I bought a new video game to play on my PlayStation, I would have to have something for her to do. Like I'd have to give her money to go shopping, or have something that would amuse her while I'm playing the game. And no, she wouldn't/couldn't find something to do on her own. She expected *me* to do that.

After a few days of trying to figure out something for her to do, #1 just agreed to go to the steakhouse with us. She wouldn't just stay home, or let us take her somewhere first, she *had* to go with us because it wasn't fair that she had to sit home by herself. I couldn't believe that she said that she would go with us. That was *extremely* out of character for her. If she's not the center of attention or we're not doing something that *she* wanted to do, she will make the experience very, very unpleasant for all parties involved. The fact that she agreed to go concerned both me and Rose.

On the night of Rose's 51st birthday, we took her out to Ruth's Chris steakhouse. Which, if you've never been, is a very nice (and expensive) place. As soon as we got out of the car, we could smell the amazingness of great steak being cooked. It must have smelled like the rotten asshole of a meth addict's cadaver to #1 because as soon as she caught a whiff of the air, she gagged a little.

This was *not* a good sign.

By the time we arrived inside and were seated, I knew things were going to be bad. All #1 could do was bitch and complain about how horrible it smelled in the place and how disrespectful Rose and I were by making her go to dinner at a steakhouse when we knew full well that she despises meat.

At one point Rose looked like she was going to remind #1 that she could have stayed home instead of coming with us, but apparently thought better of it and decided to keep her mouth shut. Which was probably for the best.

While we were looking over the menu, it was nothing but drama. The only things that #1 could order were soups, salads, bread sticks, and fries.

Even though she was a vegetarian, #1 didn't eat soups or salads. And she *refused* to eat bread sticks and fries for dinner. Even though on any other occasion they would have been fine.

Finally, Rose had had enough.

Rose: "#1, I'm begging you. Please let me enjoy my birthday dinner. I've traveled a long way and have waited a very long time for this night. It would mean a lot to me if we could order our meals and enjoy ourselves. Please."

And then it happened.

#1: "Are you fucking kidding me??? How could you *possibly* enjoy yourself here? The smell in here is absolutely disgusting and I refuse to eat here. You and Lawn Mower are completely disrespectful and awful people for making me come here. I cannot even believe that you went through with it. I figured that you would think twice about it and have some common fucking decency and respect for me and my beliefs. But noooooo. You just *had* to come here. To a bloody fucking steakhouse. Where poor, innocent cows are slaughtered for no other reason than to fill your fucking stomachs! You both make me sick, and I'm not staying here another minute! We are leaving. Now."

Me: "Are you kidding me? You can't suck it up for an hour or so for your mother? It's her birthday for fuck's sake. This is all she's talked about for *months*, and you wanna take it away from her? Come on #1. Be reasonable."

#1: "No. We're leaving right now and that's all there is to it."

Me: "No. We're not."

#1: "Yes. We are."

And then she got up and walked out the door. Leaving both Rose and I sitting there not knowing what to do. We were at least ten miles from home and knew that #1 would walk there just to be stubborn and prove her point. We also knew that if #1 *did* walk home, the night would go from bad to worse in a horrific proportion.

So, we decided to leave and ended up eating Rose's birthday dinner at Panera Bread instead. Not at the American steakhouse which Rose had dreamt about for a few *decades*. I'm well aware that I can be an epic dick from time to time, but even I would have sucked it up for my mother. Especially if she had just traveled from *another country*. But that's me.

#1, on the other hand, refused to bend even a little for her own fucking mother. She completely ruined the night and pretty much Rose's entire holiday trip over here. Why? Because #1 is nothing more than a self-centered, selfish cunt. Change my mind.

And if you still happen to disagree with me, like I told you before, go fuck yourself.

Not too long after Rose returned to England, #1 was in one of her raging bitch modes and wanted "to go do something." After being married to the vile cunt for what felt like eons, I knew that it was something that:

A: I definitely *didn't* want to do.

B: Would cause me to hate her even more for making me do it.

C: I would have to endure or risk being mutilated in my sleep.

D. All of the above.

As soon as she told me that "we would be gone for a while," I knew that I was in trouble. So I ran to the bathroom and mixed up a quick shot so I could feel normal enough to suffer through whatever intolerable bullshit was about to come my way. While in the middle of my shot, #1 just about walked in on me, so I had to quickly discard everything and I wasn't able to finish it.

Not fucking good.

Once we got in the car and I asked her where we were going, she informed me that we were going to take pictures of a lighthouse in Cape Florida.

Which was on THE OTHER FUCKING SIDE OF THE STATE!

And there was no way for me to get out of it.

Fuck.

By the time we started heading home, *five fucking hours later,* I was *really* going through it. The sweats, the shakes, the irritability, the anxiety, and of course, my IBS was acting up.

Oh, what's IBS you ask?

Irritable. Bowel. Syndrome.

IBS is a common disorder that affects the large intestine. IBS *usually* causes cramping, abdominal pain, bloating, gas, diarrhea and/or constipation.

In reality, your stomach/colon are fucked. The slightest thing can set you off (and often does) into a *literal* shitstorm. Once you feel your stomach start to bubble, you need to find a toilet ASAP or there's going to be trouble. If you don't, well......

It's *not fucking good.*

If you suffer from IBS then you already know that even Jesus hates you.

I suffered from IBS *and* I was dope sick. This is the equivalent of having a superflu, taking an entire box of laxatives, using several suppositories and chasing it all down with a gallon of apple juice.

God, the universe and even little baby Jesus hated me.

And of course, when we were just a few short miles from our house, my stomach started to bubble. I'm not talking about one of those I-can-hold-it-for-twenty-minutes-until-I-get-home sort of bubbling, either. I'm talking DEFCON-one-nuclear-war-is-imminent-global-state-of-emergencies sort of bubbling.

The problem was that I was in a completely residential area. I couldn't just pull over and do the Hershey squirts all over the side of the road. I **had** to make it home. And fast.

I floored the gas like I was a pedophile with an all-day play pass at Chuck-E-Cheese's.

And then I got pulled over.

Doing seventy in a twenty.

Through a construction zone.

Which was in a school zone.

Fuck. My. Life. I was *literally* within eyesight of my house when I got pulled over. And I know that you know, that when you've *gotta go*, the closer you get to a toilet, the harder it gets to hold it in.

I was already at the point of spontaneous combustion *before* I got pulled over. By the time the cop got to the window, my reactor core was starting to shut down. I seriously debated flooring it, getting to my house, running inside to my toilet and taking whatever followed– but I was out on several different bonds at the time and waiting to be sentenced. I knew that a Fleeing and Eluding charge on top of everything else would not go over well in court or with my attorney.

To the cop, I must have looked like Whitney Houston after a month-long crack bender. I was bouncing in my seat, sweating, breathing in and out like I was in labor (which I basically was) with a death grip on the steering wheel.

Instead of asking me the for the usual "license and registration," with the palm of his hand on the butt of his gun, he came out with:

Cop: "Sir, are you alright?"

Ha.

Me: "Actually, no, I'm not. I suffer from an extreme case of IBS and I'm about 11 seconds away from a complete catastrophe in my pants."

Cop: "Yeah, I bet. Do you have any idea how many times I've heard that before?"

Blub, blub, blub, blub, gurgle, gurgle, gurgle went my stomach.

I mustered every ounce of strength I had, squeezed my eyes and my asshole shut as tight as possible and concentrated on holding everything in the best I could.

With a very shaky and uneasy voice I said to the cop:

Me: "Sir, I can *literally* see my house from here." I pointed to it for good measure. "I need to get there NOW. Yes, I know that I was speeding. I fully....."

Gurgle, gurgle, gurgle.....

OH NO.

Me: ".....admit. That."

My breathing became more labored as my bowels started liquefying.

Me: "Please. Just. Follow. Me. To. My. House. If. You. Want. Give. Me. Ten. Tickets. I. Don't. Care. Please. I. Just. Don't. Want. To. Shit. Myself."

The cop started talking, but I couldn't hear him. My world had become completely quiet and tranquil. The sun became brighter and I saw a couple of cherubs flying in front of the car. I'm pretty sure that they were pointing and laughing at me. They knew what was coming next.

I knew that this was the calm before the storm.

And then it happened.

If you've never shat your pants before while sitting down, let me tell you: it's an unforgettable experience.

You see, because you are sitting down, the poo (or in my case, the 37 pounds of blended slop) can't just come straight out like it would if you were seated on a toilet. It needs somewhere to go. And because your ass is on a seat, it just. Goes. Everywhere.

The more poo you have coming out, the more necessity for room. The more necessity for room, the more expansion. The more expansion, the more total area covered. It's simple physics. A lot of mass quickly put into a small area is not good.

The shit went down both pant legs, covered my balls and started shooting up through my waistline within a second. I was completely covered in my own shit before my heart could beat twice. It was actually kind of impressive.

What was even *more* impressive is how fast the smell traveled.

It smelt like death warmed over.

And it filled the car *instantly*.

In mid-sentence the cop gagged.

Cop: "OH MY FUCKING GOD, WHAT THE FUCK IS THAT SMELL?!"

And here I thought that cops were supposed to be pretty quick on their feet.

I didn't say anything.

I just sat there, gripping the steering wheel with both hands, staring out the windshield.

I didn't say anything because I couldn't.

I had nothing.

But a giant load of shit in my pants.

#1 perhaps *might* have said something, if she wasn't retching her guts out of the passenger door. The cop just stood there staring at me in utter disbelief. He said nothing for a good two minutes, and I refused to make eye contact with him. If I did, I knew that I would have cried.

He opened and closed his mouth a few times before he spoke. #1 got herself cleaned up and kept looking between me and the cop, not knowing what to say.

For once, the bitch was speechless.

Finally, the cop blinked first.

Cop: "Sir, I suggest you go home and get yourself cleaned up."

I just nodded, turned the car on, and drove home in silence with the windows down.

#1 and I never spoke another word about the incident.

Ten days later, we sold the car. We had to. That fucking smell was *embedded* in it.

You KNOW HOW SOMETIMES, some people don't accept the obvious? The truth could be right in front of them, and yet they fail to either see it or admit it. Most of the time, that's me.

Even though #1 and I hadn't had sex in a long time, and somehow she'd became pregnant, I still didn't believe that she was fucking around on me.

I know, I'm a fucking idiot.

Anyways.....

#1 had been finding more and more reasons to leave the house after work for hours on end. When I asked her what the hell she was doing, she told me that she was hanging out with her friends from work or shopping or some sort of other bullshit. Her main "gal pal" was a gay dude named Mike.

It seemed like every-fucking-day after work, #1 and Mike had something to do. Now, I know that I'm not a master of the obvious, but eventually shit started to tingle my spidey senses.

I decided to take matters into my own hands and set up a little sting operation. One day while the bitch was in the shower, I snatched up her phone and installed a tracking GPS app that ran silently in the background.

I didn't do anything with it for a few days and just played it cool. Then one Friday night when she came home from work, took a shower, got herself all dolled up and told me that she was "going to go have a few drinks with Mike," I decided that it was time to see what was up.

A few hours after she had left, I got in my truck and turned on the tracker app. Luckily, she was close by. She was actually about a mile down the road from our house, and moving at a steady speed. I found her car and followed it until she pulled into a Walmart parking lot. That's when I noticed that there were two people in her car. She was in the passenger seat, and some dude was driving the car.

They pulled into the far end of the parking lot and just sat in the car. I followed and parked my truck close enough for me to see what was going on. A few minutes after they had parked, #1 leaned over towards the driver's side, and her head disappeared for a second. Then it bobbed back up.

Then back down.

Then back up.

No. Fucking. Way.

The bitch was giving him head in a Walmart parking lot!!

Well, I've got something for her ass....

I picked up my phone, dialed her number, got out of my truck and started walking towards her car. I stopped walking when she didn't answer.

So, I waited where I was and called back.

She didn't answer again, but she looked like she still had a mouthful in the car.

I decided that I wasn't going to wait for her to answer her phone, and started walking towards the car again.

By the third ring of the third call, I had reached the passenger side window and knocked on it as hard as I could without breaking it. I won't lie. I was kind of hoping that she'd bite off his dick when I startled them.

Me: "HI!"

THE LOOK on her face was priceless.

The look on *his* face was even better. It was a mixture of oh-my-god-I'm-about-to-cum and oh-my-god-this-white-dude-is-going-to-kill-me.

I couldn't make out what she was saying to him in the car, but it was pretty obvious that they both didn't want to be there. The dude turned the key and had the car in gear before the engine could even turn over. Then he hit the gas and peeled out of the parking lot like a dude who just walked into a house and found Chris Hansen from Dateline NBC standing there.

Me, to no one: "So I take it the family vacation is out this year?"

She didn't bother coming home that night.

Can't say that I blame her. If I got caught sucking a dude off in a Walmart parking lot, I'd be a bit embarrassed too. I mean, I'd at least have enough class to do it at like, Red Lobster or something.

Wait, what?

Let's forget I said that and move on.

Anyways...

I found out later that #1 was telling the truth. She *was* hanging out with Mike. Just not her gay co-worker Mike. Mike also happened to be the name of the dude she was sucking off.

Deception is a motherfucker, isn't it?

Not too long after the blow job incident, #1 and I thought that it was a good idea to spend some time apart. One day, in a generous mood, she suggested that I go back home to spend some time with my family in New York over the holidays. We didn't really want to be around each other, and I couldn't think of an argument for me *not* to go, so I booked a flight and went home.

Over the week I didn't talk to #1 much, nor did she really make an effort to reach out to me, which apparently was fine by the both of us. I spent a lot of time with my family and went out around town a few nights to have some drinks. On one of my outings, I ran into an ex of mine who I hadn't seen since we had broken up: Tina.

Tina and I parted on some difficult terms. Well, difficult for me, not her. She cheated on me and left me for the dude. But that was quite a few years prior, and I didn't really hold a grudge.

Tina and I had a few drinks and a few laughs and that was it. We exchanged numbers and said that we would get together again before I left but never did. I returned to Florida and didn't think much of it.

After being back in Florida for about a week, Tina messaged me to say hi. We talked back and forth for a few days, mainly just bullshitting. I would bitch about my home life and she would bitch about college life and her family, and that was it.

The main reason I was bitching was because I had found out #1's true motive for suggesting that I go to New York. She wanted to spend Christmas with Mike. And I don't mean the gay one. Her justification for it was:

#1: "I didn't want to be alone for Christmas."

Me: "You're fucking kidding me, right?"

#1: "No. Why?"

Me: "Why? Because you're the one who suggested that I leave for the holiday. You said that it wasn't going to be a big deal and that you'd be fine on your own. You assured me of that fact."

#1: "Well, I was lonely."

Me: "Right. Like it wasn't the fucking plan the entire time."

I was pissed, but there wasn't much I could do about it.

On New Year's Eve, we decided to go to the beach and hang out. #1 decided that it would be a good idea to drink a pint of vodka by herself while we were on the beach. There was no way that I was going to drink with her to begin with, but especially on fucking New Year's. No way I was going to risk driving.

It was while we were on the beach and #1 was good and shitfaced when Tina sent me a message and #1 intercepted it.

All it said was something to the extent of hope you have a good and safe New Year's, but that was enough for #1 to lose her fucking mind. #1 asked me who Tina was and how I knew her, and I explained that she was an ex I ran into while back home and that was it.

Apparently, that was unacceptable.

According to her cunt logic, it was okay for her to be fucking, blowing, and sending me off to another state so she could spend her Christmas with another dude, but I couldn't talk to another chick via text. Especially an ex.

Makes sense, right?

I didn't think so either.

For the entire ride home, #1 did nothing but scream at me. She decided to tell me how much of a piece of shit I was, and how disrespectful it was of me to be going behind her back and hanging out with Tina, and then continuing my adultery (yes, she actually used that word) by continuing to speak to Tina.

Like I said, cunt logic.

Once we got home though, that's when things got *really* interesting,

Prior to this day, I'd never seen #1 really lose her shit. Sure, I'd seen her mad. Hell, I've *made* her mad on several occasions. But when we got home, this was a whole new level of pissed off. She truly took my talking to Tina to heart. #1 felt so slighted by the fact that I was speaking to another woman that she became violent.

First, she started throwing things from the house around. Then she started throwing things from the house *at* me. The Keurig did some serious damage to the drywall, and I had to stop and wonder what it would have done had it made contact with my head. That's when I started to get concerned.

After the objects stopped flying all over the place, #1 got quiet for several minutes and started to get a look on her face that I'd never seen before. Her eyes had this.... glow to them and she looked like something had just *snapped* in her head.

She got up, walked to the kitchen and pulled out a butcher knife. She started walking towards me holding the knife with the blade facing down, like how a kid is taught to walk with a pair of scissors or a knife in their hand.

Then she raised the knife over her head, with the blade facing me. Right then, she could have either lunged towards me and brought the knife down in a powerful stabbing motion, or she could have slammed it down into her stomach without twisting the blade. I wasn't sure which she planned on doing.

And then she said it:

#1: "I'm going to do it. I swear to God."

Ut-oh.

Me: "#1, what are you planning on doing exactly? You need to put down the knife, or I'm going to call the police."

#1: "I'm going to fucking do it, Lawn Mower. I'm going to fucking do it."

Me: "Put the knife down now, or I'm calling the cops."

She just held the knife in place and kept repeating that she was going to do it, over and over again, no matter what I said to her.

I was in genuine fear for both of our lives, so I pulled my mobile phone out of my pocket and dialed 911. I didn't get to talk to the operator because #1 started taking a few steps and backed me into a literal corner. I kept the phone in my hand and held it so she could see that a call was in progress, and also so the operator could hear what was going on.

Me: "#1, I don't know what you plan on doing, but you need to put the knife down. I've got the cops on the phone and I'm worried."

#1: "I'm going to fucking do it."

Me: "Do what?! Are you going to stab me or yourself?!"

I figured that giving the operator a little insight into what was going on would assist in getting the cops to my house a little quicker.

Showing #1 the phone or telling her that I was speaking to the cops didn't seem to faze her, and she kept slowly walking towards me.

Me: "Stop walking towards me with that knife in your hand or I'm going to have to defend myself."

#1: "I don't care. I'm going to fucking do it!"

And then I heard the sweetest sound I've ever heard in my life:

BANG-BANG-BANG-BANG

Cop knock

Cop: "POLICE! Open up!"

Me: "It's open!! Get your fucking ass in here!!"

The cops opened the door and drew their weapons on #1. That kind of got her attention and she dropped the knife. Then they detained her and pulled me outside to talk.

I tried to explain the situation the best that I could to the cop, but in truth, I had no idea why she snapped like she did. I don't know if it was the combination of the booze and the sun or if it was the fact that I was talking to Tina. Either way, I explained it all to the cop the best that I could and then asked him what they were going to do with her.

The cop explained that it was completely up to me since this was a domestic dispute. He said that I could press charges on her for attempted assault or even attempted murder if I wanted. As much as I hated the bitch, I couldn't do that to her. He then informed me that even if I didn't press charges, she would be going in for a mandatory seventy-two hour psychological hold and examination, since it was unclear if she was trying to hurt herself or not.

Oooooohhhhhhhh shit.

It was New Year's Eve, and #1 of all people was going to have to go to the loony bin, drunk off her ass, and stay there for three days. I didn't have the heart to send her to jail, but the psych ward? Absolutely.

While trying to hold back a shit-eating grin, I informed the cop that I didn't feel pressing charges was necessary, but I wholeheartedly agreed that a psychological examination was needed.

After that, the cop went back inside and helped his partner escort #1 (in handcuffs I might add) to the patrol car. She was not impressed. It took everything I had to not record the whole scene with my phone.

The next morning, I received a phone call from a seriously pissed off #1 *demanding* that I come pick her up.

Once again, showing my maturity by not exploding with laughter, I tried to explain to her that I couldn't pick her up until the seventy-two hour hold was lifted.

I would quote her exact words here, but she started cursing at me with words I didn't understand. Remember, she's British, and they curse on a whole different level than we do over here in the States. But I can assure you, even though I didn't understand what she was saying to me, I know it was very harsh and demeaning.

Once her stay in the mental hospital was over and they released her, things didn't get any better at home. She started wearing a giant SC on her chest which stood for

Super Cunt. Getting a taste of her own medicine– even though it was nothing like what she was doing to me– only pissed #1 off more instead of making her realize that the shit she was doing was fucked-up. We started fighting even more than usual, and I increased my dope use to almost hourly.

Clearly, I had strong coping skills back then.

#1's CUNT-TASTIC ATTITUDE not only continued, but got worse. Not only did she start ruining my life, but she started fucking things up for me with my family as well. A couple months after her meltdown and mini vacation in the mental hospital, I got a call from my grandmother who asked me if I could come up to visit for a few days. A long weekend was coming up, and pretty much the whole family was going to be there. My grandfather was very sick and didn't have much time left; it was left unspoken that this would probably be the last time I was going to be able to see my grandfather alive.

I talked about it with #1 and asked her if she wanted to go. She said that she didn't but that I should absolutely go and spend time with my grandfather and family. She understood that it was probably the last time I would see him alive.

A few days later I left Florida and started on my 10-hour drive to South Carolina.

Halfway into my trip, #1 started in with her bullshit.

First it started out with a few texts saying how she was bored and lonely.

Then she started calling my phone.

#1: "Why did you leave me here all alone?!"

#1: "I can't believe you would do this to me!"

#1: "It's beyond disrespectful that you went on a fucking trip without me."

And it didn't stop there.

She kept calling and calling and calling. Finally, I turned off my phone and left it that way for the rest of the trip.

When I arrived at my grandparents', my grandmother came out to the driveway to meet me.

Grandmother: "Lawn Mower, you need to call #1, *now*. She has called here, I can't tell you how many times already and she's looking for you. Your grandfather is not impressed, and neither is anyone else."

Great.

I called #1 and it was nothing but absolute #1 bullshit. Demanding that I come home. Demanding that I leave South Carolina that instant. Telling me how horrible and disrespectful I was for leaving her. Even though she knew that it was probably the last time I was going to be able to see my grandfather alive, and the fact that *she told me to go* didn't matter. She was only concerned with herself.

I told #1 that I wasn't leaving and that she was going to have to deal with it.

That didn't go over well at all.

I even tried hanging up on her several times, but she kept calling.

And calling.

And calling.

It finally got to the point where my grandfather told me that it would be best for everyone if I left. #1 was making things very difficult for everyone there, as if it wasn't already difficult enough.

I left with my head hung low, my tail between my legs, and nothing but shame and embarrassment laying heavy on my shoulders.

That was also the last time I ever saw my grandfather alive.

Can't imagine why I'd hold any resentments against #1, right?

* * *

My MARRIAGE to Sally Super Snatch was (obviously) over. I was miserable, she was miserable, I had so many resentments towards her that I could easily write 10,000 words on them, and apparently my skin tone wasn't dark enough for her liking.

She hated me. I hated me. My family was beyond furious with me. My family was beyond furious with her. Her family was rather upset with me. And the only one that liked me was my lawyer. Each new arrest or issue meant more money for him. He was a paid attorney, and my Aunt Katie was footing the bill, so I really didn't give a fuck what it cost.

I figured that shit couldn't really get any worse.

Then it did (like it always does).

Isn't that awesome?

That October, my grandfather passed away. I knew it was coming, but it still hurt. I think it hurt so bad because I never got to say my goodbyes to him. I allowed #1 to take that away from me. I immediately flew back home to upstate New York to be with my family and lay him to rest.

And this, kids, is where Beavis enters the story.

Beavis is my first cousin. From a very young age, Beavis and I had been as thick as thieves. We corrupted each other in so many different ways, it's astounding. If I were to jump off a bridge, he'd be right behind me. If he was throwing an M-80 into the open window of a car, I was lighting the fuse. You get the idea.

Alone, he and I were bad enough. Together, we were fucking ridiculous.

Then, when you factor drugs/alcohol into the equation:

AND AS FATE would have it, at the time of the funeral, Beavis was also into intravenous drug use. He also had access to *a lot* of opiates. It was a match made in heaven.

Granted, a very fucked-up, addict heaven. But to each his own, right?

Beavis and I almost missed our grandfather's funeral– in which we were both pallbearers– because Beavis kept "missing his shot." Which is Addictspeak for not being able to find a vein with the needle. And I was way too high to help him.

It was bad enough that I didn't get to spend time with my grandfather before he passed. Missing his funeral would have been abominable, even for me. We made it to the funeral with *seconds* to spare, and caused a scene loud enough to wake the dead.

Well, almost.

Yes, I know, we're completely fucking revolting.

Can you imagine what comes next?

AFTER THE FUNERAL, the family got together and I almost went through my first intervention. My family kept telling me that I needed help, and I kept telling them that I was fine. We did this little dance for a few hours, and all the while I kept sneaking into the bathroom to shoot up.

After I shot up, I slithered into the coat room and stole money out of the purses that were in said room.

Purses that belonged to my family and close friends of the family.

Mere hours after we buried my grandfather.

I bet you didn't see that one coming.

* * *

THE DAY before I was due to fly back to Florida, my grandmother called me to see if we could go have lunch. At lunch, she dropped a bombshell on me:

Grandmother: "Lawn Mower honey, I received a phone call this morning from the Clintons...."

(The Clintons were my grandparents' closest friends in Florida, and have been for years. During the summer months while the Clintons were living in New York, I would watch over their house.)

Grandmother: "....and they told me that they had noticed several items missing from their home...."

Grandmother: "They reported the missing items to the police, and the items were discovered at a local pawn shop. They were pawned by you. The Clintons have pressed charges on you, honey, and there's a warrant out for your arrest."

I just sat there silently. I mean, what could I really say?

Believe it or not, I had actually *forgotten* that I'd pawned their stuff. How fucked-up is that? I was doing so much shit, that I had actually forgotten about felonious behavior.

Grandmother: "You're in a lot of trouble right now, honey. I suggest that you straighten out your act, and *right now*, or you're going to spend a long time in prison."

Wait...what?

Prison???

They don't send drug addicts to prison.

They send them to rehab or something, right?

THE NEXT DAY I flew back to Florida with a bit of anxiety. By the time my flight landed, I was a fucking wreck thanks to my fucking wife. The spiteful bitch decided that it was a good idea to first call the sheriff's office and let them know when and where my flight was landing. Then she took it upon herself to inform me of said previous phone call, a mere fifteen minutes before my flight was due to take off.

Lawn Mower

During the flight I had convinced myself that a full-blown SWAT team was waiting for me at the gate with the orders of: *shoot to kill*, and if you had shoved a piece of coal up my ass when the flight left New York, I would have shit out a diamond by the time it landed in Florida. Apparently #1 held a grudge over me catching her with a mouthful of cock in that Walmart parking lot.

The only solace I could come up with was that I was a drug addict. I figured that when I went to court, I would give the judge a huge sob story, tell him that I was a drug addict and beg him for help. Then he would send me to rehab– because they don't send drug addicts to prison– and I'd be home in ninety days, tops.

Even though I was figuring a ninety day stay in rehab, I still didn't want to get off the plane. I was scared shitless, and for every second that passed, the image in my head of what was waiting for me once I stepped foot off that plane kept getting worse.

Can you imagine my surprise when I got off the flight and no one was there? Not one single fed, cop, sheriff, state trooper or airport security guard. No one paid me any mind, and I was able to walk off the plane, gather my belongings at baggage claim, strut my ass right out of the airport and hail a cab without incident.

When I arrived home, I told #1 to go fuck herself, took a shower, got high, watched *Supernatural* and went to sleep.

The next day, I turned myself in on the warrant, called my family back home and told them to get a hold of the bondsman, then sat in jail waiting for someone to come and bail me out.

I waited.

And I waited.

And waited.

And waited.

And waited.

And no one fucking came.

I called my family and received the "this is what's best for you right now" speech, which didn't fucking impress me.

I even called #1.

She just laughed and hung up.

I was stuck like Chuck.

Who in the fuck is Chuck anyways?

My lawyer came to see me to discuss my "options" a few days later. Even with the new charges, I still didn't "score out" to prison, and considering the circumstances surrounding my case, he felt that my best option was an "open plea."

For those of you who have not had the pleasure of dealing with the absolute fuckery that is the Florida judicial system, I will explain what those previous terms mean.

When someone is arrested for a crime in Florida, the ADA (assistant district attorney) has to fill out a 'Criminal Punishment Code Scoresheet' pursuant to rule 3.992(a).

This scoresheet contains several different sections, such as: primary offense, additional offense(s), victim injury, prior record, etc. When the ADA inputs information about your alleged crime, said information is computed as follows:

Every crime is awarded an offense level between 1-10 (FYI a 10 is very bad). Each level has a certain number of points allotted to it. For example, offense level 5 equals 28 points. These numbers are static and do not change.

They are, however, reduced. If you are arrested on multiple charges– that's more than one for the simple people– your points for the additional charges will now be added into section 2, properly dubbed "additional charge(s)."

Whatever your charges are, the one with the highest offense level will be considered your "primary charge" (guess where the other charges go?). Anyways, for an additional offense, the level points are significantly reduced. Instead of 28 points for a level 5 offense, you'll now receive 5.4 points.

If you hurt someone– Victim Injury– as in murder, accidental death, severe, moderate, slight, sexual contact, etc., your primary charge offense level points are multiplied by a number. Example: for second degree murder they're multiplied by 240. Yikes!

If you've been previously arrested, you have what's called a "prior record." Whatever your prior record was originally, the offense level is significantly reduced as well. That level 5 offense (from your past) is now worth 3.6 points.

Then, of course, there are sections for other sorts of nonsense like violation of probation, legal status violations, firearms, prior serious felony, enhancements, blah blah blah.

Everyone still with me?

Now, the ADA will add the points from all the sections together to get your "total sentence points." If your total sentence points are equal to or greater than 44 points, then the state's attorney will multiply that number by .75 and Bob's your uncle! That new number is the *minimum* amount of time (in months) that your happy ass is going to spend in prison.

Fucked-up, eh?

With all of my charges– nine in total– I "scored out" to 39.8 points. For those of you with shitty mathematical comparison skills, 39.8 is *less than* 44. This meant possible jail time but definitely no prison for Lawn Mower.

Like I said, drug addicts don't get sent to prison.

An "open plea" is when you throw yourself at the mercy of the court, pretty much taking the ADA out of the equation. You give the judge complete sentencing discretion. This is a good tactic for those people looking at a lot of time, or who are trying to get a better deal. I mean you're pretty much gargling the judge's balls and enhancing their god complex, but fuck it, I'd rather gargle on some balls than go to prison.

Did I really just write that?

Let's forget I did and move on.

Due to my "serious drug problem," my lawyer said that it would be in my best interest to open plea to the judge, explain that I had a problem, and beg for help.

Who was I to question him? He was the seasoned lawyer, not me. Plus, he was a *paid* attorney, not some overworked, uncaring public pretender (Jailspeak for public defender) who could care less about me and my case.

* * *

I went for sentencing in early December. I had yet to go through any withdrawals because my cellmate had smuggled in a shitload of methadone.

Please don't ask me *how* he got it in.

And please excuse the pun.

I was staying high and I didn't score out to prison. Life was good, all things considered. At sentencing, I wasn't paying attention to anything being said. I was really fucking high and I didn't care. I let my lawyer handle all the lawyering stuff. That's what he was getting paid for, right? I pleaded guilty to all my charges, gargled the judge's balls and threw myself at the mercy of the court. My lawyer said that I wouldn't– his actual words were *shouldn't*– go to prison, so I had nothing to fear.

After my tear-filled open plea, the State was allowed to put in their two cents before final sentencing.

This is when things went to shit really fast.

ADA: "Your Honor, I'd like to point out to the court that following his June court appearance– when you allowed the defendant bail I might add– the defendant went directly to a pawn shop and sold more stolen property. This would be case number ABC123, which the defendant has just pleaded guilty to."

Oh, that's not good.

Right then, I heard the door to the courtroom open. I turned around to see who it was, and imagine my surprise when I saw my wife, #1, walking into the courtroom.

Holding hands with Mike, the dude she was blowing in that Walmart parking lot.

Lawn Mower

The bitch walked right in like she owned the place, sat her lily-white ass down with her boy toy, and then the fucking cunt smiled at me.

Do you remember that scene from "A Christmas Story"?

You know the one. When the tire blows on the car, and Ralphie's dad gets out to change it, and Ralphie goes out to help him. Then Ralphie fucks up, spills the lug nuts all over the place and says some shit that a kid in the 1940s should never say. Especially in front of his father

Well, I did the same fucking thing.

Except I didn't say exactly the same thing, nor did I say it while changing a tire with my old man. I said it in an open fucking court room, while being sentenced.

Me: "You've gotta be fucking kidding me."

Not one of my finest moments, I will admit.

Judge: "*Excuse me?!* What did you just say Mr. Lawn Mower?"

Oh no.

My lawyer leaned over and whispered into my ear.

Lawyer: "You better come up with something really good right now, because you're in a world of shit that I can't help you with."

Gee, thanks guy.

Me: "Uh, um, Your Honor, I *sincerely* apologize. I was completely distracted for a moment when someone walked into the courtroom, and I was absolutely beside myself when I saw my wife enter, holding hands with some strange man."

I will gladly throw that bitch under the bus at any given opportunity.

The judge looked right at #1 and called her out.

Judge: "Excuse me, miss. Is this true what the defendant here just stated, that you're his wife and that you just walked in here holding some man's hand?"

#1 looked pretty fucking sheepish right then.

#1: "Um, yea."

Judge: "And I'm going to go out on a limb here and say that this man is some sort of boyfriend?"

#1: "Yes..."

Judge: "Uh-huh. Rather distasteful, don't you think?"

#1: "Well, um..."

Judge: "That was a rhetorical question, Mrs. Lawn Mower. Now please leave my courtroom and take your boyfriend with you while I finish with your *husband's* sentencing."

This is the best judge ever.

Judge: "Now, where were we? Oh right. Is this true Mr. Lawn Mower?"

Me: "Your Honor?"

Judge: "What the ADA had previously stated about you leaving my courtroom after pleading guilty, only to go pawn more stolen property."

Me: "Oh. Right. Uhh.... I plead the fifth, Your Honor?"

Judge: "You can't plead the fifth to something that you've just plead guilty to, sir."

Shit.

Me: "Oh. Then. Um. I'm sorry?"

Judge: "Uh-huh. I bet you are. Just like you're sorry about your little outburst a few minutes ago. Mr. ADA, what does the defendant score out to?"

ADA: "County time, Your Honor."

Judge: "I see. Well in that case, due to your activities outside my courtroom and due to your outburst *inside* my courtroom, I sentence you to eighteen months in the Florida

Department of Corrections, followed by two years of probation. I'm also recommending drug treatment while in the Department of Corrections so you can receive the "help" that you so desperately begged me for. Good luck to you, sir."

I turned to face my lawyer.

Me: "What in the fuck just happened?"

Lawyer: "You were sentenced to prison."

No shit.

Me: "You said that I wouldn't go to prison."

Lawyer: "No. I said that you *shouldn't* go to prison. You went with an open plea. The judge can do whatever he wants. Plus, you just cursed in his open courtroom."

On that day I learned 3 important things:

1. Never curse in open court while in the midst of an open plea.

2. They *do* send drug addicts to prison.

3. This is not the best judge ever.

* * *

I WANTED to share the following story with y'all earlier but it didn't really fit into the storyline. Even though this happened before I met #1, I felt that it didn't really flow with the feng shui of everything, so I'm going to be lazy and just toss it in here.

Some people question if they're a good friend or not. I don't. Even though I'm a really shitty person, believe it or not, I'm a pretty decent friend.

How do I know this?

Easy!

I do the things that other friends won't do, like tell you that your new dress looks horrible on you, and that yes, you *should* lose a few pounds, or that your girlfriend is a complete fucking whore. Most people say that they want "honest" friends, but when it comes down to it, they don't. Most people want a friend that will lie to them in order to make them feel better, and I *refuse* to be that friend. I'm the friend that they *say* they want, but cringe when I come around.

Here's a prime example:

I had this friend named Kimo. Kimo's a few years older than I am, but we used to hang out with the same crowd, and eventually became close friends. Kimo had a kid with this chick named Ruby. Even though Ruby was younger than I was and a grade behind me, I still knew who she was.

Ruby was always a good-looking chick in school, and she got exponentially hotter after a few "cosmetic surgeries." Translation: she got her tits and nose done.

Shortly thereafter, Ruby did what all self-respecting, halfway-decent looking, post-cosmetic surgery young women do for work: She started stripping.

Wait I'm sorry, *exotic dancing.*

Kimo wasn't thrilled about this one bit, but there was fuckall he could do about it since they hadn't been together in quite some time. I think he was a bit salty about the fact that she got hotter after she dumped him. Or the fact that as his best friend, I fucked with him relentlessly about his baby mama being a (whore) stripper.

So now we'll fast forward about five or six years.

I was bored one day and was doing what all young men do when they're bored and alone: I was watching porn. After perusing a few sites, I came across a site that I'd never been on before and that had free access to the videos.

Jackpot!!

This was all pre-Pornhub FYI.

As I surfed my way through the site, I came across a section with this chick named Angel. I clicked on her section because something looked awfully familiar about Angel. I was watching her in action (which wasn't very impressive by any means) for a while, and then it clicked:

Ruby.

No. Fucking. Way.

Well…. maybe.

No. It can't be.

Can it?

Is that *really* Kimo's baby mama??

There was only one way to find out.

I picked up the phone and called Kimo.

Kimo: "Yo."

Me: "What are you doing right now?"

Kimo: "Not much. Bored."

Me: "Perfect. I just sent you a link to a website. Go check it out and tell me what you think."

Kimo: "It's not another fucking virus, is it?"

Me: "No dude. I *promise* you that it's not a virus."

Kimo: "Okay. Hold up."

I was so excited to hear his reaction that I almost wet myself.

Me: "You there yet?"

Kimo: "Hold on, it's loading now. Okay, it's playing, I see…. WHAT THE FUCK?!!??!"

Me: "Dude?"

Kimo: "That fucking…. that dirty……what the…… I'm going to fucking kill her….."

In the background I could hear things being thrown around and broken, along with quite a few unintelligible words.

Me: "So it *is* Ruby then?"

Kimo: "Fuck you."

See. I told you that I was a good friend.

A normal friend would only *tell* you that the mother of your first-born child was doing porn for a living.

Only a good friend would *show* you.

* * *

Ask anyone who's ever been to prison and they'll agree that the first day is *always* the worst. If it's the first day *and* your first time going to prison, then life truly sucks a hairy nut sack for you at that moment in your life.

My first day started as a *very cold* morning in January. Central Florida Reception Center (CFRC) is located in– get this– central Florida, and you can scoff all you want, but at 4:30 in the morning, it was really fucking cold.

About fifty people came with me from the county that morning. When we arrived at CFRC, we were rushed off the bus by two correctional officers (COs) screaming at us. We were ordered to get into two equal parallel lines.

This proved to be a difficult task because most of the people arriving with me that morning couldn't figure out half of fifty if their life depended on it, and even fewer people knew what parallel meant.

I could already tell that it was going to be a rough day.

Once we accomplished the monumental task of forming two lines, we stood there staring at the dude standing in the line across from us, freezing our asses off, while the COs screamed all sorts of unintelligible nonsense at us.

I had a very difficult time understanding what was being screamed at me for several reasons:

1. I'm not inbred.

2. I do not speak, nor do I understand, redneck.

3. I was too busy shivering uncontrollably to concentrate.

One word brought my attention into complete focus.

CO: "STRIP!"

Wait. What? We're outside and it's about 22 degrees out.

He's *got* to be kidding.

CO: "I SAID STRIP NOW MOTHERFUCKERS!!!"

Fuck. He's *not* kidding.

I don't know what sucked more. Being butt-ass naked with forty-nine other butt-ass naked dudes surrounding me, or it being so cold outside that my balls were slowly inching their way back inside my body.

What I can tell you is that the *combination* of the two was very bad, and that the whole situation was about as much fun as a set of sandpaper anal beads.

One guy in our group decided to voice his opinion about how much it sucked. Please allow me to introduce: That Guy.

That Guy is the guy that you don't want to be. He's the one you always hear horror stories about. He's the one who thinks he knows it all. The one who thinks he's Billy Bad Ass, and the one who *always* has to show off in front of his friends. And I can personally assure you, there's *always* one everywhere you go in prison.

I just don't think that the CO was expecting him to show up so soon that day, because when That Guy said:

That Guy: "This is fucking bullshit."

The CO shit a brick.

CO: "What the..... WHO THE FUCK SAID THAT?!!! Who's the fucking tough guy that thinks he can talk in MY FUCKING SALLY PORT?!"

That Guy: "ME. I said it, and I'll say it again. This. Is. Fucking. Bullshit."

Oh, this ought to be good.

The CO walked up to That Guy and got right in his face.

CO: "And just who in the fuck do you think you are, inmate?"

That Guy: "I don't think I'm nobody but me. Name's Wolf. Not inmate."

CO: "Well lookie here y'all, it's Billy Fucking Bad Ass! Well, it's a pleasure to meetcha Mr. Bad Ass, would you care to introduce yourself to the fellas here?"

THAT GUY OPENED his mouth to speak but never got any words out. Before he could utter a single syllable, the CO hit him with a right hook that looked like it did some serious damage. Wolf was asleep before he hit the ground.

CO: "Anyone else have something to say?"

He must have been pleased with the response because he started right back where he left off.

After a few more minutes of the spread-your-cheeks-wide-squat-and-cough bullshit, we were led inside for some more fun. We left Wolf right where he was, still asleep on the ground, in nothing but his birthday suit.

Personally, I wasn't shocked that I had just witnessed a CO knocking a dude out. I was shocked at the fact that the dude had to be pushing damn near seventy, and the CO didn't give a shit. That, above all else, frightened me.

The rest of the day went something like this:

Being screamed at.

Being humiliated

Being screamed at more.

Being humiliated more.

Being screamed at again.

Being humiliated again.

You get the idea.

We were shaved, humiliated, showered, humiliated, dressed, fingerprinted, humiliated, TB tested, photographed, humiliated, had blood drawn, ate, and were introduced to the Florida Department of Corrections in about ten hours.

Oh, and get this. The clothing they give you when you first come into prison is dirty and used. You can still *smell* the last dude who just got done wearing them. I can't even describe how disgusted I was when I noticed the giant shit stain in the boxers that they gave me to wear. And no, you cannot ask for a different and/or new pair. So don't even be like, "I'd just hand them back and ask for a new pair." Shit doesn't work like that in prison. Just ask That Guy.

It was a long fucking day.

A long fucking day that still wasn't over.

We still had to be brought to our respective housing units.

Walking into a housing unit for the first time was a surreal experience. I was the new guy, and everyone knew it. Even though I came with forty-nine other people, life had worked its fuck-you magic and saw fit that I was the only person assigned to housing unit D.

Awesome.

As soon as I walked through the door, it was like a scene out of a movie: all activity stopped and all eyes were immediately on me.

Well, isn't this just swell.

I tried to act like I wasn't a rookie to prison, but it was blatantly obvious that I was green as baby shit. Green is Prisonspeak for: fucking clueless.

Plus, I was still wearing my ID tag.

See, Florida has this fancy system of letting people know how many times you've been to prison, and they put it right on the ID tag which you're required to wear at all times.

If it's your first time in prison, you get a big "o" in front of your DC (Department of Corrections) number. If it's your second time, you get an "A" in front of your number. If it's your third time, you get a "B" in front of it, etc. I later figured out why it's a letter system and not a number system. Florida DOC employees can't count. No, I'm serious. During my stay in the Florida prison system, I must have seen hundreds of "recounts." Those fuckers couldn't count to one hundred on their first try if their lives depended on it.

As soon as I walked into the housing unit, dudes were sizing me up. My plan was to go straight to my cell and try to remain unnoticed. Out of sight, out of mind– right?

Wrong.

I'd really like to tell you that I didn't get beat up and robbed for everything I owned that day, but that would be a lie. Prior to prison I hadn't had much fighting experience, and the COs forgot to give us the memo on first night etiquette. Now I had a good understanding of how those dudes in Fight Club must have felt.

That night, I laid on my bunk beaten, bloody, and bruised, while several thoughts kept racing through my mind:

1. I'm a junkie.

2. I'm in prison.

3. How the fuck did this happen?

4. I thought junkies went to rehab?

5. Where are all the fucking drugs at?

THE NEXT DAY, new people arrived and I was no longer the center of attention. A week or so later, I was transferred to a new prison where my time started to fly by. This was for three reasons:

1. I learned how to fight, and fought fairly often.

2.I had money in my canteen account.

3. Drugs were *everywhere*.

The Florida Department of Corrections became my new stomping grounds, and its inhabitants became my new plugs, which is Addictspeak for drug connection.

It was easier to get drugs in prison than it was on the street. It was amazing. Why hadn't I realized this fact earlier and fought my case on the street for so long?

Yes, that's exactly how fucked-up my mentality had gotten due to my addiction. I thought prison was great and was mad that I hadn't gotten there sooner, like it was fucking Busch Gardens giving out free beer in the beer tent.

It really sounds like I was "learning my lesson" doesn't it?

* * *

My LITTLE GO-AROUND in the Florida Department of Corrections was a piece of cake. I only got my ass kicked a handful of times (even though I fought constantly), saw three people get stabbed, and one dude get his throat slit. Being high pretty much every day has its advantages.

I can't really tell you a lot of details about what happened during those eighteen months, mostly because they're all a blur. What I can tell you with absolute certainty is that I was a fucking asshole the entire time. I played on my family's sympathy at every turn, and I was well taken care of by them because of this. Thus, my stay was quite comfortable.

EVEN THOUGH I WAS AN ASSHOLE, I somehow made it to work release, and completed my sentence from there.

While at work release, an incident happened which really took me by surprise. It should have opened my eyes to a few things, but it didn't. This goes back to me not being able to spot the obvious.

In Florida prison if you want to be able to call someone, or someone wants you to be able to call them, they have to mail you a hard copy of their phone bill which clearly displays their name, address, and phone number. So, if your friends, family, or loved ones have a prepaid phone service that doesn't bill, you're fucked. The Florida Department of Corrections wants to know who the fuck you're calling.

Once you receive a copy of the phone bill, you have to get the copy to your counselor and they– at their leisure– have to verify that said information on the bill is accurate, at which point they can either approve or deny the number. Even if you provide a copy of a bill with all the correct information on it, if your counselor wants to be a douchebag that day, he/she can and will deny the number from going on your approved calling list.

This process can take *weeks*. And you are only allowed to make changes to your phone list twice a year. So, if you missed the cut off-date for some reason, you're fucked and have to wait about six months before you can try to make another change. That's prison for you.

When I was in work release, we were able to use pay phones in the facility and call whomever the fuck we wanted, without having to go through all the previously mentioned bullshit. Apparently now times have changed, and you're able to have a cell phone.

On my birthday, I decided to call my youngest sister, Blondie. Blondie and I had been writing each other often during my sentence, and had gotten quite close. So, I figured that I would call and say hi and hear a friendly voice. We spoke for about 20 minutes, and I told her that I'd call back in a couple of weeks.

Two hours later, I was called into the sergeant's office, put in handcuffs, and told that I was "going to jail." Going to jail is Prisonspeak for going to the box (solitary confinement).

Me: "What the fuck am I going to jail for?"

Sergeant: "Because your father just called and informed us that you violated a no-contact order that's in place between you and your sister."

Here's the thing. My father and I have never cared for each other at all. We hadn't spoken in years, and that was fine by the both of us. I knew that he didn't like Blondie and I writing, but I figured *fuck 'em,* her mom was cool with it, and that's all I cared about.

Apparently, he felt differently. So differently in fact, that he found it necessary to call a prison and tell the staff a blatant lie, which he could not substantiate, in order to get his way and his son in trouble.

And yes, this is my *biological* father I'm talking about.

Can we say douchebag??

Come on, say it with me... *douchebag.*

It took an immense amount of convincing, but somehow, I talked the sergeant into calling my grandmother (my father's mother) in order to verify that there was in fact **no** no-contact order, that my father and I hated each other, and that he (my father) was an angry, spiteful, son of a bitch who would absolutely put his own son in jail, just for kicks.

The sergeant called my grandmother and she verified that everything I said was true.

Then he called my father back asking him to fax or e-mail a copy of the no-contact order so that they could move forward with disciplinary action against me.

My father assured him that a fax was on the way.

Three hours later, the sergeant got tired of waiting and set me free. He figured out in half a day what took me over thirty years to figure out: that my father is a lying piece of shit.

Although my father is a lying piece of shit, sometimes his opinions are on par with the rest of the family's. And if he felt that I shouldn't be speaking to my little sister, perhaps there was some merit to this opinion. This fact should have bothered me, but it didn't. I simply chose to ignore the possible truth that there were people out in the world who didn't like me and wanted nothing to do with me anymore. Most addicts are good at ignoring the hard truths of life.

After that, things were fine. I kept working at my job and was able to save up almost three grand for my release back into society (it's called *work release* for a reason).

Since my marriage to #1 was over, I made the decision to move back to New York after I was released. After my sentence I still had two years of probation to complete, so I had to transfer said probation back to New York. This was not an easy task, and since New York sucks almost as much dick as Florida does, they said that I had to be placed on state *parole* as opposed to probation. What the fuck, right? New York was already bending me over backwards (without any lube) and I hadn't even stepped foot into the state.

* * *

ONE OF THE major conditions of being on parole is no police contact. This is a big time no-no. And within five hours of my release from prison, I was face to face with the cops thanks to #1. Let me explain.

My mother and Aunt Katie came to pick me up the day of my release. They flew in from upstate New York all the way to Miami (where the prison I was being released from was) and rented a vehicle that we would be driving back home in.

The plan was to go to my house (the one I still owned with #1), get whatever was left of my stuff, take care of a few miscellaneous things, then start heading to New York. We were hoping to take care of everything that day, and be on the road the following morning. I was given ninety-six hours from release to report to parole in upstate New York, and it was a twenty-two-hour drive. Time really wasn't the issue; I just wanted to get home, get my shit, and get the fuck out of Florida faster than a redneck blows his load in his sister's mouth on a Friday night.

The ride from the prison to my house was roughly four hours, and it was a *long* four hours. My mother and Aunt Katie just kept droning on and on about how badly I fucked up, how lucky I was that I didn't get a longer sentence, how disappointed everyone was with me and how long the road ahead of me was. All things that I was completely aware of, and thus didn't want to hear right then. But I was stuck in the back seat of the rental van with fuck-all to do but look out the window and try to ignore them.

A thought crossed my mind of getting a piece of paper and writing "Help! I've been kidnapped! then putting it up to the window for shits and giggles, but I decided against it.

See, I can be mature!

I was really looking forward to getting back to my house. Before going to prison, I had twenty-two parrots. By the time I was released, only two of them were left. Some were re-homed, but most of them fell to the wrath of #1. To this day I still don't have a straight answer as to what happened. She claims that they "got sick" and that there was nothing she could have done. Personally, I believe that she stopped taking care of them and let them all die out of spite. #1 *knew* that I loved those birds more than I ever loved her, and she did the one thing that she knew would destroy me. The bitch killed my birds.

When I walked through the front door, Mango, my blue and gold macaw, started to lose her mind. Mango was my favorite out of all of them. She was so happy to see me. She was blushing, and dancing, and doing things that a happy bird does. I cried like a little bitch when I picked her up. Out of everyone and everything, I missed Mango the most. Rio, a Maui sunset macaw, was almost as happy to see me as Mango was. And I was just as happy to see Rio. It was a very happy and emotional family reunion. I was over being reunited with my human family; I wanted to see my pets. Any pet owner who's been away from their pet for a significant amount of time knows exactly what I'm talking about.

After the reunion with my girls, I had to start getting my stuff together. I went into the master bedroom to get whatever was left of my clothing. When I walked into the closet, I was a little baffled. There was a lot of men's clothing in there, but none of it appeared to be mine. When I went through what used to be my dresser, I found myself in the same situation. Plenty of clothing, none of which was mine. Apparently, #1 had a live-in boyfriend and I didn't get the memo.

AFTER FINDING some dude's clothing where mine used to be, I definitely felt some sort of way. I wanted to take all of his shit out into the backyard and burn it, but I knew that that was an extremely childish thing to do. So, instead of me acting like a child, I did the adult thing and filled up a glass from the kitchen with my urine, then dumped it all over the clothes in the dresser.

Maturity is my middle name.

Contrary to what you may believe about my above action, I really didn't give a flying fuck that #1 had a boyfriend. Sometimes you just need to pour a cup (or two) of your urine over someone else's shit to make you feel better. Right?

All I wanted to do was get my shit and leave. I started looking around the house and couldn't find a fucking thing of mine. I checked every room in the house and came up empty-handed. Aunt Katie and my mother were trying to help me look, but couldn't really help much because they didn't know what was mine and what wasn't.

I started losing my shit a little, thinking that the cunt threw all of my stuff out, and my mother was trying to calm me down. I have been known to go a little overboard in my actions out of spite when I feel that I've been wronged and/or I feel the need to get someone back.

Pouring urine over someone's clothing was for shits and giggles. If #1 threw out everything that I owned, I was going to either (literally) paint the walls with my feces, or burn the house down. Possibly both. And my mother knew this. So, Mom being Mom, she tried to Dr. Phil me, while Aunt Katie did what Aunt Katie does best: ignored the situation, grabbed herself a glass from the kitchen, and poured herself a hefty glass of wine.

Aunt Katie is what we call a *functional* alcoholic. She also lives in a bubble while pretending that life isn't going on all around her. She drinks till she's sloppy, pass-out drunk on a daily basis, and yet can still manage her life somehow.

My mother decided to take it upon herself at that moment to call #1 at work. I don't know if it was to give #1 a piece of her mind, or if it was to be cordial and ask about my stuff. I knew that it was going to be bad right from the start when I heard my mom say:

Mom: "What the fuck do you mean, why am I in *your* fucking house? The last time I checked my son's name is on the deed to this place as well."

I may have forgotten to tell my mother that just before my release, I received a letter from #1 stating that she did not want me or my family to set foot inside *her* home unless she was present. I didn't read anything past that part of the letter, even though that statement was in the first paragraph and the letter was several pages long.

The conversation between #1 and my mother went from bad to worse quickly, and I really didn't feel like listening to them get into it, so I took the phone from my mother.

Me: "It's me."

#1: "Get the fuck out of my house."

Me: "Well, it's nice to talk to you, too! Listen, I don't feel like listening to you and my mother scream at each other all morning, I just want my stuff, so if you would just tell me where it is, I'll grab it and we'll leave."

#1: "I don't give a fuck what you want. I want all of you out of my house *now*."

Me: "Fuck you. It's my house as well, or have you forgotten that fact? I'll stay here as long as it takes to get my shit ready. If you don't like it, why don't you go shove a pineapple up your cunt and meditate. I'm sure it'll fit with no problems."

#1: "Real mature, Lawn Mower. I'm telling you that I want you out of my house now, or I'm calling the cops."

Me: "Yeah, okay #1."

Silence.

Me: "Hello?"

Silence.

Me: "Hello?"

Mother: "She hung up on you, didn't she?"

Me: "That fucking bitch."

Mother: "I've been saying that for years, honey."

Less than five minutes later, guess who was knocking on the front door?

YEP.

The fucking cunt called the cops.

Nothing to panic about, right? I mean it's not like I was just released from prison *that fucking morning*. And it wasn't like I was on parole and couldn't have any police contact or anything.

Oh wait...

Before I got to the door, two thoughts occurred to me.

Five fucking hours out of prison and I'm about to go back thanks to that fucking cunt.

And:.

Why the fuck does this cop look so familiar?

Me: "Afternoon officer, how can I help you?"

Cop A: "We got a call about some people breaking in and trespassing at this address. Would you mind stepping outside to talk please?"

Me: "Sure, not a problem."

I turned inside the house

Me: "Mom, Aunt Katie– #1 called the cops on us. They're here and we need to go outside."

Aunt Katie: "Are you serious?"

Cop A: "Yes ma'am, he's serious. You need to step outside now please."

When we were all outside, my mother and Aunt Katie both started talking to the cop at the same time. Being the professional that he was, he called a junior officer over to speak to them while he spoke to me. I didn't want to deal with them either, and they're my own flesh and blood.

Cop A: "So, what's going on here sir? Do you have any identification on you?"

Me: "I sure do, officer, and I can explain everything."

Cop A: "I've heard that before."

Ugh. I fucking know better than to start talking to a cop and opening with "I can explain everything."

Me: "No really, I can."

I handed him over my prison release card because it was the only thing that I had with me at the moment.

He took a quick look at it, sighed and said:

Cop A: "Alright then, let's hear it."

Me: "Okay. The bit.... woman who placed the call to y'all is my wife. This is our home that we purchased six years ago. As you can see from my ID, I was just released from prison this morning. My mother and aunt, who are over there..." (I pointed to them for good measure) "came from upstate New York in order to pick me up. We just drove from Miami to get here so I could gather up whatever was left of my stuff, and then we're leaving in order to head back to New York. I'm on parole up there and have ninety something hours to report."

Cop A: "If this is your house and your wife lives here, then why are you going to New York?"

Me: "Because I hate the bitch and want nothing more to do with her. Our marriage has been over for a long time now and I'm ready to move on. I couldn't do anything about it while I was in prison. But now I'm out, and it's time to get my shit and move forward with my life."

Cop A: "So you own this house with your wife?"

Me: "Yes, we bought it together."

Cop A: "And she doesn't have a restraining order out on you or anything, does she?"

Me: "Not that I know of."

Cop A: "Okay, well how about you give me a minute, and I'll go check. As long as everything checks out, you can get your stuff and be on your way. I can't stop you from going into your own home."

Me: "Seriously?"

Cop A: "Seriously. It's your home man, and you're not doing anything wrong. I'll be right back."

The cop walked over to his partner who was talking to my mom and aunt, said something to him, then got in his car and was doing some cop stuff on his computer. While he was doing his cop thing, #1 came flying down the road and slammed on her brakes in front of the driveway, leaving a nice patch on the road.

Oh, this ought to be good.

#1: "GET THE FUCK OFF MY PROPERTY!!!"

Cop B: "Ma'am, why don't you just calm down and step over here and talk to me for a minute."

#1: "NO! I don't want to talk to you. I don't want these people on my property! I want them gone now, and I want them arrested."

Well, fuck you too, cunt.

I watched Cop A shake his head as he got out of his car and approached #1.

Cop A: "Ma'am, I suggest you calm down and do as the officer says."

#1: "I want that man" (pointing to me) "arrested!"

Cop A: "Ma'am he hasn't done anything wrong here. This is his home as much as it is yours and he has every right to be here."

#1: "But I don't want him here!"

Cop A: "I understand that ma'am, but there's not much you can do about it. Not to mention the fact that it's to my understanding that he *is* trying to leave, just as soon as he gets his stuff together. Isn't that right sir?"

Me: "Yessir."

Cop A: "See? So why don't you go over there and talk to the other officer while Mr. Lawn Mower goes inside to gather his belongings."

#1: "NO!!! I don't want him in my fucking house!!"

Cop B: "Ma'am, you need to calm down and step over here. I suggest you do it right now, otherwise I'm going to have to detain you."

Please, if there is any sort of God out there, please, please, please let this bitch get arrested.

Me: "Yes dear, go over there like a good girl."

#1: "FUCK YOU!!!"

Cop A: "Really dude?"

Me: "Sorry, I had to. It's not every day that I get to watch someone put her in her place."

Cop A: "I get it man. Just go inside and finish up. How much time do you need?"

Me: "Not long, maybe thirty minutes."

Cop A: "Okay. We'll stay here and keep her outside so there's no issues."

Me: "Thanks, I appreciate it."

Cop A: "No problem. Get your stuff and be on your way."

Me: "Okay, thanks."

As I was turning to go back into the house, the cop approached me.

Cop A: "You don't remember me, do you?"

Me: "Um, no I don't. Should I?"

Cop A: "Well I wouldn't want to remember me either after an incident like that. I pulled you over a few years ago for speeding not too far from here..."

Oh, my fucking god...

Cop A: "You uh, had a bit of an accident...."

Me: "Yeah... I remember that day."

Cop A: "Yeah, me too. I'll never forget that day as long as I live. Or that smell. I must have told that story a hundred times. And you know what? It gets funnier every time I tell it. Did you ever get that problem taken care of?"

Me: "Not really. It sort of comes and goes as it pleases."

Cop A: "Well, sorry to hear that. Best of luck to you in New York."

And just like that, life comes along and kicks me in the balls.

After that, I went inside, got my shit, took a shit, got my birds, got into the van and got the fuck out of Florida.

* * *

UP UNTIL NOW, I've only intermittently discussed my family. This isn't due to a lack of involvement in my life. It's just that I moved to Florida to get *away* from my family (not to mention the dude I may have ripped off for the cocaine).

Unfortunately for me, since I was on parole and moving back to New York, being away from my family was no longer an option for me.

My mother and I had some seriously deep-seated issues that went back a couple decades (fuck that makes me sound old). She did her best to raise me (and my sister) right, and she tried to provide a good life for us, but her own issues got in the way more often than not.

Now, I want to make one thing clear right fucking here: ***I DO NOT BLAME MY MOTHER FOR MY MISTAKES AND BAD DECISIONS***. I made them. I own them.

But I'm also not foolish enough to believe that she didn't contribute to my dysfunction and overall (un)well-being

And no,; I was never touched in my "special place" by some twisted fuck while my mother covered it up or anything like that. I just had a really fucked-up childhood/adolescence.

My mother was an addict and vacillating alcoholic. She also suffered from bipolarism and depression, which made for some really interesting nights at home. Between her purse, medicine cabinets (notice the plural), and hiding spots around the house, at any given time one could easily find well over a hundred different prescription bottles around our house.

I'm not going to go into details about growing up with my mother for personal reasons. And I don't want to hear any shit about it either. It's not like I haven't told all of you gossip whores enough personal shit as it is already, though I will say that Dr. Phil would have had a fucking field day with my family. We would make the people from *Running with Scissors* blush.

* * *

For those of you with short-term memory issues, I'll remind you that my *probation* in Florida was transferred to and mutated into *parole* by New York State. I emphasize this because personally, I'd rather hear someone tell me that they're on probation than on parole. Parole has a stigma surrounding it. Don't you think?

When I transferred my probation to New York, I had to file what's known as an "Interstate Compact for Adult Offender Supervision." Which is a bunch of legal bullshit for New York is my babysitter, but Florida is still my daddy. So, if (Odin forbid) something happened while I was in New York, Florida was going to whoop my hairy ass.

I've mentioned that I hate Florida, right?

One of the mandatory criteria of the interstate compact was that I had to live with immediate family, and Mommy Dearest drew the short straw on that one.

Actually, that's not entirely accurate. The only immediate family I had left that were still speaking to me were my mother, Aunt Katie, and my sister. My sister was too young for me to live with and Aunt Katie simply wasn't an option. So off to Joan Crawford's I went. And I was absolutely looking forward to putting wire hangers in the closet.

My mother and I had difficulty getting along during the best of times. We both knew that us living together under strenuous conditions was just asking for trouble. But she was my mother and she loved me, so we both had to suck it up.

What I didn't know at the time– but quickly figured out– was that my mother was still using, had fallen off the wagon, started drinking heavily, and had a live-in boyfriend (KFC).

KFC was a raging drink-till-you-black-out-then-say-and-do-mean-offensive-and-violent-shit-then-pass-out-and-forget-about-everything-from-the-night-before type of alcoholic.

Fan-fucking-tastic.

Throw into the mix the facts that I was just getting out of prison, still using drugs, hadn't learned a damn thing during my incarceration– except how to be a better liar and con artist– and that I was ready to fucking party. And what you get in the end is an epic fucking disaster.

Within the first three nanoseconds of meeting KFC, I fucking hated him. He was belligerently drunk and spitting huge wads of green phlegm on the wall. It was completely disgusting. My mother had failed to warn me about KFC on the trip to New York and instead of doing so, she got higher than a kite about two hours before our trip ended. After about ten minutes of being home and meeting KFC, I went looking for her stash(es).

It didn't take me very long to find what I was looking for, and I was off to the races before I even reported to parole.

Don't you just want to bring me home to meet your parents?

I HAD a job within my first two weeks of returning home, was jumping through all the mandatory hoops necessary for parole, and my parole officer didn't really give a shit about what I was doing, so I assumed that he was just really cool and didn't give a fuck.

It wasn't until later that I realized he was only giving me enough rope to hang myself.

* * *

I MET A GIRL, Not Fucking Gwen, and fell in love. I thought that she was the one for me. I thought that I could finally settle down and move forward with my life. I thought that I could control my using and that things would be okay. I thought that as long as I stayed away from heroin, that everything would be fine.

I was very wrong. Nothing was fine. And I couldn't stay away from heroin.

I was acting as if I was Mr. Rehabilitated, when really, I was Mr.   I-should-be-going-to-rehab-and-getting-help-or-I'm-going-to-find-out-what-rock-bottom-really-looks-

like-very-soon.

An example of how hard and fast I was falling towards rock bottom was when I invented the game Riggy roulette.

Let me explain...

One day, Kimo (y'all remember Kimo, right? Baby mama. Stripper. Porn star. Etc.) called me up and asked if I wanted to hang out. Before he even got the question out of his mouth, I knew that it was going to be one fucked-up night. Whenever Kimo and I got together, shit got real.

I don't mean real as in we talked about life issues and tried to solve them like mature adults.

I mean real as in I don't know how either of us never ended up going to the hospital or the morgue.

See, at the time, both Kimo and I were on parallel paths of self-destruction, and we were equally clueless to the fact.

You can only imagine where this is going, right?

That, or you really don't care, but you've invested too much of your time reading this nonsense to turn back now.

Either way, I'm going to tell you.

When I pulled into the driveway, Kimo came running out of his house jumping up and down like a little school girl who just gave her first blow job and couldn't wait to tell her friends about it. He had the biggest shit-eating grin that I've ever seen in my life and he was so giddy I thought he might die from lack of oxygen. I'd never seen the fucker so happy.

His happiness only made me happier because I knew that very few things on this planet could make Kimo *that* happy. And there was only one thing that would make him that happy when I was around.

Can you guess what it was?

Come on. I bet you can.

Yes, that's right, kids. Drugs.

But what *kind* of drugs, you ask?

All. Fucking. Sorts.

Kimo literally dragged me out of my car and into his house, where sitting on his table were five separate Ziploc bags. Each bag was about half full and contained a different looking substance.

When I saw everything that was laid out on the table, my jaw hit the floor and my eyes bulged out of their sockets like when you put it in a chick's ass without telling her first.

Me: "Dude, what in the fuck is all that?"

Kimo: "Our night."

Me: "Do you know CPR?"

Kimo: "Nope." Insert shit-eating grin. "Do you?"

Me: "Fuck no."

Kimo: "Cool."

Me: "We're so fucked."

Kimo: "Yup."

I looked at each bag and discovered that Kimo had been a good boy and covered all of the basic food groups: Heroin. Cocaine. Crack. Molly (MDMA, not this fake shit going around these days). And Meth.

There was enough dope sitting in front of me to impress Motley Crüe.

I have to admit, I was torn. Half of me was scared shitless while the other half was ready to fucking party.

I only had one problem.

It wasn't the fact that there was enough dope on the table to send us both to prison for life. Nor the fact that Kimo was expecting to dabble into each bag on this very night. My problem was that I lacked the proper tools to embark on the wild journey laid out before me. I had only brought one syringe with me.

At this point in the story, I feel confident that everyone knows what a fucking syringe is by now, right?

So, I posed my problem to Kimo.

Me: "Dude, I only brought one rig with me."

Kimo smiled, reached into his back pocket and pulled out two brand ten packs of rigs. The man was prepared.

Me: "There is a god."

I found myself staring at the bags of dope, sort of lost in a trance. I was both scared for my life and as giddy as a chomo (child molester) at Chuck E. Cheese. I found myself pondering a single question: *Which one of these is going to kill me tonight?*

And that's when the idea hit me.

Riggy roulette.

Me: "DUDE! I've. Got. An. Idea."

Kimo: "Oh boy."

Me: "Nonono dude. This is fucking epic. I think this is my best, worst idea ever!"

Kimo: "Better than when you decided to drop acid in the mouths of passed-out drunk people?"

Me: "That was a great idea. But I will admit that waking them up later on with the air horn was a bit over the top."

Kimo: "What about the time you were walking around that party giving people bumps of "coke" when it was really special K?"

Me: "Umm..."

Kimo: "Or what about that time when you dropped that roofie in a beer, and mixed it in with a bunch of other beers, then had everyone standing around slam a beer. What was that shit called again?"

Me: "Roofie roulette."

Kimo: (snapping his fingers) "That's it!"

Me: "Well this idea is better than all those ideas. Combined. I call this one..... *Riggy* roulette."

Kimo: "Oh god."

Me: "She's not going to save either of us bro, so let's not start that nonsense."

Kimo: "Fuck me. Okay, how does this "Riggy roulette" thing work?"

Me: "It's simple. We each fill up all of our rigs. Two rigs for each bag that's laid out on the table. Then we mix 'em up so we don't know which is which. Once that's done, I'll point to a random rig on the table and that's the one you've gotta use. You'll do the same for me. We won't know what we're shooting up until it hits us! It's going to be fucking epic!"

I must have had a seriously sinister face on at that moment because Kimo actually took a step away from me.

Kimo: "No. Fucking. Way."

Me: "Dude."

Kimo: "I'm not doing that shit. That's fucking insane bro. Even for us."

Me: "Dude."

Kimo: "There's no fucking way."

Me: "Dude."

Kimo: "Seriously??"

Me: "Dude."

Kimo: "No way."

Me: "Dude."

Kimo: "One of us is going to die tonight you know."

Me: "Dude."

Kimo: "Is there any way of talking you out of this is?"

I hesitated like I was actually thinking it over for a minute.

Me: "Nope."

Kimo looked at the floor and shook his head in total defeat. He obviously didn't see this coming when he decided to obtain all that dope. And he definitely didn't see this coming when he called me and told me that it was time to party. I could tell that he was trying to understand how I just managed to take an already out-of-control situation and turn it into an absolute disaster, even before we got started.

He called me with a shit ton of free drugs and a let's party attitude. What the fuck else did he expect was going to happen?

Kimo: "Fuck it. I'm down for the cause."

Me: "That's my boy!"

Now no matter how bad you think the *idea* of Riggy roulette is, I can assure you, its *application* was a thousand times worse. All we were doing was one giant speed ball. All. Night. Long. Not only were we doing a giant speed ball, but neither of us knew what drug was coming next.

First it was the dope (heroin).

Then it was the crack (And yes, even though crack comes in a rock form, it can be put into a needle. All you need is a little lemon juice. It's basic chemistry. Acids and bases. Didn't anyone watch Breaking Bad?).

Then it was who the fuck knew.

Shot after shot after shot after shot after shot.

Like I stated previously, I have no fucking clue how neither of us overdosed that night. Well, *night* doesn't really describe it. It was more like two days. With all the different types of drugs going through our systems, sleep was not much of an option. So, we did what we knew how to do best: we got fucked-up.

Half the time, I didn't know if I was coming or going. One minute, my heart was ready to beat out of my chest. The next, I had this high-pitched ringing in my ears. Then I'd get really paranoid and would start staring out the window thinking that the cops were about to bust the door in. Then I'd start telling Kimo my life story, over and over again.

It was absolute in-fucking-sanity.

We were playing Russian roulette with ten fucking bullets and walked away without a scratch. Any single one of those shots could have killed us. The combination alone *should have* killed us. Out of all the bullshit and shenanigans I've ever been a part of, out of all the insane fucking ideas that I've ever had, to this day, Riggy roulette is the one that still makes me sit back and think: *Wow. What in the fuck was I thinking?*

OF COURSE, I did nothing about my problem. I fell for my own bullshit that I was telling everyone and believed every word I said.

Does any of this sound familiar?

I was already on the fast track towards rock bottom, and because it was obvious, I couldn't see it. It only took a few steps for me to get started, but once I was moving, I was like the motherfucking Juggernaut. There was no stopping me.

Step 1: Steal my mom's prescription medication.

Step 2: Steal other family members' prescription medication.

Step 3: Start hanging out with old buddies.

Step 4: Make some new "friends."

Step 5: Wake up with tattoo on back of my head.

If you recall, the story started out with me going drinking with my buddies because I had a particularly difficult morning. What had happened was I had come home after working the overnight shift as an electrician, remodeling a Walmart.

Working the overnight shift sucks.

Working the overnight shift and coming home to a door that had been busted in sucks even more.

Working the overnight shift, coming home to a door that had been busted in, finding the kitchen in complete disarray with medical paraphernalia all over the floor and not being able to find your mother is enough to send someone over the edge.

Well, isn't it just my luck that I'm highly experienced in stressful and traumatic situations?

Most people would have flipped their shit at that point. Me? I just called the hospital and asked if my mother had been brought in during the night. They told me that she was there, but that's all they could tell me.

Next, I called the police station to find out what the fuck happened. About fifteen minutes later, an officer showed up at my place and informed me that my mother had tried to kill herself by taking an abundance of prescription pills. Sometime after she had swallowed all the pills, she had called 911 and said that she was having trouble breathing and needed immediate help. Emergency responders received the call and had to break the door down in order to get into the residence. They found my mother unresponsive and had to rush her to the emergency room.

All I could do was roll my eyes and groan. Call me insensitive if you want (and I know you will), but this isn't the first time something like this had happened. If I had to count how many times my mother has tried to kill herself throughout my life, I'd have to start using my toes because I'd run out of fingers. So go fuck yourselves, you judgmental pricks.

The cop told me they had found my mother's journal with a suicide note written in it, but that it was being held as evidence. He informed me that once my mother was conscious and the doctors figured out what to do with her, then the journal would be returned.

After digesting everything the cop told me, I started drinking. Mind you this is around eight in the morning.

Forty-five minutes later there was a knock on the door. I got up to answer it with a beer in hand, and opened it up to see none other than my parole officer standing on the front porch.

HE INSTANTLY LOOKED DOWN to my hand and saw the beer. He looked back to me and said:

PO: "Rough morning?"

Me: "You could say that."

PO: "Uh-huh. Care to enlighten me a bit?"

As I took a sip of the beer, because at that point I was already fucked and didn't care...

Me: "Sure. Come on in. Want a beer?"

PO: "You're fucking kidding me, right?"

He took two steps into my place and saw how the kitchen was destroyed and the medical shit laying all over the floor and said:

PO: "On second thought, maybe I will take one. This could get interesting."

I walked to the fridge, grabbed myself a fresh beer and one for the PO and told him what I knew about what had happened. He drank his beer and listened to the story with utter disbelief. All he could do was shake his head and sip his beer while I told him about it, along with a little family history.

After he finished his beer and I finished talking, he surveyed the scene one last time and told me:

PO: "This is your one get out of jail free card. I suggest you use it wisely."

And that's exactly what I did!

After taking a shower and going to the hospital, I called some buddies and told them to meet me at the bar. I said fuck you to sleep and decided to heed my parole officer's advice regarding my get out of jail free card. The fact that my mother was on life support in the ICU was of little concern to me right then. I was going to get fucked-up and that's all that mattered.

And we *all* know how well that turned out for me....

Step 6: Start shooting heroin (again).

Step 7: Start pawning shit (again).

Step 8: Start scrapping wire (again).

What is that saying about repeating the same thing over and over while expecting different results?

But wait!

In the spirit of not disappointing anyone, I get worse.

Step 9: Steal blank checks from my stepdad.

Step 10: Forge signature on said checks and cash them.

My family found out about the checks and ended up sitting me down for a *What the fuck are you doing? You need serious help,* conversation. I didn't listen to a word that was said beyond "we're not pressing charges." Once I heard that, I gave them my best *I'm going to get help,* speech.

And of course, they believed me.

And of course, I did nothing of what I promised.

My solution?

I decided to move in with Not Fucking Gwen and her kids in a place far away from my family's prying eyes.

By now, I had been out of prison for almost a year. I had already lost one job, was on my way to losing a second, and had committed several felonious acts (which I never got caught for) all due to my heroin use.

Moving in with Not Fucking Gwen and taking on all the responsibilities that come with living on your own and helping to raise someone else's children was obviously the smartest move I could make, right?

Well.......

It lasted 42 days.

Which brings us back full circle to the winner of the epically fucking bad night award: When I woke up hand-cuffed to a bed in the ICU.

I woke up that Friday morning to Not Fucking Gwen screaming at me. It was seven in the morning and I hadn't had my morning "get right" shot yet, so I wasn't really feeling the situation.

Not Fucking Gwen was screaming at me because the night before, her aunt, Big Red, had called and said that most of her jewelry was missing. Not Fucking Gwen immediately asked me if I knew anything about it– she was aware by this point that I was getting high, but was clueless as to how bad it had truly become– and I did exactly what the situation called for at that moment: I lied and denied.

The next morning (this would be the morning Not Fucking Gwen was screaming at me), Big Red called again and told Not Fucking Gwen some interesting information. That her neighbors had seen me at her house, in the middle of the day, when no one was home. They didn't think anything about it because they'd seen me there all the time with Not Fucking Gwen.

Well, it didn't take Shaggy and Scooby to put together what had happened.

Jewelry is missing.

Lawn Mower was there, alone, when no one else was home.

Lawn Mower used to have a serious drug problem.

Lawn Mower is currently using drugs.

Lawn Mower has a history of stealing and pawning things in order to feed his drug habit.

Therefore: Lawn Mower must have stolen the jewelry.

So Big Red and her husband, Andre, called Gwen, informed her of their super sleuth deductions and that they were in fact on their way to our house to confront me.

Not Fucking Gwen (rightfully) went ballistic.

I (rightfully) got up, tucked tail, and got the fuck out of Dodge.

Life was shit for me at this point. I was in trouble with parole for failing a urine screening (or two), I had just gotten fired from *another* job, and I was shooting up a few grams of heroin a day.

I knew that I was in some serious fucking trouble because as I was (literally) running out the door, I heard:

Not Fucking Gwen: "You're in some serious fucking trouble Lawn Mower, they've already called the cops."

It took me less than two seconds to compute what that meant:

1. That's a *new* charge.

2. I'm already on parole.

3. I just violated my parole with a new charge.

4. I'm going back to prison.

Fuck. That. Noise.

Just in case you're not really paying attention, this is the point when I hit rock bottom at full fucking speed.

Now I'm running from Not Fucking Gwen, Not Fucking Gwen's family, my family, parole, and the cops. Just a typical Friday in the life of Lawn Mower. When I get caught, I'm going back to prison for a long time. I'm a heroin addict going through withdrawals, and I'm too much of a coward to face anyone or anything. I needed to do something.

My solution:

Self-homicide.

Yes, I've already stated *multiple fucking times* that I'm a coward. I don't need your smart-ass side comments.

Instead of running away from something, I was now a man on a mission. The plan was already formulated somewhere in the back of my head, and I was on autopilot. I drove across town to my Aunt Katie's house and kicked in the front door. I knew that both Aunt Katie and her fiancé Cyclops were at work. I also knew that my Aunt Katie had copious amounts of prescription medication in her medicine cabinet, and I was fully aware of the fact that Cyclops owned many guns. One way or the other, I was going to die that day.

Once inside, I ran straight for the medicine cabinet and started swallowing pills. *A LOT* of them. While swallowing a large number of miscellaneous medications, I also did a huge fucking shot of heroin. I was going to go out with a *bang*. No pun intended.

Next, I ran into their bedroom and saw one of Cyclops' guns laying out on the bedside table with a loaded clip right next to it (he must have known that I'd be coming).

I picked up the gun, slammed the clip into place, slid a bullet into the chamber, put the gun to my head and......

The next thing I knew, I was in the ICU, and I was *fucked*.

It wasn't until later that I found out everything that happened.

Obviously, I lost the nerve to use the gun.

What I didn't lose the nerve to do was take my aunt's jewelry and run out of the house.

While I still had the gun.

For those of you who aren't well-versed in New York state penal law, I have now elevated my crime status to a first degree, armed burglary. Which is a violent felony offense. Let us not forget that this is an armed burglary by a *convicted felon* (on parole) no less.

I'm really racking up the points, aren't I?

Somehow, I managed to make it to a pawn shop, pawned all of the jewelry, and found the dope man.

Don't ask me how because I have no fucking clue.

Meanwhile, while all of this was going on, Aunt Katie's neighbor had seen me come and go and decided to call my aunt at work about it. When she described the vehicle that was in her driveway, my aunt immediately knew that it was me. Aunt Katie rushed home, saw what I had done, and called the cops.

That's how I became wanted for *multiple* felonies.

Because of the missing firearm, I was also considered *armed and dangerous*.

But wait! There's more!

Not Fucking Gwen had called The Sister to tell her about what had happened that morning. While The Sister was still on the phone with Not Fucking Gwen, Aunt Katie also called The Sister to tell her what *else* I had done.

Naturally, my sister *freaked the fuck out* and called me. I spoke with her briefly and told her that I wasn't going back to prison. I told her to tell everyone that I loved them and that I was sorry.

This information was relayed to the authorities, and that's the point when I was considered to be armed, dangerous, AND suicidal.

By this time, every cop in town was looking for me, and find me they did. I was driving down the road, shooting up heroin and refusing to pull over. The cops shut down the highway as I took them on a "low speed chase" across town.

At 33 MPH the whole way.

No bullshit.

This continued for a while until I simply pulled over. My sister told me that she was talking to me the entire time and somehow convinced me to pull over. My mother told me that she watched the whole thing on the news. Including the part when I was ripped out of my SUV and hit with a taser.

I remember NONE of this.

Fortunately for me, since I was considered a 'suicidal party,' the news couldn't broadcast my name.

Unfortunately for me, I was in a shitload of trouble, with one more problem to add to the mess: no gun. The gun wasn't on my person nor in my vehicle. When the cops asked me where the gun was, I opened my mouth to speak, and dropped dead. Literally.

For a little over a minute, I was clinically dead.

Gold star to me for reaching my goal!

The medics on hand brought me back to life. I wasn't conscious, but I was alive. And I was ***fucked***.

If you're reading this and thinking to yourself *this guy is a complete fucking scumbag*, wait until you read what I *haven't* told you yet.

My mother and Aunt Katie lost both of their parents at a very young age. Between them, they only had a handful of things that belonged to their parents. The majority of these items were in the form of jewelry.

Which were kept at my Aunt Katie's house.

This was the same house I just burglarized.

And the same jewelry I had just pawned.

FYI: These items were never recovered. But that's only because the pawn shop owner was a shady cockmonger.

Now, if you think that I can't sink any lower, you're wrong. Because what you don't understand yet is my *relationship* with Aunt Katie.

Aunt Katie had *always* been there for me. She had always been a pillar of support for me throughout my entire life. She had never, not once, turned her back on me, nor denied me anything I needed or asked for. She paid for my lawyer in Florida, ensured that I always had money in my commissary account, and made sure that there was always money on the phone so I could call home.

She came to pick me up from prison when I was released and drove me back to New York. She bought me new clothes and tools for work, and even loaned me the money to buy my vehicle.

Without Aunt Katie, I would have been fucked a long, long time ago. I'm indebted to her in so many ways it's unbelievable. These are debts that go far beyond anything of monetary value.

And now she's a victim of one of my crimes.

I always hurt anyone who means anything to me. I don't just burn my bridges– I drop atomic bombs on them and then I piss on the ashes.

And then, when I was at absolute zero, the lowest possible point that I could reach in my life, the point at which I needed someone the most, I had no one left that I could turn to for help.

There was no one to blame but myself.

Ladies and gentlemen, in case you're wondering, this is what rock bottom looks like.

* * *

WHEN YOU'RE a kid and you get into trouble, you know it's serious when an adult throws your middle name into the mix (Lawn-Fucking-Mower).

When you're an adult and you get into trouble, you know it's serious when the judge comes to see *you*. I don't mean you were in their courtroom and they came out from the chambers, or they walked to the back of the courtroom where the cells are. I'm talking about when the Judge travels across town for the sole purpose of meeting with you.

On a Saturday night.

For a little while, I thought the cop was just fucking with me. So when the Judge walked into my room (sadly without his robe on) in the ICU, I knew I was fucked.

When he read off the laundry list of charges, adding statements such as: "which carries a maximum sentence of life in prison," "fucked" no longer seemed like a strong enough word.

If you want to know exactly what my charges were, eat a dick. I'm not going to discuss that abortion. Just know that I had a couple of violent felonies (by a parolee no less), and what I was looking at was the actual possibility of spending the rest of my nights cuddling with Bubba, and the rest of my days wearing adult diapers because my asshole would be nothing more than a gaping hole.

Which, if you've never been in that situation, I can assure you, it's not a good feeling.

And I'm talking about the situation of looking at life in prison, not having your asshole reamed out by a big black man, you twisted fucks.

When the Judge finished describing just how fucked I was, and the court proceeding was "officially" over, he leaned a bit closer to my bed and said something to me.

Judge: "Son, you're in a lot of trouble here, and I'm not just referring to your charges. From what I understand you're extremely lucky to be alive right now, and you shouldn't take that for granted. Most people don't make it back from where you just were."

And with that, he left.

Pretty solid advice from a guy who just told me that my life is basically over.

IF YOU WANT to experience hell on earth– I mean *true* hell on earth– become completely addicted to heroin, rack up a bunch of felonies, get arrested, go to jail, and detox.

Detoxing, in and of itself, is undoubtedly fucking horrible. There's nothing to even compare it to. Having a superflu with AIDS, combined with an aggressive form of SARS, on top of stage four colon cancer is a semi-close description of it, but I still feel that even that lacks the true flavor of what a heroin detox is like.

This detox, however, took things to a monumental level.

What made it so monumental, you might ask?

Two words: turtle suit.

A turtle suit is an anti-suicide smock. It's a tear-resistant, single-piece outer garment which is used to prevent someone from forming a noose with it. It's a sturdily quilted, collarless, sleeveless gown that pretty much looks like a Fred Flintstone dress. It's thick, heavy, itchy, green, and awkward as fuck to wear.

I was a little confused when the cop threw the turtle suit at me and told me to put it, and only it, on. No socks, no underwear, no nada.

Me: "What the fuck is this for?"

Cop: "You're on suicide watch."

Me: "Suicide watch?"

Cop: "Yup."

Me: "But I'm not suicid....."

Oh. Right. The whole felonious-car chase-overdose thing.

Me: "Never mind."

I put on the turtle suit, felt far worse than I did five minutes prior, and was led to the elevator where we went up to the fifth floor.

* * *

I HEARD the screaming before the elevator doors even opened.

Me: "Where the fuck are we?"

Cop: "Fifth floor."

Ohh that explains it.

Me: "Oh. Well, what the fuck is 'the fifth floor,' and is all this screaming normal?"

Cop: "This is the mental health and PC floor. And the screaming is actually pretty mild right now."

Mental health and protective custody.

Fucking awesome.

If you want to know what *completely fucking eerie* feels like, be the new guy walking onto a mental health floor. Trust me, it's great. When the floor goes from absolutely fucking bananas to dead silent because everyone is staring at you, it's really fucking creepy.

The setup of the mental health floor was pretty typical– similar to any jail you've ever seen on TV. Two tiers with around thirty cells on each tier. Single-man cells with a solid door instead of bars, and a small window in the door about five inches wide and three feet high.

There were two separate sets of stairs on either end of the pod that lead up to the second tier. The stairs and the second tier were completely enclosed in security glass, which I found odd.

Me: "What's with the Plexiglass?"

Cop: "So nobody can do a swan dive off the second tier."

Makes sense.

Cop: "Yup, we don't want one of you nutbags hurting yourselves, now, do we?"

It wasn't lost on me that I was included in the "you nutbags" statement, but I decided to leave it be. At the time I had bigger issues to deal with.

I was led to the far corner of the first tier where there were several tables set up in front of several cells. Each table had a cop sitting at it, literally staring into the cell in front of him.

I walked into the cell and the door closed behind me. The cop who brought me to the cell sat at the table in front of my cell door, sat down, and just stared at me.

Right, "suicide watch."

There was nothing in the cell but your standard issue sink/toilet combo and a mat on the floor. There was no pillow, no blanket, no toothbrush, no nothing. I didn't even get a roll of toilet paper. I had to ask for some each time I had to use the toilet.

And yes, when I had to shit, someone was there watching. It's an awkward experience having someone you don't know stare at you while you're dropping a deuce. The experience is only heightened when they watch as you wipe. One time, I even showed the cop the poo on the toilet paper just for good measure.

Because that's me, Mr. Maturity.

I'd never been a guest in a nuthouse before, nor do I deal with "crazy" well. I'd had some experiences dealing with some off-kilter people while growing up, and it was *not* pleasant. So being in a mental health unit, in jail, while detoxing, didn't sit very well with me.

When the guy in the cell next to me brought out his "home-made" teddy bear collection to show everyone, I knew I had to get the fuck off of that floor immediately. I'll let you piece together where he got something brown and pliable to make the bears with.

It took me a week to get out of the turtle suit, and about a month to get off of the mental health floor. It didn't really take Sigmund Freud to figure out that I wasn't A) crazy or B) suicidal. I was just a coward who didn't want to pay the consequences for his actions.

I was only thirty days clean and still going through post-acute withdrawals. I had a lot of anxiety and was only sleeping a couple hours a night. I had no idea what was going on with my case, and I was freaking the fuck out.

The only thing that was really keeping me going was Not Fucking Gwen. Don't ask me why– because I still don't know why– but she was standing by my side, which gave me hope for the future. And in jail, hope can be a powerful thing. Trust me.

I saw both my lawyer and my parole officer on the same day. It was a good news, bad news type of day. The good news came from my lawyer, who told me that Cyclops' gun had been recovered and that the state wasn't pursuing any further charges in that area. I was yet to receive any sort of plea offer but she (my lawyer) was working on it.

My parole officer came with the bad news. He informed me that I had been violated and that he had contacted Florida about my violation. He let me know that Florida would be issuing a warrant for my arrest for the violation of probation.

Great.

* * *

AFTER A MONTH on the crazy floor, I was moved to general population. The classification officer that moved me said that I'd be much happier in gen pop.

She was very wrong.

General population was filled with complete fucking animals. I'm talking the absolute dregs of society. The reason stereotypes were created, all sardined together in the same fucking place. When dudes are locked up in jail and they're facing some serious fucking time, shit gets real. One day I received a couple of cracked ribs and then some pepper spray to the face. After that I decided to move to where I heard it was a bit calmer.

They called it the "clean and sober pod," and it was definitely one of the best decisions I made while I was in county jail. Besides it being a calm area to be in while fighting your case, the jail offered a multitude of programs and courses that one could partake in, including AA, NA, and anger management. Not only was I able to start working on my recovery, I was also able to get my OSHA 10-hour card and a few other state-recognized certifications.

Fighting my case proved to be much more difficult than working on my recovery (which was no fucking picnic either). I was charged with a few felonies and was facing a lot of time, the maximum being twenty-five to life.

When my lawyer came to me with my first plea offer, I almost shit myself. Ten years. Five in prison and five on parole, if I plead guilty to two counts of burglary in the second degree. Not a bad deal considering everything involved in my case. But even so, I turned it down.

I turned it down for three reasons:

1. Burglary in the second degree is a violent felony offense. I'm not a violent person, I have never been a violent person, nor did I want any violent felonies on my record.

2. I was a drug addict. I needed a program, not prison. (Gee, does that sound familiar?)

3. It was the first offer. You *never* take the first offer.

My lawyer was a tad frustrated with me for not jumping on the deal. She said that my charges carried a maximum of fifteen years. I told her that I wasn't a violent person and that I wasn't copping out to a violent charge. She countered with the fact that I broke into a house and stole a gun, and that that's very much a violent act. I parried by saying that I was a drug-crazed, suicidal coward, not a violent felon. And she concluded that this offer was a plea offer only. I didn't have to take it, and if I piss her off, the ADA could bring back the first-degree felony at any time, take the plea offer off the table, and take me to trial. As scared as I was, and against the advice of both my family and my attorney, I stood my ground and said no to the deal.

The rest of my plea offers went like this:

Lawyer: "Okay, the ADA is offering two non-violent burglaries, with three to six for each."

Me: "Perfect!"

Lawyer: "Ran consecutively."

Me: "Wait. That's six to twelve years in prison. That's *more* time than my first offer."

Lawyer: "Yes, I'm aware of that."

Me: "Well fuck that."

My lawyer just sighed and left.

(A few days later....)

Lawyer: "Eight years in prison, with five on parole."

Me: "What the fuck? Absolutely not."

(A few weeks later....)

Lawyer: "Ten years prison, five years parole."

Me: "This isn't how it works on TV. The offers are supposed to go DOWN, not up."

Lawyer: "This isn't TV."

Me: "No shit."

(And a few weeks later....)

Lawyer: "You're going to love this."

Me: "We finally got a good offer?"

Lawyer: "Yeah. Twelve years prison, five years on parole. Or trial."

I just sat there blinking.

Me: "Can we go back to that first offer?"

Lawyer: "No, you fucked that up."

Me: "Fuck."

I was stuck between a rock and a hard place. I didn't know what to do, but I knew that I couldn't just agree to throw away twelve years of my life. I needed more time to think, so I told my lawyer that I wanted to take it to trial. My lawyer told me that we had no chance *whatsoever* at winning in a trial, and that I'd be looking at a minimum of fifteen years when (not if) I was found guilty. I informed my lawyer that I understood, but I was going to take my chances. Plus, it's not like I was actually paying my lawyer, she was court-appointed, so fuck it.

What the fuck was I thinking, right?

Honestly, I still can't answer that question. I just knew that I couldn't say yes to what was being offered. I was scared shit-less of what was going to happen when I lost in trial, but *you* try agreeing to twelve years in prison and see how you feel about it.

So, I waited for my lawyer.

And I waited.

And waited.

Until finally, the American-fucking-dream came in to save my ass.

My lawyer strolled in on a Friday afternoon and informed me that the ADA working my case had quit the prosecutor's office in order to start her own defense practice. Apparently working for the state paid shit, and she wanted a better life for herself and her family. My case got dumped on another ADA who had an ass load of his own work to do, and in the spirit of getting my case off his fucking desk, he was willing to offer me two non-violent charges, with three-and-a-half to seven years each, ran concurrently (which is Legalspeak for: at the same damn time!), if I agreed to the offer right there and then.

God. Bless. America.

Me: "Why of course I'll accept that offer."

Can't you just see the shit-eating grin I had on my face?

I'm pretty sure my lawyer wanted to punch me right then.

Even though I was going to prison (again) and not a drug program (again), I was fucking ecstatic. If I behaved myself in prison, I could be out in a couple of years, instead of a couple of decades.

I chalked that up to a win in my book.

Only an asshole like me could call going *back* to prison a win.

What I really couldn't call a win were the visits I was getting while all this legal bullshit was going on. Yes, Not Fucking Gwen would come see me, and that was great. What was far from fantastic was the visits I would get from Mommy Dearest and Beavis (my first cousin with whom I almost missed my grandfathers funeral).

They would come together, *high as fucking kites.* At one visit, Beavis was actually nodding out– Addictspeak for: being so high that you actually start falling asleep in place– during the visit. Mommy Dearest wasn't quite at that level, but she was really fucking close. I couldn't believe their audacity. I mean, there I was sitting in jail, waiting to go to prison because of my fucking heroin habit, and those two would come strolling in, practically wearing neon signs that said "I'm high on heroin." I almost wished that I had grown up in a trailer park just to make the scenario complete.

I finally had enough one day and told Mommy Dearest not to visit me anymore, and to make sure that Beavis didn't come either. Neither of them could understand why, and I wasn't about to break it all down for them. They weren't ready for that conversation.

Nor was I.

I wasn't much for being honest and direct back then, and I would avoid conflict at every turn.

I was a giant vagina, I know.

* * *

THIS WILL BE another prime example of my amazingly creative writing skills. This incident happened in New York shortly before I got arrested, but the opportunity to weave it into this masterpiece that you've been reading never really presented itself, so once again I decided to just toss it in at the end of the section and not care if you agree with my decision or not.

And since I'm airing out pretty much all my dirty laundry for everyone's personal amusement, why stop now, right?

Of course, you'd agree with me. They're not *your* personal secrets we're openly discussing here, are they?

Anyways...

I was working for a local electrical contractor and I had to do a lot of traveling for work. On this particular day, I was mid-swan dive into the abyss of my rock bottom. Naturally, since it was blatantly obvious to everyone else, I was completely clueless as to what was unfolding in my life.

It was a Friday– which for most of the working class means that it was payday– and I had skipped out of work early in order to meet up with the dope man. I hadn't had any dope in over twenty-four hours and I wasn't feeling very well.

Translation: I felt like ten pounds of hammered shit in a three-pound bucket.

I was sick, anxious, jittery, irritated, and of course, in a life-or-death battle with my IBS.

My IBS is a funny thing, and I don't mean humorous either. It seems to come and go as it pleases. I could go months without any sign of it, and then all of a sudden:

Hello my friend.

This was one of *those days.*

What made it worse were the facts that I:

A) Was dope sick.

B) Had money on me.

C) Was on my way to get dope.

For those of you who lack basic addict math skills, A+B+C = **NOT FUCKING GOOD.**

When you add IBS into the aforementioned equation, the result is the equivalent of having an IV line of coffee, laxative, prune juice, apple juice, and refried beans.

No fucking bueno, señor.

My stomach started bubbling and I knew that I was in trouble. I was in code black, which meant that I was beyond the point of no return. The clock was ticking and I only had seconds remaining before a fecal explosion would ensue.

Once again, I found myself in an all-too-familiar situation. I was in desperate need of a toilet, I was in the middle of a residential neighborhood where I didn't know a fucking soul for miles, and I had an immediate need for a toilet.

The clock was ticking....

10. *What the fuck do I do?*

9. *Oh my god. Oh my god. Oh my god.*

8. *Should I just pull over and shit in the road?*

7. *Should I just shit my pants?*

6. A small fart slipped out and it was *very* wet...

5. My breathing became very labored and rapid...

4. *I hate my life.*

3. I started sweating profusely and clenching my asshole closed as tight as I could.

And then......

2.

1. With lightning-fast speed, I reached into the back seat of my vehicle and grabbed a box that had a few parts and pieces still in it from the job that I had just skipped out on.

I pulled my pants down in less than a tenth of a second and had the box under my ass in less time than that.

0. ....

Remember that scene from *Dumb and Dumber* when Lloyd was in the bathroom after drinking the Turbo Lax?

Well, this was just like that.

Only, I wasn't on a toilet in a house. I was driving.

During the middle of the day.

In a residential neighborhood.

I was *that fucking talented.*

After I emptied the entire contents of my bowels into the box, a brief period of relief washed over me. It was right then when I realized that I now had a small dilemma on my hands.

What the fuck do I do with the box?

I wasn't going to leave it in my SUV. It fucking reeked. And of course, there were no garbage cans anywhere in sight.

So, being the mature, responsible, and upstanding citizen that I was, I did the only thing a situation like this called for:

I pulled over, left the box full of my feces on the side of the road, and went about my business.

I mean, that's what Jesus would have done, right?

Minutes later, I got my dope, got high, and went about my day, completely forgetting about the entire incident.

Monday morning, I reported to the shop like usual in order to get material for the day. While I was talking to a coworker, my boss walked up to us and asked if he could have a word with me. His *exact* words were that he had "something to show me."

He brought me to the far back corner of the warehouse, where, sitting on a stool, was a box in a clear garbage bag. He looked at me with a look of complete disgust and asked:

Boss: "What's in the box, Lawn Mower?"

Well, I didn't need to look in the box to figure it out. It was the same exact box that I had shit in, discarded, and forgot about on Friday afternoon.

At this point you're probably wondering how in the hell did the box get there in the first place? Because I know that I sure as shit was. Excuse the pun.

You might have a hard time swallowing this. I lived this shit and even I have a hard time believing it......

Everyone has or knows someone who has a neighbor that likes to stick their nose into *everyone's business.* No matter where you live, what city or state you live in, there's always *someone* sticking their nose into your business or watching you. It's like some unwritten law of the universe.

This neighborhood was no different. Plus it had a neighborhood watch group, with a little old hag who I'll call "Cuntrag" posing as the self-appointed CEO.

Cuntrag was some retired old widow with nothing better to do than stare out her front windows all fucking afternoon.

So naturally when some strange SUV stops practically right in front of her house and drops off a box on the side of the road, Cuntrag just *had* to investigate.

Well, imagine her surprise when she looked in the box and discovered that it was full of miscellaneous construction material and human excrement.

Still, that doesn't explain *how* the box ended up in the back of the warehouse at the shop on Monday morning, does it?

The answer to that little riddle is actually quite simple. The company's name and address were printed on the "ship to" label on the top of the box.

Of fucking course. Right?

Well, when Cuntrag discovered the lovely box of brown porridge I had left in her neighborhood, she was "so beside herself" that she *just had to report it.*

But report it to whom? The police? The FBI? The EPA perhaps?

No. She had to report it to the fucking *company* silly.

And instead of just looking the company up online and calling them, Cuntrag felt obligated to bring said box right to the source.

Fucking bitch.

Cuntrag brought the box to my boss and told him what she had witnessed. She described the vehicle that left the box on the side of the road, and my boss assured her that he knew *exactly* who drove that vehicle.

My boss then apologized profusely for the inconvenience and assured her that he would personally handle the matter.

Which brings us back to the warehouse, with my boss and I staring at a box full of my shit, while he awaited an explanation from me.

But honestly, what could I say in such a situation?

Nothing. Absolutely nothing. Because there was nothing to be said. There were simply no words.

My boss, however, did have some words to say.

Boss: "You're fired."

I kind of figured as much.

Boss: "And, you owe me $75.37 for the destroyed material. You can keep the box if you like."

This was by far the most expensive shit that I've *ever* taken.

After this happened, I seriously debated purchasing Depends.

IF BY SOME chance you happen to know who Cuntrag is, and she ever happens to tell you the story of the time she found a box of shit someone left in front of her house one day, please let her know that every night since this incident I have prayed and prayed that she contracts leprosy and/or Ebola.

IF I HAD to give you an analogy about prison, I would say that prison in Florida was **_prison,_** whereas prison in New York was more like summer camp. But even so, that doesn't mean everything was all peaches and chocolate kok the entire time.

This is what went down (is that a bad phrase to use?) in the New York State Department of Corrections and Community Supervision, henceforth known as: DOCCS.

ON A SIDE NOTE, this section of this book consists of three and a half years of my fucking life. So before you go and bitch about how long and drawn out it is, just remember something: _you_ chose to read this shit. I didn't fucking ask you to.

To those of you who are still at a third grade reading level, I'll dumb that down for you: this is the "meat and potatoes" of the story. So it's really long.

* * *

ELMIRA CORRECTIONAL FACILITY, AKA "THE HILL," was opened in 1876 as Elmira Reformatory. It houses roughly 1,800 inmates, and it's a complete fucking shithole.

Inappropriately placed at the front entrance to this (all-male) prison, a reception prison at that, is the lovely statue pictured below:

THE TITLE OF THIS MASTERPIECE, you ask? "Elmira, Builder of Men."

When I look at this statue all I can think is that the standing dude is trying to comfort the sitting dude because it's the sitting dude's first day in prison and he needs a moment to gather himself. Plus, the standing dude just informed the sitting dude of the unwritten rule in prison: "If it's your first night in prison, and you've got a cellmate, you're gunna be fuckin' or suckin' by the end of the night."

When I saw it upon my arrival to the prison, I didn't even know what to think.

I mean seriously, what the fuck?

When I got out of the van, I was expecting a whole bunch of screaming, yelling, and other miscellaneous bullshit to occur, just like in Florida. Yet none of that happened.

I was stripped, showered, and changed into prison attire relatively quickly. Once that was done, I was told to sit in a giant cage in the middle of the room where all the other inmates were sitting. When I got into the holding cell, I noticed a flat-screen TV hanging from the bars, and a movie was playing.

A fucking flat-screen TV.

I hadn't been yelled at once.

I had new underwear on (not that old, dirty shit they give you in Florida).

And I was watching a new release movie on a flat-screen TV.

A fucking high-definition, flat-screen TV!

Lawn Mower

So far, this New York State prison shit wasn't so bad.

The one thing that bothered me was the fact that every single officer had a billy club hanging from their belt.

* * *

ONCE THE FINGERPRINTS and photos were done, we were given our bed rolls and were led off to the cell block area.

The CO leading the group gave us a little pep talk before we left.

CO: "Gentlemen, welcome to Hell. I'll be your guide on this magical tour, so call me Virgil. And I've got just a few rules for everyone to follow:

Number one, around here, I AM GOD.

Number two, no talking in my fucking line.

Number three, yellow lines have been clearly marked along all walkways. Walk between the lines, and keep your hands and feet inside the lines at all times.

Number four, never *ever* get caught picking something up off of my floors.

If you fail to follow these rules during this ride, I will happily introduce you to the business end of my good friend here, Mr. Widowmaker."

To emphasize his point, he held his billy club up with his right hand, while he gingerly slapped the palm of his left hand with "the business end."

CO: "Now, does anyone have any questions? No? Good, let's go."

Note to self: he's bluffing. He can't use that thing. This isn't
The Shawshank Redemption.

* * *

We were led down a hallway or two, then outside so we
could cross over to the "prison" side. We went in through a
door big enough to drive a tank through, and judging by the
size of the place I figured that that's exactly what they would
do if there was ever a riot.

We went down another hallway, past the chow hall, down
some steps, then into cell block B. My first thought was:

Ho-ly shit.

My second thought was:

For once, the movies have it right.

"B-block" is Elmira's housing unit for all inmates going
through reception. And it's nothing but absolute insanity.

It's really fucking long, really fucking wide and really
fucking tall. In B-block there are a total of 352 cells. Four
tiers high, two sides per tier separated by a catwalk every
hundred feet or so, and forty-four cells on each side.

Each cell is your standard 6' x 9' size with vertical bars in
the front.

There were hundreds of men behind those bars, and pretty
much every one of them was screaming like animals. Fire-
balls were being thrown at us from every direction. "Fish-
ing" lines were being flung across the floors and flown
through the air. All sorts of name-calling and catcalling was
going on.

Lawn Mower

There were birds flying through the air, rats running across the ground, bars being shaken to the point of teeth rattling, and it smelled like stale cigarettes, weed, piss, puke, and dirty, dirty armpits all rolled into one.

Everything was surreal. I felt like I was in a movie.

I'm pretty sure that all the first-timers going through reception that day were thinking the same thing: *what the fuck did I get myself into?*

There were lighters, cigarettes, tobacco and God knows what else being thrown all over the floor in front of us, just outside of the yellow lines which were conveniently painted on the ground. Ahead of me in the line, I could see a guy keep looking from left to right, then back left again, trying to scope out where the CO was. It was obvious to Helen-fucking-Keller what this dude was about to do.

What wasn't so obvious to *him* was the CO walking just behind him in his blind spot.

Just as Ricky Retardo scooted a hair to the left and started to reach down to grab a couple of cigarettes off the ground, Mr. Widowmaker came crashing down on the dude's wrist. If they didn't hear the *crack* of his bones or his girl-like screams in the International Space Station that day, I'd be surprised.

New note to self: he isn't bluffing.

AT THE FAR end of B-block and down another short hallway was A-block. This is where we were going to stay for the next few days. I knew that because the CO told us.

CO: "This is A-block. This is where you'll be housed for the next few days before you're moved to B-block. Except, of course, for the feller with the wrist problem. He'll be in the infirmary. He he he."

I'm pretty sure I can speak for everyone there that day when I say that his joke really wasn't that funny.

If B-block was night, then A-block was day. The blocks were polar opposites. You could hear a mouse fart in A-block all day and all night, where B-block was absolute insanity pretty much 24/7. It wasn't for a lack of people either. A-block had sixty-four cells in it, and as far as I could tell, they were all full. For some reason though, no one said a fucking word, and I wasn't about to be the one to upset the status quo.

For me, the reality of it all didn't set in until the next day when I got a letter at mail call. It was a carbon copy of a letter sent to Florida, acknowledging the detainer that was lodged against me. The letter stated that my *earliest* possible release date was over two and a half years away (I had spent almost a year in county), and that DOCCS would notify Florida thirty days prior to my release.

I had *at least* two and a half years left in prison.

Then I still had to go and deal with Florida.

I couldn't find my happy place. I didn't see any light at the end of the tunnel. All I could see was a bleak and dark future ahead of me. "They" were winning already.

As promised, I was only in A-block for three days. I was moved to a cell on the fourth tier in B-block, and I was graced with a window that was stuck in the open position and a radiator that didn't work.

It was mid-January in upstate New York.

I was *not* a happy fucking camper.

The reception/classification process went rather quickly and within three weeks I was "on the draft." DOCCS Speak for: being transferred.

Other than a con getting stabbed to death by another con, a con getting beat to death by the COs, and a dude with a set of DD tits hitting on me in the shower, reception went pretty smoothly.

* * *

OUT OF ALL THE prisons in New York State (fifty-four in total), I somehow ended up at the closest prison to my home. How the fuck I got that lucky I have no idea, but I was definitely grateful. Not Fucking Gwen would be able to come see me as often as she wanted, and so would anyone else. But I told Mommy Dearest not to worry about it because I didn't want her to strain herself financially (the truth being that I was still pissed about that bullshit with her and Beavis on that visit in county). But we spoke on the phone all the time and wrote often.

One would have thought that being in a jail close to home would have been the best thing for me.

Well, it only took me ninety days to end up in the box.

I do believe that I told you in the beginning of this mess that I was an asshole. Asshole or not, *sometimes* my bad decisions end up having beneficial outcomes, and this ended up being one of those times. Even though in the beginning (when I had no idea how things would eventually turn out) I was seriously kicking myself in the ass.

In the box, I was able to take a good look at my life, and I thought long and hard about where I'd been and where I wanted to go in life. I figured that since I was "in jail" (Prisonspeak for the box) while I was already incarcerated, I probably had a lot of fucking work to do in order to reach my goals.

Working on yourself is never easy. I'm great at giving advice and telling you exactly what *you're* doing wrong and how to fix it, but when it comes to myself, well.... my superhuman advice-giving abilities always prematurely ejaculate.

It didn't take Athena-like powers to deduce what was wrong in my life. *Everything* was wrong in my life. And I needed a serious fucking overhaul in every department, otherwise I was going to end up doing life on the installment plan.

So that's what I did. I utilized the time I had been given, and started to work on every aspect of myself that I was able to. If I wasn't an asshole, this would be the part where I would start telling you all the details of my hard work, but fuck you. If you're someone in recovery, or know someone in recovery and think that I'm going to give you all the trade secrets, you've got another thing coming. You're not going to receive recovery vicariously through me. Go out and do your own fucking work, you lazy fucking millennials.

And I really hope that my millennial statement offended one of you walking vaginas.

DURING MY TIME in the box, I did take a few difficult hits.

The worst was when my good friend, Alex, came to visit me one Saturday night. I didn't think it odd because we wrote often, and she had been continuously sending me books, different odds and ends, and always said that she was going to visit me. So when I saw her, I wasn't too surprised.

I realized about halfway through our visit that Alex had something that she wanted to talk to me about. I had figured that she was going to tell me that she couldn't write or visit anymore due to her boyfriend. I finally got fed up with her dancing around this unspoken issue and I told her to spit it the fuck out, or leave. And that's when she dropped a bomb-shell on me.

Alex: "Your mom is in the ICU. She tried to kill herself by overdosing on her prescription pills a few days ago. And no one was planning on telling you because they're nervous about how you might react."

Sometimes I'd really like to punch my family in the face.

It was rough news, yes, but I've been down this road before. It bothered me, yes, but my childhood was fucked-up, and my mother trying to kill herself (again) wasn't very shocking. According to my calculations, this would be attempt eight or nine. So after Alex gave me the news, I did what I did best: I bottled that shit up and started a new line of conversation.

How fucking sad is that? Being able to react to hearing that your mother just tried to kill herself with the same indiffer-ence as if someone had told you it was raining outside.

Makes you wonder what the fuck happened to me as a child doesn't it?

Anyways....

What Alex told me next *did* elicit a reaction out of me.

My mother had also been shooting up heroin.

Apparently, my mother had thrown KFC out and needed a housemate. Since they were all buddy-buddy now anyways and getting high together, Beavis and my mother decided that it was a good idea for him to move into my mothers' place with her. Somewhere down the line, curiosity took over and my mother asked Beavis to teach her how to shoot dope.

Let me break that down for the retarded readers.

My younger cousin taught my mother, ***his fucking aunt***, how to stick a needle in her arm and get high with heroin.

Beavis, if you're reading this, ***THIS IS WHY I FUCKING HATE YOU***.

Up until then, I only harbored a few resentments towards Beavis. After that day, I had nothing but raw and primordial hatred for him.

There I was sitting in prison due to my own fucking issues with heroin, and Beavis is out in the real world showing my mother the ins and outs of shooting dope.

Fucking awesome, isn't it?

As pissed off as I was at the news, I was grateful that Alex brought it to me in person. Had I received said news in a letter, I don't know how I would have reacted. But I'm fairly certain that it wouldn't have been good.

By the time I got out of the box, I was more focused than ever. I had goals that I was going to reach and nothing was going to deter me from them. Not Not Fucking Gwen, not Beavis, not my mom. I was going to make my parole board and take my fucking life back.

* * *

BECAUSE I HAD RECEIVED MORE than forty-five days in confinement, I had to be sent to a different facility. Somehow I ended up at the *second* closest prison to home, and I was grateful for that. I told myself that I wasn't going to fuck it up this time.

Within the first three days of me being at my new jail, I saw six people get cut/stabbed. Then the administration shut the prison down for a search of every square inch of the facility and found close to 200 weapons.

Awesome.

Can you imagine how safe I felt?

I HAD ONLY BEEN at the facility a little over a month when I received another devastating blow. I was called to the Chaplain's Office where I met with Rabbi Jerk-off. No, I'm not Jewish, it's just how prison works. You get stuck with whatever chaplain is on duty. After introducing himself, Rabbi Jerk-off then informed me that my Uncle John had passed away.

Uncle John had been fighting cancer for several years and had finally succumbed to the disease. Even though his death was expected, it tore through me like nothing I'd ever felt before.

Uncle John was like a father to me. No, he was more than that. He was my idol. I loved and respected him more than any other person in my life. Out of everyone in my family, I was closest to Uncle John. Uncle John and my grandfather (the one who had passed away a few years prior), were the only people I would call for advice when I needed it.

Losing Uncle John was like losing a part of myself, and I will never be able to express the shame and regret I carry for letting him down like I did, time and time again. I know that he was disappointed in me when I was arrested, and now I'd never have the chance to show him who I really am.

While I was in Rabbi Jerk-off's office, I was allowed to make a phone call. I called my mother and she gave me the roundabout details. She told me that she would be sending the funeral information to the facility so that I could attend the services. I thanked her, and told her that I would call her later.

Once I was off the phone with my mother, I cried like a little bitch. In that moment I felt as if I had hit a new bottom. Even though I had been clean for over a year and a half by then, everything felt as if it was raw and new. I was supposed to be there with my family, not sitting in some shit-hole prison. I hated myself more on that day than I ever had before.

After I composed myself, I spoke with Rabbi Jerk-off for a few minutes before I left, and he acted like, well, a jerk-off. Hence his name. He was cracking jokes while playing solitaire on his computer instead of trying to offer some sort of grief counseling or emotional support. He treated me and my family with absolute indifference to our loss, and wore this indifference on his sleeve.

He really pissed me the fuck off.

I left his office fuming, and returned to my housing unit to call my mother back. We spoke, and she calmed me down. Two days later I was called back to the Rabbi's office. I had assumed it was to discuss the funeral trip, and well, you know how the saying goes about assuming anything.

The Rabbi had summoned me to his office to inform me that I would *not* be attending my uncle's funeral service, because an anonymous family member had called the facility to contest my attendance. This family member had told the facility that it would cause a "serious issue" if I was to be in attendance.

Rabbi Jerk-off then voiced his opinion about how shitty of a person I must be if my own family was calling to say that they didn't want me going to a funeral.

Somehow, I was able to maintain my composure and not rip his eyeballs out of their sockets and skull fuck him to death. I left his office without saying a single word, returned to my housing unit and unleashed my fury on paper in the form of a formal write-up.

It was seven pages of pure fucking epicness. I quoted and cited everything and everyone from George Washington to the Torah. I left no stone unturned, and I directed all my anger, hatred and frustration towards Rabbi Jerk-off, with the sole intent of getting him fired. I completed my masterpiece and sent it off to Albany, the Governor, the ACLU, and even the NAACP for good measure. Then I sat back and waited for the shit to hit the fan.

WAITING for the shit to hit the fan got boring, so I occupied myself with other things. Mainly, I was trying to keep myself sane while going through the holiday season, which wasn't working for me so well. You see, even though I had a lot going on and was making a lot of life changes, I was still pretty hung up on Not Fucking Gwen.

Each weekend, I would convince myself that she was coming to see me. I'd get up early every Saturday and Sunday in order to take a shower and get ready for a visit because I just *knew* that she would be coming to see me, even though I had nothing to base said belief on.

I spoke to Not Fucking Gwen sporadically over the phone, but I wrote her every single week, with no response from her. Somewhere along the line, I started to believe my own bullshit that *she was just really busy working and taking care of her kids.*, and told myself that every day when I didn't receive any mail from her.

On the weekends when she *didn't* show up for a visit, I told myself that she'd be here next weekend because she *must have* been really busy this weekend.

Fucking pathetic, aren't I?

It gets worse though.

The prison I was in is literally eight minutes down the road from the local casino. There were several weekends that I had found out that Not Fucking Gwen was going to the casino on a Friday or Saturday night and she'd be staying over. Those weekends were the worst because I **knew** she was less than ten minutes down the road from me and I had convinced myself that the only reason she was staying overnight was because she was going to come and visit me the next day.

Spoiler alert.

She never fucking came.

I was so focused on what I wanted my future to be like that I couldn't see the obvious.

On New Year's Day I got into a **HUGE** fight with my mother over the phone because I wanted her to place a three-way call to Not Fucking Gwen so I could speak to her and her children. My mother only had the one phone call left on her prepaid account, and told me that she wanted to speak to me and not waste her last call on Not Fucking Gwen (she had a serious distaste for Not Fucking Gwen).

My mother lived on a fixed income from a disability and couldn't put money on the phone often. I knew that she would be receiving her monthly check in a couple of days and that she could put more money on her account then, and that was the counter I used to each and every argument she came up with. She said that if Not Fucking Gwen wanted to talk to me, then she could put money on her own phone. My mother kept pushing the issue that she really wanted (her exact words were *needed*) to talk to me. And me being blind to the obvious, I told my mother to stop being a bitch just because she didn't like Not Fucking Gwen. After that, my mother acquiesced and called Not Fucking Gwen.

That was the last time I ever spoke to my mother.

My mother received her disability check around the third of every month. A few days after the third, I tried to call her several times, but I never got through. I shrugged it off, figuring that she must have had some bills to take care of, and thought that I would just talk to her next month.

In the early part of the afternoon on January 22nd, I was summoned to the Chaplain's Office. I didn't think anything about it, and was actually very excited to be called there because I was thinking that the shit was finally hitting the fan over my write up of Rabbi Jerk-off.

When I walked into the Chaplin's Office I was as giddy as a school girl about to give her first blow job. When I saw Rabbi Jerk-off, I actually wet myself a little with excitement. I figured that he had called me to his office to beg and plead with me to withdraw my write-up.

He didn't seem to be angry or upset, which made me slightly worried. I put a lot of serious accusations in that write-up, and he appeared to be completely indifferent to my being in his office. I knew for a fact that he had received a copy of the write-up, and that he was aware of how many different offices I had sent it to.

And then he uttered five words that changed my life forever.

Rabbi Jerk-off: "Your mother has passed away."

It took me several minutes to speak. I asked him how, and he said that he didn't know, but that I could place a call home to my family if I wanted. I called my sister and heard the three words that I've always known I'd hear for so very long.

Sister: "Mom killed herself."

Even though death is a natural part of life, it's still not easy to deal with. Suicide, on the other hand, is almost impossible to understand, and exponentially more difficult to deal with. Especially while incarcerated.

Finding out that a friend or loved one has taken their own life is something that I hope you never have to experience. There are so many unanswered questions and so many "what ifs" that it's not even funny. The unexpected and unfair hole that it tears through you is almost impossible to bear.

Hearing that my mother had killed herself, *while I was in prison*, was the single most traumatic and painful experience in my life to date. Years later, there are still absolutely no words that could even remotely categorize how I felt after receiving that news.

Even though I was almost two years clean by then, I still seemed to be finding new lows. My drug use and my actions due to my drug use had just cost me more than I was willing to pay. Had I been home, had I gotten my shit together sooner, perhaps her suicide could have been avoided. Perhaps if I'd spoken to my mother on New Year's, instead of fighting with her so I could speak to Not Fucking Gwen, she'd still be alive.

Perhaps......

Perhaps......

Perhaps......

The fact of the matter is that I'll never know.

And that's something I have to live with for the rest of my life.

* * *

ANOTHER SHITTY PART of the whole situation was that I didn't even get a chance to tell my mother that she was no longer a mother-in-law. A few days prior to my mother's suicide, I finally received my divorce decree from #1. I had taken it upon myself to file for divorce. I no longer wanted to be married to the cunt nor she me. My mother *hated* #1 and would have been so happy to hear that I was no longer tied to her in any way, shape, or form.

* * *

WHETHER YOU WANT to believe me or not– I really don't give a shit either way– there are some really good people in prison.

If it weren't for some of these people, I know for a fact that I never would have made it through everything while incarcerated. Five such people I'd like to mention here, because I owe them all such a huge debt of gratitude.

Fat Boy: You were the first person I talked to about my mother, and you embraced me in the longest and most important hug of my life. You didn't care that I was crying like a little bitch in the middle of the dorm or that everybody was watching. You showed me a compassion the likes of which I'd never seen before.

Disco Nights: Without your help, or the help of Mrs. Disco Nights, I wouldn't have been able to go to my mother's funeral and lay her to rest with my family.

Mac: Our talks kept me sane. On numerous occasions, you saved me from jumping off a cliff. Your insight has helped lead me in the right direction countless times. Had it not been for you and our talks, I would have done something very stupid that would have impacted the rest of my life.

Pretty Pretty Princess: We weren't friends prior to my mother's suicide, but became friends afterwards. You helped me through the darkest aftermath that I've ever experienced and I don't think you even realized it. Nonetheless, you were there for me, and you were a friend.

Douche Bag: There is nothing more I can say other than thank you. And you know why (you still fucked a man though). You are a true friend, and my life has been significantly enhanced since you became a part of it.

THE NEXT COUPLE of days were beyond shitty. Because of Fat Boy, Mac, Disco Nights and Douche Bag, I not only made it through everything, but I did it clean. Later on, it was only due to Mac, Pretty Pretty Princess and Douche Bag that I was able to make it through everything.

Due to a difference in last names, I had to prove that my mother was my mother– how fucked-up is that? Naturally, my mother had a *different* last name when she had me than when she died. And since she had never visited me since I'd been in prison, documents had to be found proving her name changes, and then they had to be faxed to the facility. My sister and Mrs. Disco Nights worked hard to get everything together that the facility required to ensure that I was able to attend my mother's services. Without them, I never would have been able to attend.

Thank you both.

***

MY MOTHER's funeral was a mix of emotions for everyone. It was a combination of happy, sad, awkward, disbelief, anxiety and a lot of *what the fuck*.

Happy, because I hadn't seen my family in almost two years.

Sad, because of the reason we were there.

Disbelief, because it was difficult to comprehend that my mother was truly dead.

Awkward, because I was handcuffed and shackled.

It's kind of hard to hug someone when you're pretty much hogtied.

And *what the fuck* because, well, what the fuck?! My mother fucking killed herself. How would you react in that situation?

Some of my family members didn't know how to respond to me. They weren't sure if they wanted to hug me or slap me. Which was understandable. The fact that I was escorted by two armed prison guards probably didn't help the situation either. But fuck 'em. She was *my* mother. Not theirs. I had a *fucking right to be there*.

If you felt "uncomfortable" with me being there, you could have walked your happy asses right outside the funeral home and played a game of hide and go fuck yourselves

And you know who you fucking are.

LEAVING the funeral wasn't easy. I had so many emotions going through me right then that I didn't know if I was coming or going. It was such a bittersweet experience, and one that I'll never forget.

As I was leaving, an unprecedented change happened within me. It was something that I'd never experienced before then, and that I haven't experienced since. Sort of like how the Grinch started to feel things at the end of the story. He realized something, a great truth, and then a major change came about within him. (Now, I could have used the metaphor of when a boy jerks off and blows his load for the first time, but I'm trying to show my maturity here).

It took stealing from my family, losing everything, two prison sentences, my uncle's death, my mother's suicide and almost two years of clean time for this change to happen. Once that change happened, I wasn't the same person anymore. I felt different inside. Like one door had closed and another had opened. And in that moment, I *knew* that I'd *never* be the same person again.

* * *

THE DAY AFTER THE FUNERAL, I called my sister to see how she was holding up. After we spoke for a while, she said that she had something she wanted to talk to me about.

Oh boy.

The Sister: "Your father called me the day before yesterday and asked if he could come to mom's funeral..."

This was not what I was expecting.

Y'all remember my father, right? The guy who blatantly lied to the Florida Department of Corrections in order to get me in trouble, just so I wouldn't call my sister again.

Yeah. That guy.

The Sister: "...but I told him no because I didn't know how you would feel about it. Plus, I didn't think that anyone else would have wanted him there either."

Me: "Especially mom."

The Sister: "No shit. Anyways, Aunt Sara said that she saw his car drive by the funeral home a few times during the services. That's fucking weird, right? Who the fuck stalks a funeral? Besides, they haven't spoken to each other in like, what, ten years?"

Actually, my biological parents hadn't spoken civilly for the better part of two decades, so it was definitely odd that he would want to attend to my mother's services. They basically hated each other.

After I digested the information, I decided that it was time to try and bury the hatchet with dear old dad. He was now my only living, biological parent after all. So, I decided to put on my big-boy pants and write him a letter. In the letter, I expressed my gratitude for his wanting to be at the services and I also suggested that perhaps we could attempt to put the past behind us, and maybe start fresh.

The letter I wrote him was one of the most mature, adult-type letters I have ever written. I was open, honest, and direct. I expressed a great interest in finally getting to know my father and leaving the past where it was. What better opportunity for a father and son to reunite than the death of the mother, right?

Wrong.

The letter he wrote me back was unbelievable. The hate and anger that radiated from the six pages was almost contagious. The first time I read it, I felt physically ill, like I had just swallowed the ending of a bukkake party. The second time I read it, I was in complete denial that a father could actually write that to his first-born son. The third time I read it, I wanted to mount a giant dildo to a reciprocating saw and pay some unsavory people to kidnap my father, tie him down to a bed, insert the business end of said saw where the sun doesn't shine and have them go to town. The fourth time I read the letter.... well, you get the idea.

Here are some of the highlights from his letter:

"I wasn't going to write this letter. But after receiving yours, I wanted to set the record straight."

"I don't believe for one second that your mother's death struck a chord with you on any level. Of this I am truly sorry."

"I'm sure that you were upset in missing your uncle's services. I don't want you to think for one minute that your grandfather would be your buddy. He wouldn't and neither would my brother."

"If you knocked on your uncle's door today, he wouldn't want to let you in. He would never trust you. If someone broke into his house, he would pick you for the number one suspect. That's what your uncle thought of you!"

"Your uncle didn't believe that you got in trouble because of drugs. He went to his grave telling all of us that drugs didn't cause you to rob your aunt and whatever else you did. I also believe this. You may have been doing drugs, but that wasn't the cause. You're just a bad person. I really don't want to waste any more paper on you, but you should know that your grandfather was thinking along the same lines when he took his last breath."

"I do not want a relationship with you. I want nothing more to do with you."

"No one believes a word you say, and no one will for a very long time. Everyone believes that you will be back in prison in less than three years once you get out. Even your mother thought this."

"I just wanted to let you know what everyone thought of you. And I wanted you to know what my brother thought of you before he died. He knew that you would end up back in prison and that you'd be a lifelong failure."

"I'm sure that your mother is a lot better off without you in her life now."

Let me break this down for the slow motherfuckers out there.

My biological father wrote that shit to me.

While I was in prison.

Five years after my grandfather (his father) had died.

Five months after my uncle (his brother) had died.

And a mere month after my mother had killed herself.

Yes. My father is an *epic* douchebag. I know that I've already established this fact, but I just wanted to reiterate it for y'all.

It takes a special type of asshole to write a letter like that and luckily, I knew just what a situation like that called for!

I made a copy of the letter and mailed it to his mother.

After that, I never received a letter from my father again.

Did I mention that I'm my grandmother's favorite?

* * *

IF I TOLD you that I wasn't angry at my mother, I'd be lying. Anyone who's ever dealt with suicide will tell you that once the initial shock wears off, anger will surely follow. There might be a few emotions prior to anger, but trust me, anger *will* rear its ugly head. Even to this day, a small part of me is still very angry with her. Like all wounds though, time has a way of working on it.

To help me cope with everything, I decided that I had to view her suicide as something different from what it was. So, instead of viewing it as a selfish act, I viewed it as a self*less* and sacrificial act.

Her death was the catalyst for a plethora of changes both internal and external in my life, and the lives of those closest to me. Without this spark, perhaps these changes never would have taken place. I (have to) believe that in some small way, my mother knew that.

A huge change was my relationship with my sister. Even though she is six years my junior, she is far more grounded and mature than I could ever dream of being. She is someone that I absolutely look up to.

Did I really just fucking admit that?

Growing up, my sister and I hated each other. We always fought and tormented each other (I mainly tormented her). Now, however, I don't think that two siblings could be closer. Unless, of course, they were from central Florida, in which case they'd naturally be married or some shit. Sick redneck fucks.

Today I know that without a doubt, my sister will be there for me one hundred percent. Even if she's furious at me, if I need her, she will be there. For someone like me, with serious abandonment issues (gee, I wonder how that's possible), that knowledge is beyond priceless.

THE INTERNAL CHANGES I went through were sudden, and almost overnight. I felt focused and determined. I felt as if I had a purpose (even if at the time I didn't know what it was). I wanted a better life for myself, and I was willing to put in the work to get it. I didn't feel as if the world owed me something anymore. I felt as if I owed the world. I started making a plan and setting goals for myself. At thirty-two years of age, I was finally starting to become a man. Whatever that meant exactly.

There are hundreds if not thousands of books written about being a man or manhood. Every *man* has his own opinion on what makes *him* a man. If you ask someone what makes them a man, some will tell you that you measure a man by how much he'll sacrifice for his family, or the quality of his work, or by the strength of his word. Others– the more ignorant type– will tell you it's how much pussy he gets, how much money he has, or how much dope he sells (I *promise* you that this is true. I couldn't make that shit up if I tried).

If you want my opinion (which you're going to get whether you wanted it or not), I think that the measure of a man is simple. I think that the measure of a man isn't in his superiority to another man. The measure of a man is in his superiority to his former self.

That's pretty fucking deep for a guy like me, eh?

* * *

My determination led me into a new lifestyle. I had set a goal for myself to be a runner. Growing up, I was always the fat kid. I hated sports and any sort of physical activity. I never ran the mile in school and I had absolutely no desire to do anything but play video games and watch TV.

When I told Douche Bag about what I wanted to do, he laughed at me. Laughed until he cried. Douche Bag worked out all the time, was a wrestler in high school and college, rode pro motocross and was studying to be a personal trainer. Looking at him though, you'd never believe it. He looked like a kid who had yet to hit puberty, or get laid.

I, on the other hand, looked like a fat, overweight slob. I was 270 pounds and I ate nothing but honey buns and pancakes all day. Bread and soda, cookies and cakes. That was my diet. I needed to change it.

The first day of running was about as much fun as jerking off with sandpaper. I'd heard the expression "he's turning green" before someone pukes, but thought it was only that–an expression. I found out the hard way that it's not just an expression.

I made it two and a half laps around the track before I started blowing chunks everywhere. Douche Bag found this hilarious. I told him that I didn't find it quite so funny, and then proceeded to inform him that I hope he catches chlamydia.

Even though it sucked, I didn't give up. Which surprised the hell out of me. All my life I'd been a professional quitter. If something proved difficult, I'd give up on it and move on without a second thought. But instead of giving up, I went back for more punishment.

And thus, my endeavor with running began. We would run pretty much every day or do some sort of calisthenic work-out. Douche Bag was teaching me about eating right. Good carbs vs. bad carbs. Muscle twitch. Recovery times. Shit like that. Pretty much everything that he was paying to learn, he was teaching me for free.

Dumbass.

In my off time from running, I had a lot going on. My first priority was to get out and *stay out* of prison. So, I needed to make my board and have a plan for after release. This was the first time that I wasn't trying to fly by the seat of my pants, and I was a little out of my element. But I did the best I could. Thanks primarily to the help of Mac.

Mac had been incarcerated for almost thirty years. He had a lot of insight into parole and the parole board, and he went out of his way to help me with preparing for mine. It would be impossible to quantify how much his assistance truly helped me.

Next, I had to address the issue with Florida. They still had a detainer lodged against me for the violation of probation, and I didn't want to do all this time in New York, and get released early on parole, only to end up being extradited to Florida in order to do more time down there. Fuck all that noise. Who in their right mind would want to put up with all that bullshit? Not me!

With just those two issues on my plate, I had a lot to deal with. Yet, I decided to add more onto it. I still had bridges that I had to mend with family and friends. I had to stay vigilant in maintaining my recovery. And I had to find more ways to keep bettering myself, so I decided to teach myself a second language and enhance my reading.

With all that nonsense going on, time *really* started to move for me. My days were spent working on the issues at hand, and my nights were spent working out and learning. Within a few months I had an exact plan of attack for my parole board, I had filed a couple of motions in the state of Florida, I was able to run multiple miles without stopping, I could have a short, simple and direct conversation with someone in Spanish, and I had a few literary classics under my belt. I was over two years clean, and for the first time in my life, I didn't hate who I was.

When I refer to "literary classics," I mean authors such as Milton, Dumas, Steinbeck, Shakespeare, Dostoevsky, Max, Keller, Melville, Dante, etc. And yes, I've read *at least* one book by each of these authors.

Now, just because I've *read* them, it does not mean that I completely *understand* what I've read. Personally, I'd like to punch Shakespeare in the face, throw Dante down several flights of stairs, and take a ball-peen hammer to the nut sack of whomever proclaimed *The Grapes of Wrath* to be a literary classic.

I was going to read *The Catcher in the Rye*, but I wasn't in the mood.

Get it??

* * *

BY THE TIME 2016 came around, I was a Spanish-speaking, book-reading, plan-having, running fool. By January first of that year, I had lost close to seventy pounds. I was a new fucking me.

I hadn't spoken to Not Fucking Gwen much after my mother passed. She wrote me a Dear John letter and I laughed when I read it. I mean, it was pretty fucking obvious that she had moved on. Not Fucking Gwen was no longer a priority for me, and so I wasn't too concerned with her bullshit.

Alex wrote and visited as often as she could. She had gotten married and she and her husband were working towards their first child, so it was hard for her to visit, but I was grateful for what I got. Like I said before, she taught me the meaning of friendship.

My upcoming parole board became my main focus. Even though it was still six months away, I was a nervous wreck. I had put together a packet to provide the parole board which contained all sorts of goodies. I had letters of support from family and friends, proof of employment, my plans for the future, shit like that. I even threw in the kitchen sink for good measure. I left no stone unturned for this venture. I was *not* going to walk in and "wing it" like I normally would in every other situation in my life.

I still faced one small dilemma: my speech.

On paper, I write as I think, and somehow I come across as intelligent. One time I even had a judge tell me *on the record* that I was a highly intelligent and extremely articulate young man, and that he even had to use a dictionary for some of the words I had used in my letters. What the fuck, right? (If you don't believe me, I'd be happy to provide you with a copy of the court minutes from that day for your reading pleasure, and then you can go eat a giant bowl of cock soup.)

When I spoke, however, I tended to have a mind/mouth clusterfuck. I either stuttered and got hung up on my words, or I spoke entirely too fast. Things never came out as I intended them to and it was fucking fr- fr- fr- frustrating. I knew that I had to do something about it before I went in front of the parole board.

I signed up for a program where I had to facilitate convict-run (I hate the word inmate) programs. For four hours a day, I had to keep a bunch of convicts engaged in some sort of conversation. The courses were really fucking boring, and the administration didn't give a fuck what was being said as long as everyone behaved themselves. So, I got to talk about whatever the fuck I wanted. It was perfect! As long as someone was up in front of the room speaking, the convicts passed the class and the administration left us the fuck alone.

By the time I had to go in front of the parole commissioners, I could articulate myself very well. I was confident in my speech, and public speaking no longer bothered me in the slightest. I was ready.

My parole hearing itself was fucking weird. The parole commissioners asked me questions that I *never* anticipated and that had *fuck all* to do with my case. One line of questioning in particular was just fucking insane.

Parole Commissioner: "Who was the first person you ever got high with?"

Me: "My cousin Beavis."

Parole Commissioner: "And where is he now?"

Me: "I have no idea; I've heard Florida, but I don't speak to or associate with him."

Parole Commissioner: "I see. And is he still chasing the bag?"

Fucked-up, right?

There were other similar lines of questioning which had fuck all to do with my case. It didn't matter what they asked me though. I was honest, direct, and sincere when I spoke to the parole commissioners. I didn't just give this hearing the old college try; I put everything I had into it.

I finished with the board around noon on a Wednesday. I wouldn't find out if they let me go until late Monday afternoon at mail call. (Yeah, they sent you your decision in the mail because they didn't have the balls to tell you to your face in the event that they denied you and you lost your shit).

Those were the longest five days of my life.

* * *

BEFORE WE PROCEED, I feel that I should give you a little insight into the New York State Board of Parole. In all reality, it's a bunch of cockamamie bullshit. Pretty much everyone who goes to prison leaves on parole in one form or another. It's just a matter of *when* you leave prison and how much time you're going to spend on parole.

The sentence I was given (3.5 – 7 years) is what's known as an indeterminate or "split" bid. I was eligible to be released when the first part of my sentence was completed, which for me was three and a half years. This is why I was appearing before the parole board. They were deciding if they would let me go, or keep me in prison to complete my sentence. You see why I was so hell-bent on preparing for it?

When you appear before the parole board, they have complete discretion on what to do with you. The fate of your life is literally in their hands, and most of the commissioners think of themselves as gods because of this.

There is absolutely no rhyme or reason to their decision-making process. Of course, there are rules and guidelines that they have to follow, but they govern themselves. If they don't follow their guidelines, they only have to report to themselves. It's complete fucking horseshit.

They alone hold the power to interpret executive law as they see fit. Once in a while a convict can get a parole decision overturned in the courts because the parole board did something really fucked-up. Then that convict will get a reappearance date and will have to go in front of the parole board again. But the parole board is like a fucking casino: it's their house, their rules, and the house *always* wins.

If they don't like your face?

Denied.

If they don't like your crime?

Denied.

If they don't like your answers?

Lawn Mower

Denied.

If it's raining outside?

Denied.

The panel of parole board commissioners are essentially a bunch of fuckbags, and perfectly good assholes were wasted when teeth were put in their mouths. To me, the parole board commissioners actually fall lower on the scale than Florida DOC employees. And I've already made it perfectly clear how I feel about those fuckers.

BY THE TIME Monday evening came I was ready to lose my shit. I was an absolute fucking wreck all day long. I can't even begin to imagine how it would feel to wait for your decision after a decade or more, because after only three and a half years, the waiting was fucking torture.

The general rule of thumb when you get your decision back is that if the envelope is heavy, you were denied. If it's light, then you're being released. This is because if you were denied parole, you have the right to appeal the decision, and they will automatically send you the necessary appeal paperwork with the denial.

When I was handed the letter, I thought that it was the heaviest piece of mail that I'd ever received.

I was so sick to my stomach that I couldn't open it after I felt its weight.

I stared at it for a solid hour before I got the balls to open it.

When I finally opened it, I couldn't believe what it said.

YOU'RE GOING HOME, ASSHOLE!

Well, not in those *exact* words, but you get the idea.

Fifty-two people appeared before the parole board that month in my facility. I was one of the *four* released.

They only let four fucking people go home.

And I was one of them!

It was one of the happiest moments in my life. It was even better than getting my first hand job on the school bus! For once in my life, something went right for me. After three and a half years of incarceration, I was going home.

Or so I had thought.

* * *

THE ISSUE with Florida was yet to be resolved. If the courts didn't rule in my favor, I wouldn't go home and I'd be extradited to Florida for the violation of probation. It's not that I didn't want to take care of the violation, it's that I didn't want to go through with the whole extradition process.

For years, I'd heard horror stories about extradition and I didn't want to find out if any of them were true or not. I was scared to death that I was going to get fucked over and find out that reality is far worse than all of the stories combined.

I had filed multiple motions fighting my extradition to the Florida courts. Now, it was just a matter of time waiting for a decision on what Florida would do.

The next couple of months went by in a blur. I was running every day at least five miles, and reaching more and more personal goals. By the time I was about to leave, I was 185 pounds, and could run a half-marathon without stopping. Before then, I'd never really been proud of myself.

The month before I was going home, my sister had a lot on her plate due to having her first son. Since she had so much going on, I didn't want to bother her with stupid prison shit, so I asked my buddy Disco Nights if his wife could buy me a pair of jeans to be released in. I had money in my account, so paying for them wouldn't be an issue. I just didn't want to leave in prison release clothes. He told me that it wouldn't be an issue and once again he came to my rescue.

Or so I had thought.

* * *

EVERYTHING WAS GOING SMOOTHLY until about two weeks before my release date when I got some bad news.

I wasn't going home.

Florida was definitely coming to get me.

* * *

Now BEFORE WE go on with our story, I wanted to tell you about something that happened to me before I went to my parole board. It didn't really fit into the chain of events that you've already read about. If I had added it in somewhere else, I feel that it would have fucked up my feng shui, hence why I'm just throwing it in here.

If you don't like it, fuck off. You've already paid for the book so I don't really give a shit at this point.

* * *

BY NOW I feel confident that I've established how shitty a person I've been in my life. Haven't I?

I mean, I've stolen from my friends, I've stolen from my employers, I've stolen from complete strangers, and I've stolen from my family. I'm not really someone you want to bring home to meet your parents. I get that.

I also get that I'm not liked by a healthy number of people.

So, I pose a question to you.

How much does that shit need to be crammed down my throat?

How much cock do I have to eat before enough is enough??

Honestly– do people really need to go out of their way to ensure that I know that they don't like me?

When did a simple "Lawn Mower, I really don't fucking like you" cease to be enough?

Very few people have ever gone out of their way to make sure I know that they don't like me. One person in particular went above and beyond any necessary measures to ensure I knew that I was *extremely* disliked by him, without ever saying a word to me or my family. Here's how he accomplished this task.

My sister and I share the same mother. For my not too bright readers, that means that we have different fathers. The only person that I'm actually close with on her side of the family is her father, who is my (ex) stepfather. Regarding everyone else on her side of the family, it's always been awkward between us.

My sister's grandmother passed away while I was still living in Florida. Her grandfather passed away while I was in the midst of my sentence in New York.

Before he passed away, one of his other grandchildren stole thousands of dollars in cash from him that he had hidden around his home. This grandchild did this in order to feed his heroin habit (and no, it wasn't me. I've never taken anything from that man). This thievery went on for quite some time and everyone knew about it. They just didn't want to do anything about it because they don't like to make waves and they had to protect their precious family name.

This grandchild's antics were definitely up there with mine, except they never got into any serious trouble for anything they did.

Yes, I'm fucking bitter about this.

Anyways, the grandfather passed away and life went on. I wasn't very close to the man but I mourned with my sister because I'm a good brother. Except for the whole thievery and heroin junkie thing.

Then one day I got called for legal mail. I was waiting on several motions to be heard by the courts in Florida, so being summoned to legal mail wasn't unexpected.

What *was* unexpected was the fact that the letter came from a *New York State* law firm.

When I read the document, I just about shit a long-lost set of anal beads. Sometime before he passed away, my sister's grandfather had changed his will to specifically include me in it.

What did he want to leave me?

Cash maybe?

A precious family heirloom?

A car?

Or the family jewels perhaps?

Negative.

He wanted to leave me with fuck all.

And for the morons who can't understand what that means......

Nothing.

He wanted to leave me nothing.

His will stated: "Mr. Lawn Mower, his ex-step grandchild, is to receive absolutely nothing from Mr. Grandfather's estate."

This man had four biological grandchildren and one great-grandchild (all of whom he was close to), and none of them were even *mentioned* in his will once.

Let's process this for a moment. The man disliked me so much that he went out of his fucking way to **AMEND HIS WILL** to ensure that when he died, someone of no relation to him whatsoever would receive absolutely nothing that he owned. Not even a ball of pocket lint.

Forget bequeathing this to little Sally. Or that to little Tommy. I want to make sure that that motherfucker Lawn Mower doesn't get jack shit.

Now, I'm going to let you decide: who's a bigger asshole here, him or me?

* * *

I'VE ONLY COME across three guarantees in life:

Death.

Taxes.

And extradition to Florida.

Anyone who lives in Florida can recite the state motto: "Come on vacation, leave on probation, come back on the violation" Aphorisms like this exist for a reason. In the case of Florida, it's because they'll extradite you if you fail to return a library book.

I'm not fucking kidding here. If you owe the state any *shred* of time or money (due to being on probation), and they find a reason to violate you, such as unpaid parking tickets, pulling the tag off your mattress, or jaywalking... They. Are. Coming. And you are fucked.

Why is this?

Because Florida, being "the penis of America," likes to fuck people.

In reality, it's because one of the largest prisoner transportation entities in the US is based out of the Orlando area, and Florida has an ironclad contract with the fuckers.

Yee-fucking-ha.

I SIGNED my official release paperwork on a Friday afternoon with my Offender Rehabilitation Counselor (ORC). He told me that I was being released that coming Tuesday (because that coming Monday was a holiday and New York doesn't release on holidays) and that Florida would be there to pick me up.

I was fully expecting to be extradited to Florida. I had just spent the past three and a half years fighting with the fuckers over my VOP warrant, so of *course* they would want to pay me back for all the aggravation and paperwork I'd caused them.

What I wasn't expecting was what came next.

Normally, when someone is being released, the phone call always comes first thing in the morning between seven and eight, informing the dorm officer to have the inmate ready and to send them to "draft" by nine.

Tuesday morning came and I said all my goodbyes and gave everything that I wasn't taking with me away. In prison, one tends to collect a lot of shit (because you never know when a paper clip or a rubber band might come in handy) and traditionally, when someone goes home, they give everything away. I wanted nothing more to do with New York State prison, so I gave away ***everything***. My personal sheets, clothing, toothpaste, etc. If it wasn't what the state gave me when I first came through reception, then I didn't want it. I was ready to fucking go.

And then I waited.

And waited.

And waited.

And waited.

By 9:30 a.m., I was a little antsy as to why the phone call hadn't come in yet. Mind you, in a dorm, the phone rings constantly. So each and every time the phone rang, my asshole puckered up, thinking that my ride was here.

By noon, my blood pressure was a bit high.

At 3:00 p.m., I started to lose my shit.

At 5:00 p.m., I lost my shit completely. Something was definitely wrong. And no one was telling me a goddamn thing.

When the Captain came through doing his rounds, I tried to speak to him about the situation, but he told me in no short of words to get fucked. They don't release anyone past 3:00 p.m., and obviously I was mistaken on my release date.

Well, fuck you too.

Meanwhile, Pretty Pretty Princess found me losing my shit completely hilarious. Not the fact that I was still in prison, but because for once it was *me* losing my shit, and he had something to fuck with me about. Considering that I would fuck with him pretty much all day, every day, he was enjoying his chance to do the same.

At 12:01 a.m., Pretty Pretty Princess came to my cube and tapped on my bed.

Me: "What?"

Pretty Pretty Princess: "Dude, you're still here? Weren't you supposed to be released yesterday?"

Me: "I hope you get raped in the shower tomorrow."

THE NEXT MORNING CAME, and I was far from being in a good mood. On my way to chow, all I heard was:

Guy 1: "What the fuck are you still doing here?"

Guy 2: "I thought you were being released yesterday?"

Guy 3: "Dude, what the fuck?"

Guy 4: "What, you like it that much here you decided to stay?"

Grant me the serenity to accept the things I cannot change, the courage to change the things I can, and the strength not to kill one of these motherfuckers.

CO: "Umm, you do know that your release date was yesterday, right?"

Me: "I hate you."

AFTER CHOW, it was more of the same bullshit.

Guy 5: "You know it's Wednesday, right?"

Guy 6: "Who the fuck stays *past* their release date?"

Guy 7: "How much does your life suck right now?"

Breathe in through the nose, one, two, three, four.... Out through the mouth, one, two, three, four.

By the time they called programs, I was on the precipice of a complete fucking meltdown. I knew that it shouldn't matter– I was already in jail, waiting to be brought to another fucking jail– but it was the principle. My sentence in New York was complete. I did my part. And. I. Wanted. Out.

Plus, if one more person asked me what I was still doing here, I'd never leave because I was going to fucking kill them.

During the time when they allowed movement for programs, I all but sprinted to the ORC's office, avoiding everyone.

I was in the hallway in front of the ORC's office, pacing back and forth making it abundantly clear that I wanted to speak to no one. I was waiting for my ORC to come around the corner so he and I could have a few words.

Fifteen minutes later, I saw him.

He gave me a look that was half confusion, half constipation and asked:

ORC: "What the fuck are you still doing here?"

I was so stunned, all I could do was blink at him. My jaw was clenched so tight that I cracked a tooth and my fists were clenched so tight that I drew blood.

When he saw the murderous rage boiling behind my eyes, he actually took several steps backwards. A very pregnant pause ensued between us while I gathered control of my emotions.

Me: "We need to talk. Now."

Another long pause.

ORC: "Um, why don't I figure out what's going on and I'll call you back here when I know something."

Me: "Why don't we figure it out now, together, before I really lose my shit and someone has to do a lot of paperwork."

Another really long pause.

ORC: "Only if you promise not to lose your shit in my office."

Me: "Sure."

ORC: "Really?"

I held up three fingers in the Scout salute

Me: "Scout's honor."

It only took a quick phone call to figure it all out. A major hurricane had just passed through Florida and they were running two days behind schedule because of it. They had called the facility to pass on the information, but apparently someone had forgotten to give me or my ORC the memo.

Because my release date had suddenly changed, my ORC had me sign some forms acknowledging said change. On the form he drew up, it stated something about my date being changed and blah blah blah. What drew my attention was that it said "I understand that I am being picked up by the US Marshals Service...."

The motherfucking Marshals were coming to get me!

The Marshals don't drive. The Marshals **FLY!**

That meant that I wasn't going to ride in that horrible fucking van that I'd heard about!

I signed the form and went on my merry-fucking-way, thinking that an extra couple of days was well worth not having to ride in that van.

Just as I was walking out the door:

ORC: "Were you really a Boy Scout?"

ME: "Fuck no."

ORC: "You know I can write you a ticket for lying to me."

Me: "Go ahead. By the time it gets processed, I'll be long gone from this shithole. Have a nice life."

ORC: "Have a nice time in Florida."

Touché

* * *

THURSDAY MORNING CAME, and I was ready to fucking go. My bags were packed, and all the other nonsense was taken care of (again). All I had to do was wait for my ride.

So I waited.

And waited.

And waited.

And waited.

And, what the fuck.

By the time the call for me to leave finally came in (after 5:00 p.m.), I was a fucking basket case. Doing time in prison is one thing. Doing time in prison two days *past* your release date while you're waiting to be extradited? I could write thousands of words about the range of emotions I experienced that day, but I'll dumb it down to save on printing costs.

It really fucking sucked.

When I got up to the front of the administration building, I was *beyond* ready to hop on a plane, get the fuck out of New York and get my Florida shit over with. I was sick and tired of dealing with New York State prison and all of its bullshit, and was ready to start the next chapter in my life.

There were several officers in the administration building when I arrived, and they all had shit-eating grins on their faces. When I asked for my parole clothes, they all lost their shit.

What the fuck?

The Lieutenant on duty gathered his composure and said:

LT: "I think you'd be better off staying in your state greens."

Me: "Fuck that. I just spent three and a half years wearing this shit. I want to wear *my* clothing. Not these fucking rags that y'all provide."

LT: "You sure about that?"

Is this guy retarded or something?

Me: "Of fucking course, why wouldn't I be?"

LT: "If I give you your clothing, you do know that you have to return all state property, right?"

Sometimes– actually it's *most* of the time– I can't see the obvious.

Me: "You think I wanna keep this garbage?"

As the Lieutenant tossed me the box with my clothes, all the other officers were snickering like little school girls talking about some poor schmuck's little dick.

What the fuck?

LT: "Okay. Here you go. Spanky."

Me: "Yeah, uh…whatever."

You would think that after three and a half years in prison that I'd be able to pick up on any disturbances in the force.

Something was definitely wrong here; I had no idea what and my Spidey-senses were doing fuck all

Sadly, subtle has never been a language that I've understood. And when I opened the box, I hated myself more than I ever thought possible.

The box contained two items. When I saw them, I simultaneously wanted to kill myself for trusting Disco Nights, and Disco Nights for being such a cock monger.

You know the old axiom "be careful what you ask for"? Well, I should have known better than to ask Disco Nights to send me in a pair of jeans. The jeans that he sent me were jeans, yes, but they were also the tightest pair of *skinny jeans* that I've ever seen. I cannot even begin to explain to you how much I loathe skinny jeans.

I grew up in the grunge/skater era of the 90s and 00s. I wear baggy/loose fitting jeans. I don't wear jeans that are so tight that you might as well be wearing a leather gimp suit. I don't wear jeans that cut off the circulation to the lower half of your body. I don't wear jeans that come with their own castration kit. I am a firm believer that anyone who wears skinny jeans *by choice* should be punched in the face repeatedly just on general principle.

The second item in the box was the stone that sank the ship.

Disco Nights had sent me a pair of underwear as well.

But not just any plain old pair of boxers or briefs.

He sent me in a pair of fucking booty shorts.

Black male booty shorts.

With two handprints on the back side.

One on each ass cheek.

And the words "SPANK ME" written above the hand prints.

Need a visual?

As I held them up in disbelief, the mental wheels started spinning.

The LT called me "Spanky."

He'd seen the booty shorts.

The officers were laughing their asses off when I asked for my clothes.

They'd seen the booty shorts.

LT told me that if he gave me my clothing, I had to return all state-issued items.

I'm wearing state pants and boxers.

I HAVE TO WEAR THIS SHIT OUT OF HERE!

A knock at the door...

LT: "You alright in there, Spanky?"

Laughter erupted from behind him.

I hate my life.

LT: "You need to hurry up in there, Spanky; your ride is here."

In the end, I did what any self-respecting man would have done in my position. I put on the booty shorts and skinny jeans, and walked out of the bathroom with my head hung low to the ground. I refused to make eye contact with anyone, while they all exploded with laughter.

So THERE I WAS, being released from prison in a pair of booty shorts that said *spank me,* jeans so tight that my voice went up an octave, and my dignity nowhere to be found. The only reassuring thought that I could muster was that a direct flight to Florida was only a few hours long.

When the laughter finally died down, I took in a deep breath and gathered as much courage as I could before I picked my head up and looked for the Marshals.

Except, I didn't see any guys in suits.

I saw one dude, dressed in full combat gear, short of a face mask and helmet. His bulletproof vest said USC across it, and his utility belt would have made Batman jealous.

In his left hand he held leg irons, handcuffs, and a waist chain.

In his right hand he held a piece of paper which had my picture and information on it.

Hrm......

Gordo: "Mr. Lawn Mower, my name is Officer Gordo with US Corrections. You are being placed into my custody for extradition to Florida for a felony violation of probation warrant. Until we reach Florida, you are being held under Federal custody. My partner, Officer Braces, and I will be escorting you on your trip. Do you have any questions?"

Me: "Yeah, what time is our flight?"

Gordo: "Flight?"

Ut-oh.

Me: "Uh, yeah. Flight. We are *flying* to Florida, right?

Gordo: "No sir. We're driving."

He gestured with his thumb towards the van in the parking lot.

Fuck.

Can this day get *any* worse?

Me: "Straight through?"

Gordo: "No. Our itinerary changes every few hours. Legally, we can hold you in the van for up to thirty days. We stop every six to eight hours for a bathroom break and after five nights of being on the road, we stop for a courtesy hold in a jail overnight. As of right now, I have no idea when we will be getting to Florida. I would probably guess that we'll be there within a week or two."

Me: ***"A FUCKING WEEK OR TWO??!!"***

Gordo: "Yes sir. Now, there's two ways we can do this. The easy way, in which you cooperate with me, be a good boy, and everything will go nice and smoothly. Or the hard way."

To this day, I have yet to be that mad again. I've come close, yet haven't been able to cross that threshold again. But if you could for one second, imagine yourself in my position: being released from prison two days late, being extradited to another state for who the fuck knows how long, being completely humiliated and having to wear booty shorts with skinny jeans, and *then* finding out that the one thing you'd been dreading (the infamous van ride) had just come true: how would you have reacted?

I turned to face the LT.

Me: "Am I out of your custody?"

LT: "Yeah."

I turned back to Gordo.

Me: "Fuck you, we're doing this t...."

In about a tenth of a second, Gordo had me on the ground and hogtied. He put a gag in my mouth and called for his partner. Gordo and his partner Braces then carried me to the van and tossed me in the back like a sack of potatoes. I landed in a wet pile of what I can only describe as a mixture of piss and vomit, then watched them close the cage and doors behind them while my world was engulfed into total fucking darkness.

* * *

MY EXTRADITION to Florida was the second worst experience of my life. To this day, I still have nightmares about riding in the back of that van. To anyone who's ever been extradited before, I feel your pain. To anyone who's never been extradited before, do yourself a favor and never get into a situation where you have to be extradited. Trust me on this.

* * *

First, I need to explain how the van is set up so we can be on the same page.

Imagine a regular cargo van.

Now imagine a wall going down the middle of the van, lengthwise.

Now imagine a metal bench on either side of the wall, about the length of a standard park bench, against the outer walls of the van.

Now imagine a cage door facing the outside.

Now imagine the outer doors to the van, with blacked out windows.

Starting to get the picture?

Good.

But I'm not done.

Let's go back to the benches for a minute. A park bench isn't that long. It's roughly six feet.

At the end of the bench, imagine *another* wall, only this time it's going the width of the van.

And on the other side of that wall, imagine another metal bench against the wall.

They claim that each compartment "fits" four. And by "fit" they mean barely enough room to breathe. They pack people in like human sardines. Twelve in total. Four on the left side, four on the right side, and four in the front.

You're crammed in there like this:

THE ONLY DIFFERENCE between the van pictured above and the van I rode in was that the wall separating the front and back sections was solid.

Looks comfy, doesn't it?

Well, it fucking wasn't.

But I'm still not done! Let us not forget the fact that everyone has on handcuffs and leg shackles which are both attached to a waste chain.

And now you get the *full* picture.

* * *

My extradition lasted ***ten fucking days***. For the first several hours, I remained hogtied until we got to Connecticut where we were picking up another poor soul. When Gordo opened the door, the conversation was very short:

Gordo: "You wanna try this the easy way now?"

Me: "Mhmm."

Gordo: "Thought so."

My Mr. Tough Guy act went right out the window.

I lost part of myself on that six-hour ride to Connecticut. Being hogtied and gagged for any extended time period is one thing. Doing it for six hours, in the pitch black, lying in a puddle of bodily fluids, while wearing booty shorts and skinny jeans, is life altering.

* * *

I left New York on a Thursday afternoon. I didn't get to my Florida destination until 11:45 p.m. the following Sunday night. We were on the road the entire trip, short of twelve hours when we had to stop in Atlanta, Georgia.

Before we made it to Georgia, there were multiple stops. Our route went something like this:

New York to Connecticut.

Connecticut to Manhattan (yes, back to New York).

Manhattan to New Jersey.

New Jersey to Pennsylvania.

Pennsylvania to West Virginia.

West Virginia to North Carolina.

North Carolina to South Carolina.

South Carolina *back* to North Carolina.

North Carolina *back* to South Carolina.

Then from South Carolina to Georgia.

In every state there was at least one stop. If not two. Sometimes three.

By the time we made it to Atlanta, it had been over fifty-six hours since I had been out of the van for more than five minutes for a bathroom break.

We were fed three times a day. We received two items off of the dollar menu from a fast-food drive-through, and a small cup of water. And no, they didn't remove the cuffs, or unhook us from the waist chain in order to eat or use the bathroom. Figure that one out.

When we got to Atlanta, there were nine of us. Eight men, and one woman. We were tired, miserable, cranky, sweaty, smelly, and pissed off. Somewhere between Spartanburg, SC and Atlanta, one of the dudes on the other side of the wall had to take a shit. We still had at least four hours before we were going to stop again for a bathroom break.

He tried yelling to the officers through the walls but they acted like they couldn't hear him for the longest time. After he finally started getting on their nerves, they flat out told him to get fucked. That's when he decided to take matters into his own hands.

Somehow he managed to get his shirt off, get his shirt underneath himself, and drop a deuce in his shirt. Even though the sound was disgusting and the smell was horrific, I gotta admit that I was kind of impressed. I had trouble sitting up straight, and yet this dude was able to remove articles of clothing and take a shit in them.

Several of the dudes in the van were screaming and yelling at Shitty McGee. Two other dudes threw up. And one dude cried like a little girl.

The smell was so bad that even Foxtrot (the chick on the other side of the wall) started to gag.

If I didn't live through this, I'd be calling bullshit, trust me.

The only satisfaction any of us got out of the situation was when Braces opened the door to the back of the van in Atlanta. When the smell hit him, his face got all scrunched up like when a chick tries anal for the first time, and then he barfed. Gordo just stepped back and shook his head laughing.

* * *

WHEN WE GOT TO ATLANTA, nothing else mattered. I needed to get out of that fucking hellhole we were traveling in. I needed to stretch my neck and legs, I needed to sleep, I needed to get out of the cuffs and shackles, and I needed to see Foxtrot (I'll get to that later).

I was so happy to arrive at the jail that it didn't even dawn on me that there would be some sort of intake process. That is until a deputy brought all eight of the dudes into a room and said six words that made me want to die.

Deputy: "Strip down to your boxers, y'all."

Disco Nights: 2

Lawn Mower: ○

You got that one buddy.

How does one even begin to explain to seven convicts and a cop why you have on booty shorts with spank me written across the ass, and still save your dignity?

Easily.

You don't.

I just stood there and didn't say a word. Not because I didn't want to, but because I couldn't. At that point, I had nothing.

Even though everyone looked at me like I had three heads, and the deputy almost died because he forgot to breathe during his fits of laughter, no one said a word to me about it. Which was a good thing, because I'm fairly certain that I would have cried if they did.

After that, we were put in a holding cell, given mats, fed, and left alone. I put my mat in the corner, ate, then curled up into the fetal position and cried myself to sleep. That night I had dreams about Disco Nights contracting AIDS and dying a very long, painful, and horrible death.

The next morning, we got up, were fed, and headed out on our merry way to Florida. The rest of the trip was uneventful and uncomfortable, but it didn't matter. After five days of hell, I was about to arrive in Florida and start my next adventure.

DID you think that I forgot to tell you about Foxtrot?

Well don't worry, I didn't. Even though this happened during the extradition trip, I felt that the topic of Foxtrot should be discussed separately.

I'm sure you'll understand why. If not, oh well.

DURING MY LITTLE adventure down the Eastern Seaboard, I found further proof that if there is a "God" (as in one all-knowing, all-powerful, almighty-type being), he hates me.

One of the pickups that we had to make was in Manhattan. Most anyone living in New York City, can tell you that 100 Center Street is nothing but absolute in-fucking-sanity all day, every day. When the court system runs twenty some-thing hours a day, you already know that shit's fucked-up. You can almost set your watch by the times of the bus arrivals from and departures to the island. Yes, I'm referring to Rikers.

We had to park the van on the street because there was nowhere else to park. Braces must have picked the short straw, because he had to stay and babysit us while Gordo went to pick up the newest contestants for "your life's really about to suck."

Braces got bored playing the *Cops* theme song on the radio (I can't even make that shit up) because he came back to fuck with us a bit. He opened the back door of the van a little and let some of the "fresh" air in. I really couldn't see much through the cunt hair-sized opening in the door, but I could definitely *hear* a lot. And all I could hear were Hispanic people.

Now, before we continue, I feel that there's a small fact y'all should be aware of. For years I had a thing for the Spanish culture. I loved everything about it. The language, the food, the history, the ethics, and especially the *women*. At one point in my life, I was completely fucked-up over Hispanic women. I had spent years of my life learning the Spanish language and watching Univision & Telemundo for the sole purpose of (hopefully) one day having a conversation with a hot Hispanic chick. Think me shallow or callous, I really don't care. It is what it is.

We were parked in front of the courthouse for a good couple of hours. Even Braces was starting to get antsy because he was coughing up information about who we were picking up. He said that we were picking up two people, one who would be going to West Virginia, and the other who would be going to Florida with the rest of us. Yippee.

And then I heard her.

Braces forgot to mention the fact that one of the people we were picking up was a female. Her name was Foxtrot.

And she was *Hispanic*.

There *IS* a god.

By law, women and men cannot be transported in the same area together, so all females have to ride in a different section of the van. This section was towards the front of the van and separated from my area by the wall that I was sitting next to. This was probably the one time in life where not getting the window seat actually paid off. And because I was next to the wall, I was elected to engage in conversation with Foxtrot, which was fine by me.

The second she opened her mouth, I was in love. She had the sexiest voice and accent that I'd *ever* heard, and after about thirty seconds of speaking with her, I was ready to confess my undying love and propose to her.

Except for the fact that she was being an absolute fucking **cunt**, and on an epic scale. She actually took "Hell hath no fury..." to a whole new level. And I can't blame her. Finding out that you're being extradited somewhere really fucking sucks. That being said, she was taking superbitch to a whole new level.

Imagine taking twenty-five alpha females on their periods and combining them together to get one huge super alpha female, with a raging river of menstrual blood constantly flowing. Sprinkle a little essence of Regan (from *The Exorcist*) and a splash of Nancy Grace, and *voila!* You have Foxtrot.

Did I neglect to mention that Foxtrot was 100% Boricua? Translation: Puerto Rican. And in case you're not "in the know," Puerto Rican women are certifiably fucking crazy.

When I attempted to speak to Foxtrot, she pulled the "no English" card on me.

Sorry chica, but this white boy can habla.

When she realized that I could (passably) speak Spanish, she gave me the silent treatment.

Well fuck you too, bitch!

Then, after several hours of the unrelenting, unabated and incessant boredom that the van provided, Foxtrot (slightly) dropped her attitude and started to speak.

To me.

In Spanish.

Foxtrot: "Are you the only guy back there that can speak Spanish?"

Me: "Pretty sure."

Foxtrot: "You know that I can speak English, right?"

Me: "Yep."

Foxtrot: "If I start speaking in English then I'm going to have everyone back there trying to holla at me, ain't I?"

Me: "Yup."

Foxtrot: "We'll just stick with Spanish then."

The guys: "Yo what's she sayin', bro????"

Me: "That she can't speak a lick of English."

I'm an asshole, I know. But after three and a half years in prison, I'd much rather be talking to an unknown female than the sausage party that I was sardined with.

Foxtrot: "Smooth."

* * *

FOXTROT and I talked for hours. Nothing serious, just your run-of-the-mill basics. Plus, my Spanish wasn't that great for any in-depth conversation. I did find out that she was forty, from the city, had two kids, was being extradited for a violation of probation (isn't that a bitch?) and that she *loved* white boys.

I should have known right then and there that this was a trap.

But most of the time, I never see the obvious.

And I always forget the fact that God hates me.

So did I see the situation for what it really was?

Of course not.

When we stopped for bathroom breaks– as infrequent as they were– we all tried to catch a glimpse of Foxtrot, but it never panned out. Gordo and Braces found it amusing.

Once we even asked Gordo if she was as hot as she sounded, and he replied:

Gordo: "You wouldn't believe me if I told you."

Still, I didn't see the obvious.

See, in my mind, Foxtrot had to be the most beautiful woman alive. I just *knew* that she looked exactly like Rosario Dawson when she played in *The Rundown*, and somewhere around North Carolina I decided that I wanted to marry her.

You can't even begin to imagine my excitement when I found out that we had to make a stop in Atlanta, and that we would be staying overnight. The fact that I was going to be able to lay down (albeit on a concrete slab) and get out of the handcuffs and shackles that I'd been in for over a hundred hours was only a small contribution to my excitement. What I was really excited for was the fact that I was going to see the future Mrs. Lawn Mower for the first time.

The anticipation kept growing as we got closer. I was so excited about seeing Foxtrot that I'd even forgotten about how bad it smelled from all the shit and vomit in the back of the van. Well, that, or I'd just become immune to the smell by then.

* * *

Lawn Mower

In Atlanta, I was the last guy out of the van. Gordo and Braces had us all out and lined up against the wall before they went to get Foxtrot out of the van.

I was like a little kid at Christmas waiting to open up *the big present*. You know which one I'm talking about. The special one that Santa always hid so it would be the last present you opened. The one thing you'd talked about all year. The one thing that you *really, really,* wanted. The one thing that you just had to have. The one thing that... you get the idea, right?

When Braces opened up the side door, I actually held my breath. I could hear her chains as she moved. I could hear her voice as she bitched to Braces about how horrible the van smelled. I could see her in my mind's eye.

Then, I saw her with my real eyes.

And then I threw up in my mouth.

Foxtrot was by far the ugliest woman that I'd ever seen in my entire life.

She looked like Sloth and Mama Fratelli had a child, and that child was born with both lupus and cerebral palsy. Then, the inbred Fratelli baby grew up and had a child of its own with one of the Garbage Pail Kids, which produced Uber Slothette.

Uber Slothette was then gang-banged by the child version of Jason Voorhees, the Leprechaun, and the dude from *Mask* (the movie with Cher in it). Somehow the sperm from all three dudes merged together and formed a Captain Planet "super sperm" and that super sperm was the one mother-fucker out of 10,000 to reach the egg inside Uber Slothette.

Nine months later, we have baby Foxtrot.

Forty years, two kids, and copious amounts of sex, drugs & who the fuck knows what else later, we have adult Foxtrot.

Gordo and Braces were laughing so hard at my reaction to Foxtrot that another officer had to come over to make sure that they didn't need some sort of medical assistance.

I should have seen it coming, I know.

But I didn't.

So, fuck off.

And tell God to go fuck off with you.

AND FYI: I never spoke another word to Foxtrot after that.

AFTER TEN LONG and grueling days of traveling in what can only be described as hell on wheels, I'd finally arrived at my destination. Not many people can say that they were ever happy to go to jail. But I can. Without a doubt, I was the only person in that jail with a smile on my face.

I owed probation eleven months. I just did three and a half years in prison, and still had three and a half years of parole to complete. I felt confident that this was going to be a short stay, which was another reason why I had a smile on my face. My time in jail was almost over.

Or so I had thought.

Lawn Mower

When I walked through booking, I got quite a few funny looks. I knew I looked like I just came off a month-long meth bender, and I was kind of wobbling when I walked because there wasn't enough room in the fucking skinny jeans for me to bend my knees, but at that point I couldn't have cared less. I was tired, hungry, in pain, and I just wanted to get everything over with.

I went through the booking procedures and a final humiliating strip search (fuck you very much, Disco Nights), and was given a pair of oranges, Jailspeak for.... I'm pretty sure you know what I'm talking about by now.

Within a couple of hours, I was booked, fed, and given my phone call. I called my sister for my "one free phone call" which lasted all of ten seconds.

Literally.

After that, I was led to my cell where I immediately passed out. I don't think I've *ever* slept that good in my life.

The next morning, I went to first appearance and the judge placed my case on the fast track because it was only a violation of probation. My next court date was a mere ten days later. I couldn't have been happier. I even gave myself a motivational pep talk:

Me: "Ten more days Lawn Mower, and you'll be a free man!"

Guess what?

I was wrong.

The day before my scheduled court appearance, my public defender called me to tell me that my court date had changed. She had *just* received my file and didn't know anything about my case. She told me that she'd contact me just before my next court date, which was twelve days away.

Okay, twelve more days. That's not so bad.

Eleven days went by and my public defender *finally* contacted me.

Public Defender: "Okay. So we've got court tomorrow. Did you receive your discovery that I sent you?" (A discovery is Legalspeak for the evidence the state's attorney has and plans to use against you.)

Me: "No."

Public Defender: "Okay. No problem. I'll give you a copy of it tomorrow. Let me give you the basics. You score out to prison time. The state's attorney is offering you six years with credit for time served. The state's attorney said that if you decide to not take the plea offer and try for an open plea (*remember these terms?*) that he'll recommend ten years in state prison."

Me: "I'm sorry, can you please use smaller words when you speak. I thought I heard the words six, ten and years somewhere in there."

A brief pause.

Public Defender: "The state's attorney wants you to go to prison for six years. If you try to fight him on this, he's going to push for ten years."

Me: "You've got the wrong client. I'm only here for a violation of probation."

Public Defender: "Yes I'm aware, and no I don't."

Dumbfounded doesn't even come close to how I was feeling at that moment. Six years for a violation of probation?! How the fuck is that even possible? If you recall I only received eighteen months on the *original fucking charges!*

Here's how:

First off, the Florida judicial system is a fucking joke.

Second, all the lawmakers in Florida are inbred and enjoy the use of anal beads.

Now that I've covered those two points, I can further explain.

In a violation of probation situation, Florida brings back your original charges and resentences you. The state's attorney does a whole new score sheet and everything, but this time they can add in anywhere between 6 – 24 points for the violation.

Then you get resentenced according to the "new" score sheet. Any sane (or non-inbred) person would call this double jeopardy. Florida calls this a "sanction" and gets away with it.

The fact that I was originally sentenced to two years of probation was meaningless. The fact that I had already completed thirteen months of said probation prior to the violation meant even less.

The only thing that *did* mean something was the fifteen and a half months that I had spent in prison in Florida. The three and a half years I had just spent in New York meant fuck all.

And there I was thinking that this was going to be a short stay in Florida.

Silly Lawn Mower.

I could almost *hear* fate laughing at me saying "ha ha stupid!"

My public defender did have some impressive lawyerly advice:

Public Defender: "I don't recommend that you take that offer."

Well, no shit.

* * *

EVEN THOUGH I wasn't going to take the deal, I still had to go to court the next day, where I got to meet ADA Shit Stain.

Prior to entering the courtroom I met with my public defender to discuss my options, few as they were. The offer hadn't changed, and ADA Shit Stain was being a douchebag. My options were simple. Take it or leave it.

Well, I damn sure wasn't going to take the fucking deal. I mean, who in their right mind would take a shit deal like that? If you just said that you would have, please put my book down and eat a bag of dicks.

What really chapped my ass about the whole situation was that the only reason the violation even existed was because of my charges in New York. I had just spent three and a half years in prison for said charges, during which time I'd been trying to resolve this whole violation issue. None of that fucking mattered. And that pissed me off.

It definitely felt like someone was bending me over and wasn't using any lube.

Not that that's ever happened to me before.

* * *

ADA Sнıт Staın carried himself in the courtroom like a man who has a nightlife that involves copious amounts of Astroglide, and someone who's asshole has to be at least ten inches in diameter. At one point in the proceeding, I actually had to glance over at him to make sure he didn't morph into a teenage girl, because he was speaking and acting just like one.

You know the type:

Teenage Girl: "Well Sally's sister Brenda has one, and so does everyone else, and I really want one too! I don't understand why I can't have one! My life is going to end if I don't have one! I'll be the laughingstock of the school! You can't do this to me!" *Stomps foot for emphasis.*

ADA Shit Stain spoke in the same exact manner as he blatantly lied to the Judge, telling him that I'd been convicted of armed burglary in New York, and all sorts of other heinous bullshit.

ADA Shit Stain: "Your Honor, the defendant is a violent, violent criminal and a threat to society; he needs to spend his remaining years behind bars!"

He even stomped his foot to get his point across.

I really wish I had that shit on video.

The judge must have been accustomed to ADA Shit Stain's antics because he didn't seem fazed by them. The only thing that he cared about was the fact that we (the state's attorney and I) couldn't come to an agreement and now we had to go through a tedious violation hearing which just took up more of the court's time. Fuck 'em though. I had rights, and one of those rights was the right to a trial. I wasn't about to let ADA Shit Stain act out his wet dream on me.

What really sucked though was that the next open hearing date wasn't for another forty-two days. Not really what I wanted to hear, but fuck it, it was better than agreeing to six years in prison.

Two things happened during those forty-two days:

1. I was able to prove ADA Shit Stain wrong on his "violent, violent criminal" accusations. After proving this, ADA Shit Stain realized that he made a mistake and now he had to inform the Judge of said mistake. His mistake also meant that my score sheet had to be recalculated because he had me down as a violent offender, which brought my score to just under twenty-seven months. As a nonviolent offender, I scored out to just under eighteen months. A big fucking difference for such a simple mistake, eh? And people wonder why the justice system is so fucked-up.

2. Aunt Big Red had given Not Fucking Gwen a message to relay to me: that she wished me well, and that she forgives me.

That message was more than I could have ever dreamed of hearing. I didn't know what to say. All I could do was cry. When you wrong someone, and they forgive you for that wrong, it's one of the most beautiful and freeing things you could ever experience. Not only for you, but for them as well. Her message changed a lot of things.

Prior to hearing Big Red's message, I had been toying with the idea of forgiving Beavis. I still held him responsible for my mother's suicide. I blamed him for introducing her to the world of heroin and for her subsequent downfall

I had been thinking about forgiving him because in order to be forgiven, you must be willing to *forgive*. After hearing Big Red's message, I knew that it was time to nut up or shut up.

Believe it or not, I nutted up.

Forgiving Beavis wasn't easy. Nor was telling him that I forgave him. Beavis was (and still is) an active user. He'd always thought (and still does) that he was better than me because he'd never broken the law to get or maintain his high. For the most part, he'd always gotten his drugs through doctors and prescriptions. Only once in a while did he have to go to heroin, and that was usually because his scripts had run out.

The sad part was, Beavis didn't even understand how I could *possibly* be mad at him.

Beavis: "How could you have been mad at me? I only showed her how to shoot up once, it wasn't like I put the needle in her arm every time."

Grant me the serenity to accept the things I cannot change, the courage to change the things I can, and the wisdom to know the difference.

FORTY-TWO DAYS WENT BY, and it was time for court again. After a lot of deliberating, I decided to go with the open plea option. Even though it fucked me before, I felt that it was my best option. I wasn't going to lie down and accept six

more years in prison without a fight. Plus, the circumstances were different this time around.

ADA Shit Stain did a little song and dance on how he previously erred in his original assessment of my case. He told the judge that even though my total sentencing points had changed, he still stood by his original offer of six years.

When he said that to the judge, I said a small prayer asking for his children to be born with cerebral palsy.

Once he was finished with covering his ass while simultaneously trying to bury mine, it was my turn to speak. I spoke about everything from how I first got arrested to how I was just released on parole, and everything in between. I spoke about my mother, my addiction, my recovery, my plans, my goals, my job, etc. I spoke for quite a while, and the judge paid attention to everything I said. I apologized for wasting the court's time and not taking the original deal offered to me, but I just couldn't throw away my opportunity on parole.

I felt confident that he was going to release me. I scored out to 17.85 months (which I already had in from my first prison bid in Florida, plus the almost two months I'd just spent in county jail), I'd just finished doing three and a half years in prison in New York for the reason that the violation even existed in the first place, I had a job waiting for me, I had a home to go to, I had immense family support AND I was still under supervision for the next three and a half years. The judge could easily give me "time served" and let me go be New York's problem.

So can you imagine my surprise when the judge said:

Judge: "Mr. Lawn Mower, it appears that you have come a long way during your incarceration in New York. I think that you've got a great plan for yourself and your future, and believe that you'll be able to succeed. You will be going home Mr. Lawn Mower, just not today, and not from here. I'm sentencing you to two years in state prison with credit for all time served here in Florida. None of the time you served in New York will count towards this sentence. Good luck to you, sir."

You've got to be fucking kidding me.

This is the **same fucking shit that happened before!!!** I did an open plea to the court and I got fucked by receiving more time than I even scored out to!

Fuck you, Florida. You ass-backward, inbred, redneck shithole.

* * *

And this is how I went to prison for the *third* time.

Prison in Florida no less.

Where the only way a guy can get circumcised is when you kick his sister in the jaw.

And this is why when taking a tally of my prison bids, I don't think this one should fully count. Yes, I was going to prison again, but I was brought from the gate of one prison, straight to the gate of another one. Without going home. Without committing a crime. Without passing Go, and without collecting $200 dollars.

ALRIGHT, I admit, it wasn't as bad as I make it out to be. Yes, I was sentenced to two years in prison. But! I already had in eighteen months (fifteen and a half months from my first bid in Florida and the two and a half months that I had just spent in county jail), so all I *really* had to do was another six months (four and a half with good time) and I was home free!

Even so, I still didn't want to go back to prison and deal with all the fucking bullshit. But I had no choice in the matter, and a week later I was on my way (back) to CFRC.

At least this time I knew what to expect.

Or so I had thought.

THERE WERE ONLY ten of us coming in from county that day, so the ride to CFRC wasn't that bad. We all got off the van and lined up outside. There was no screaming or yelling, and that really surprised me. And even though it was the ass end of December, it wasn't that cold out. Don't get me wrong, it was *cold*, but not *ball-shrinking cold* like my first time coming through reception.

Two COs came out to meet us, trying to look intimidating. They were clicking their handcuffs around while walking up and down our line staring at us with "menacing" faces. That type of shit. One of them would stop in front of each one of us and stare into our eyes seeing which one of us would blink first. The Other CO kept walking, then stopped at the middle of the line to speak to all of us.

The Other CO: "Gentlemen, welcome to the Florida Department of Corrections and the Central Florida Reception Center. This will be your new home for the time being, and this is *MY* world."

Here we go with this shit again

The Other CO: "Now. We here at CFRC understand that some of you may have hearing problems. We also understand that some of you may have a learning disability..."

Eye Fucker kept up his intimidation act.

The Other CO: "Fellas, let me tell you something: today is **NOT** the day to have a hearing problem or learning disability and fuck up the basic shit. Today is ***NOT*** the day to fuck up your left from your right, or to call a ma'am, sir. Today is ***NOT*** the day to try us. Do you understand me?"

Us: "Yes sir."

Even I'll admit it. For ten dudes, it was a weak response.

The Other CO: "Are you fucking kidding me?! Say it like you've got a set of fucking balls between your legs. DO YOU UNDERSTAND ME?"

Us: "YES SIR!"

The Other CO: "Much better. Now. Before we get started, we have some preliminary shit to take care of. Now strip. Take off all your clothes and put them in a pile in front of you. NOW. NOW. NOW. You have three fucking seconds!!!"

Everyone got out of their clothes faster than your daughter did on prom night.

The Other CO: "Now, lift your hands in the air."

The Other CO: "Now let me see the backs of your hands."

We all showed him the backs of our hands.

The Other CO: "Okay, good. Now. Take both hands and spread your nuts. Your left hand on your left nut, your right hand on your right, and spread."

Easy peasy.

The Other CO: "Now. Open your mouth and rub your fingers across your gums. Then lift your tongues with your fingers."

You. Fucking. Cocksucker.

The Other CO. "That's right boys. Savor the flavor of dem nuts. Don't chew worry, boys. By the time you leave our fine establishment, y'all are gunna *love* the taste of cock and balls. You're gunna be writin' home to yer mama tellin' her how much you love the taste of cock."

The twat waffle was really getting a kick out of this.

The Other CO: "Now. Everybody turn to (I swear he said *my*) the right and face the fence."

While everyone turned to the right, I turned to the left. Which would have been *his* right.

AND JUST LIKE THAT, I became "that guy" and my life turned to shit.

Eye Fucker was on me in less than a second. He had my back on the fence, his left hand around my throat and his right fist smashed into my stomach. The fact that I was in my birthday suit was of little concern to him.

The Other CO: "What the fuck did I just get done telling you pansy-ass fucktards?!! I thought I had made it perfectly clear that today was **not the fucking day** to fuck up. Did I or did I not make that clear, inmate?"

Me: (*Between fits of coughing*) "Yes sir."

Eye Fucker: "LOUDER!"

Me: *Cough* "YES SIR." *Cough*

The Other CO: "And what the fuck do you go and do? You go and have a fucking hearing problem and fucked up some basic shit. Well don't you worry *boy*, I've got somethin fer ya."

This is when I figured a serious ass beating was on the way, but what actually happened was far worse. The Other CO had me walk about fifteen feet away from the group and turn to face the other guys with my hands behind my back. Then, he handed me a pair of hot pink Speedos, told me to put them on, and had me stand on a small platform which was conveniently stashed away in the corner.

I was on display for the world to view, in nothing but a man thong, on a cold December morning.

When I sit back and reflect on all of this, I always have to ask myself: *how the fuck do you get into these situations involving underwear?*

The ambiguously gay duo of Eye Fucker and the other CO had me standing on that platform **all fucking day long.**

Each time a new group of guys arrived from county, the first thing they saw was me. On the platform. Looking like a douchebag. In pink fucking Speedos. And every time he gave his little speech about today *not being the day*, he'd gesture to me and ask:

The Other CO: "Inmate, what's today?"

And I'd reply:

Me: "Today is not the day. Sir."

For anyone who happened to be at CFRC that morning, and went through the reception process, I'd like to state two things for the record:

1. It was cold that morning.

2. I'm a grower, not a shower (that's show....er. Not the thing you take to wash your body).

AROUND THREE IN THE AFTERNOON, I was finally relieved of my modeling duties– *eleven fucking hours after my initial arrival*– and I finished the rest of the intake procedure. I think some of the staff took pity on me that day, because I got through all the bullshit relatively quickly.

I got to the housing unit around 5:30 p.m., completely ready for some more first day shenanigans, but nothing happened. No one said a word to me. No one bothered me. And no one really even looked in my direction. I took that as a good sign because I was definitely not in the mood to be fucked with.

IF IT WASN'T for the New Testament and toothpaste I might have starved to death while I was at CFRC. It wasn't because they didn't feed us (by law they have to serve three meals a day); it was because of how and when the meals were served.

Breakfast was at 5:30 a.m.

Lunch was at 10:30 a.m.

Dinner was at 2:30 p.m.

Who the fuck serves someone dinner at 2:30 in the fucking afternoon?

The cockmongers at CFRC, that's who.

And just like a bad infomercial, there's more!

180 seconds (that's three minutes for my mathematically slower readers). That's how long you were given to eat your meal. The second you sat down you were told *"tighten up, you're on the clock,"* so you started shoveling shit in your mouth faster than a Catholic altar boy at Sunday school. If you didn't finish your meal before the time was up: Tough. Fucking. Shit.

By 7:00 p.m. my stomach was touching my backbone, so I was forced to improvise. I decided upon the New Testament for three reasons:

1. It was readily available.

2. The God of the New Testament is a pussy. If He did get pissed at me for eating His book, all I'd have to do is tell Him *"I'm sorry,"* ask for forgiveness, and ***wham!*** Clean fucking slate.

3. The God of the Old Testament is one vengeful mother-fucker. He would condemn people to Hell for eating meat

on a Friday, what the fuck would happen to me if I ate His precious book?

To all you fuckers who just got their panties in a bunch over that previous statement, this is for you:

A BAG OF DICKS.

Go eat one.

To those who knew me before all of this prison shit happened, isn't it amazing how much I've grown and matured? I mean, the old me would have eaten the Old Testament while using the New Testament to wipe his ass as he sang "Runnin' with the Devil."

My newfound maturity amazes even me.

* * *

EVEN THOUGH I'VE (clearly) grown and matured by leaps and bounds, I'm still constantly tested by life. When these little tests arise, I either pass them with flying colors...

Or fail.

Epically.

Once in a while, it's hard to tell whether I passed or failed. The following is an example of one of those times.

I was standing in line at the medication window waiting to receive my sunblock. I'm from New York and don't do well in the sun. Eat me.

The nurse inside the window had said something that I didn't hear, so I leaned my head down towards the window so I could hear her better.

CO: "Eh! Eh! Eh baw, git chur hed outta dat winder."

Three seconds later....

CO: "Eh, baw! Ain't chew listenin' ta me? Git chur hed outta dat dare winder!!"

What the fuck?

Nurse: "I think you're being yelled at."

Oh. Right.

So I turned around and was face-to-face with a woman who looked **_exactly_** like Mama Fratelli from *The Goonies*. If you don't know what *The Goonies* is, please do everyone in the world a favor and drink a gallon of antifreeze because you seriously fucking suck at life.

Me: "Oh. Were you speaking to me, ma'am?"

CO: "Yea I wuz talkin' to yew. I done told yew twice now to git chur hed outta dat dare winder."

Me: "Um. What's a *winder* ma'am?"

CO: "Are you sassin' me baw?"

Me: "Ma'am I don't know what *sassin'* is either, let alone if I'm doing it."

CO: "Oh. We's gots erselves a funny feller ere."

Me: "A what, ma'am?"

CO: "Don't chur eers werk, baw?

It took everything I had not to tell her that my ears had been laid off and were currently looking for work. But that's me: maturity master.

Instead, I just blankly stared at her.

CO: "Where yew from baw?"

Me: "New York, ma'am."

Complete disgust and contempt washed over her face.

CO: "Baw, dis eere ain't no Noooo York. Dis ere is Flor-ri-da. Chew ain't too bright are ya Yankee? My daddy hused to tell me....."

This was the point where I turned on my selective hearing. I couldn't understand a word she was saying in the first place, and in the second place, I knew she was talking a lot of shit and I didn't care what this inbred piece of trailer trash had to say.

And then it happened.....

CO: "Dew yew know who my daddy is, baw?"

Me: "I'm guessing either your uncle or your brother."

It just came out. No hesitation. No thought. No skipping a beat. No mind/mouth filter. It just came out.

Her one eye squinted at me even more while her other eye practically bulged out of her head. Her jaw was clenched so tight I thought I heard a tooth crack, and I swear I saw smoke come from her ears.

Even though she *had* it coming. She definitely didn't *see* it coming.

Nor did I see her right fist slam into my solar plexus.

I did however see my lunch come back up.

And so did about a hundred other people.

The bitch even kicked me in the gut while I was down. Then she walked away while I was gasping for air and lying in a pile of my own vomit.

So, did I pass or fail?

I'll let you decide.

*   *   *

A FEW DAYS AFTER THE "WINDER" incident, I found myself in another one of life's little fuck-you predicaments. This time, however, I definitely walked away with a W.

I was still in reception on an uneventful and boring Monday afternoon. I was reading a book in my cell and I had the sudden urge to take a piss. Not really that big of an issue, right?

Wrong.

This is what a typical prison cell looks like in Florida:

THE PROBLEM WAS that I had a jerk-off for a cellmate who refused to leave the cell unless he absolutely had to. He slept on the bottom bunk, which made it awkward when I had to use the toilet.

Since it was the middle of the day, the cell door was locked in the *open* position like in the picture. I was faced with two options.

Option 1: Expose myself to my cellmate while pissing.

Option 2: Expose myself to the entire cell block while pissing.

Not really great choices, are they?

But since I'm part genius, I had a simple solution: hold a towel with one hand in front of little mower, and hold my pants with the other. I could piss freely without exposing myself to anyone, thus solving my problem. The pants you get in reception are the elastic waist kind, so I figured that my solution would work. In theory.

My litmus test started out smoothly, until life decided to throw me a curve ball.

Seconds after I started pissing, I felt a sneeze coming on. This wasn't one of those little sneezes you can put off for a couple minutes. This was one of those throw-your-back-out-while-having-a-whole-body-convulsion type of sneezes.

I couldn't hold it in.

Nor could I stop pissing while I was midstream.

Oh no.

AH-CHEW!

I sneezed so hard that I had to brace myself against the wall, and I used my right hand to do so (this is the same right hand that was holding my pants, by the way).

When I released my grip on my pants, the elastic band did exactly what it was intended to do: it snapped the fuck back in place.

All the while, the urine stream just kept on flowing.

Translation: I pissed my pants while standing in front of a fucking toilet.

When I looked down, there was a huge, wet stain running right down the leg of my 65% polyester, blue stretchy pants. Ray Charles would have fucking noticed it.

In the same moment that I was admiring the giant piss stain on my pants, the CO boomed over the loudspeaker:

CO: "Everyone, right now! Class-A. Inspection!! Get in front of your cells! Warden's coming boys."

Are you fucking kidding me?

Let me break all that gibberish down for you:

Class-A: Fully dressed in your prison uniform with your ID showing.

Inspection: Someone's coming into the housing unit to inspect shit. You fucking idiot.

Warden's coming: Pretty fucking self-explanatory.

Once again, a*re you fucking kidding me?*

The worst part about all of this is that when you're in reception, you're only given **one full set of clothing**. I literally had **nothing else to change into.**

I had no choice. I had to stand in front of my cell, hands clasped behind my back, with a nice, giant, fresh fucking piss stain all over the front of my pants for the world to see.

If there was an available hole, I would have gladly crawled inside it to die right then and there.

And now enters the warden.

The warden was six feet tall and *easily* 350 pounds. He wore cowboy boots, had a mouth full of chew, and wore a fucking Stetson. He was the epitome of backwards-ass, corn-fed, and country blumpkin. When I first saw him, two words came to mind: *Big Hoss*.

My cell was on the top tier. Big Hoss was a massive fat-ass, so while he was doing his rounds on the bottom tier, I was promising any god, elf, nymph, leprechaun, fairy, unicorn or other mythical creature that I would personally blow them as long as Big Hoss decided that burning a few extra calories that day wasn't very important, and he stayed =off the steps to the second tier.

But of course, the gods, life, and every other fucking creature in existence hates me, and Big Hoss waddled his cornfed ass up the stairs. On his most laborious and exhausting trip up the fifteen steps, he turned his head to face the first cell on his tour (which of course was mine), and stopped dead in his tracks while looking at my crotch. This wasn't because he was gay or anything like that, it's because I had a big fucking neon sign pasted on me.

Big Hoss: "Well what in de fuck doo wee have eere? Dis baw's gone an pissed in his britches."

I remained silent, staring at nothing in particular but making sure that I didn't make eye contact with him.

Big Hoss: "Eh, baw. Yew eere me?"

Still not making eye contact with him.

Me: "Yes sir."

Big Hoss: "What's de matter baw? Yer mama didn't teech yew to take yer pecker outtayer britches before you piss? Or is yer pecker so small that you just can't find it??"

Most everyone got a chuckle out of that one.

Except me of course.

Seeing as how my mother's suicide was less than two years prior, it was still a raw subject, and I really didn't take too kindly to mother jokes at that particular place and time. Still, I decided not to respond. Big Hoss did happen to see the anger flash across my face at the mention of my mother, and he decided to stay with it. He was the warden and I was in his house. I wasn't shit to him.

Big Hoss: "Ohh. What's de mattabaw? Don't chew like me talkin' bout chur mama?"

Silence was all he got from me.

Big Hoss: "Well don't yew wurry. She don't like me talkin' bout yew either when's I bees fuckin' er."

Seriously, how does one get a job of any notoriety with speech and grammar like that? Oh. Right. We're talking about Florida. Never mind.

Big Hoss saw that I wasn't going to bite, so he moved in for the kill.

Big Hoss: "Yer mama's gotta be ashamed of a baw like chew. Skeert to def an pissin' himself in prison. Baw da best part-o-yew ran right down yer mama's asshole. Yew shouldt'a been an e-bor-tion."

When he said that, I snapped. I finally looked at that fat, inbred hick, right in his beady little pig eyes, and I retorted with the most disrespectful, spiteful and hateful inbred-redneck comment that I've ever conceived.

In my head.

Come on. I'm not a complete fucking idiot. I wasn't about to talk uber shit to the warden. At least not to his face.

I just stared the fat fuck down until he saw that I wasn't going to say anything and he decided to move on. Leaving me alone.

Fuck you, life!! You're not going to get one over on me again with some inbred hick.

Even though I was covered in my own piss and everyone in the housing unit now knew it. I still feel like I came away triumphant in this situation. I didn't let Big Hoss get to me, and I'd shown my maturity at the same time. Despite all the details, it was a proud moment for me.

Just as I was in the middle of praising myself and telling the gods of the universe to suck my hairy balls, the warden was making his exit. Right before he walked through the door to the housing unit, he turned and pointed at me while telling the housing sergeant:

Big Hoss: "Dat baw don't get no clean britches fer a week."

Well played, life. Well played.

Truthfully though, the joke's on that obese pile of pig cocks. The next morning, I got transferred and I got a clean set of clothes at my new facility. So:

* * *

HAVE you ever driven down the highway in Florida and wondered who cuts all that fucking grass on the side of the road?

Lawn Mower

No?

Well, I'm going to tell you anyways.

Prison inmates cut that shit.

Florida prisons have what are called "work camps." At these prisons, most of the inmates are cleared to work outside the gate. Some of them are assigned to the DOT or a city work crew, and for eight *long* fucking hours a day, they cut the grass and pick up the trash on the side of the highways.

All those slopes that you see on the side of the on- and off-ramps?

Inmates cut that shit too.

And I can tell you from personal experience that it fucking sucks.

The worst areas to cut, however, are retention ponds.

If you've ever been to Florida and you've driven down a road or highway and thought to yourself that the retention pond you just saw looked beautiful, please go to your local produce stand, purchase a pineapple, take it home, take of your pants and underwear, then sit on said pineapple and rotate counterclockwise.

All that tall-ass grass on the edges of the retention ponds doesn't cut itself. And most of it has to be cut from *inside* the ponds. So some unfortunate inmate is handed a weed whacker and told:

CO: "Get in that fucking pond and cut that fucking grass."

There's not really much of a choice in these situations. You may think that there is. But there isn't. It's either get your ass in the pond, in nasty, dirty, smelly-ass water that's up to your chest, or go to the box. So, what do you do? You get into the water with all the snakes, gators, rats, and every other creature imaginable, and you cut that shit down.

It's not fucking fun.

And I fucking hate the state of Florida.

If you work for the Department of Corrections in the State of Florida, I just want you to know that I pray nightly that each and every one of you cock-gobbling, backwards-ass, hillbilly, inbred fucks contracts an incurable flesh-eating virus and dies a long and painful death.

I also hope that your children become drug addicts and rob you blind of all your money and savings, so that you have nothing left to pay for the medical bills accrued from your flesh-eating virus, and thus you are unable to purchase any sort of pain medication, which will only intensify the amount of pain you are in before you die.

Then, I hope that once you're in hell, Lucifer and his minions place you in *their* prison, where you are ass-raped nightly by Hitler and a herd of elephants with tree bark covering their dicks.

And if somehow you escape hell and are reincarnated, I hope that you're reincarnated as some sort of bacteria and end up in someone's septic tank where you do nothing but eat shit for the remainder of your pathetic life.

Lawn Mower

LUCKILY FOR ME, I didn't have to put up with the donkey show of horseshit in Florida for very long; just five short months later I was *finally* on my way home.

There was only one small catch.

My father would be picking me up from prison and bringing me to the airport.

Isn't that wonderful news to be getting just prior to release? After enduring all of that bullshit. After taking all of those physical and mental hits. After all that loss. After all that pain and suffering. After everything, I had to be picked up by one of the two people on this planet who I absolutely despise.

I mean, y'all remember my father, right? The piece of shit who tried to fuck me over during my first prison sentence and the same fella who wrote that wonderful letter to me right after my mother had committed suicide. The guy who took it upon himself to inform me of exactly how everyone else in the family felt about me, when I was at the lowest and most difficult emotional state that I'd ever been in.

How's that for a kick in the balls?

Yes, I did have another option; I could have taken a bus home. I could have had the State of Florida purchase me a Greyhound ticket and ridden the bus home. A ride that would have taken about three days and who knows how many bus swaps. A ride that would have been almost as horrible as my extradition trip, because I would have had fuck all to do to occupy my time. I had no phone, no money, no clothing short of what the facility gave me to go home in. I did *not* want to sit on a bus for three fucking days looking like and feeling like a fucking bum. My superiority complex simply wouldn't allow it.

But then again, I knew that the other option was going to be just about as much fun as giving a horse a blow job.

In the end, I just wanted all of this shit to be over with and behind me as quickly as possible.

So I ended up sucking off the horse.

I GUESS this is the part where I'm supposed to tell you how great and prosperous my life has been since I've been home. Where I'm supposed to tell you how I implemented the plans I had made while I was in prison, how I have been reaching, or on my way to reaching, all the goals I had set for myself during my incarceration, how the rest of my life has been one big Swedish massage with an explosive happy ending, and how I never walked down that path of addiction, relapse, self-destruction, and incarceration ever again.

Well.........

But Lawn Mower, what about the "great change" that happened to you after your mother's funeral?

All I can say about that is, change takes time.

* * *

FOR THE RECORD, *this* wasn't part of "the plan."

"This" was supposed to be the start of a second book, not the beginning of a new section in this book. So clearly, my plans have changed.

But like Napoleon said, "Man plans. God laughs." Or maybe it was Vanilla Ice. I don't remember.

Either way, I'm fairly certain that The Old Fucker gets his kicks out of fucking with me. Yes, I just referred to God as "The Old Fucker." It's okay though, we're cool. You, on the other hand, are probably fucked for laughing.

I have this theory that I'm his personal cure for boredom. Whenever he gets tired of smiting sinners, doing fuck all for humanity, watching farm animals get raped by L****, and watching innocent children die from horrible things like starvation, AIDS, and gluten, he just checks out what I've got going on in my life and throws a huge fucking wrench in my plans so he can watch me squirm. So if you happen to make it to Heaven and meet the old geezer, and he happens to have a big, yellow stain on his holy roller robe, you'll have me to thank for that.

To put all this in layman's terms (because I'm still painfully aware that most everyone reading this book needed "a little extra help" in school, which is a nice way of saying that you're fucktarded) I fucked up pretty good. Again.

I would have simply said *retarded* there, but I'm trying to be less offensive.

This is the part where you may voice your unwanted opinions and comments about me.

Go ahead, I'll wait...

Feel better?

Good.

Because now if I get an e-mail, text, tweet, postcard, messenger pigeon, smoke signal, or any other form of communication about how I'm a total fuck-up, I'll track you down, beat up your significant other, pop your blow-up doll, then I'll rape your dog after burning down your home. Be it an apartment, condo, house, trailer, or cardboard box. Although if you're living in a cardboard box, you really don't have any room to be telling me about my life choices.

But Lawn Mower, I thought that this book was supposed to show your personal growth and what not?

Well, fine reader, it is! The "old Lawn Mower" would have simply done all of that without thinking. This is the "new and improved Lawn Mower," and now I think things through and plan them out, which in Legalspeak means "premeditated."

See? Personal growth.

Now, where were we?

Oh, right... Florida.

Here we go.

And you better strap on your seat belt, 'cause once this thing hits 88 mph, you're going to see some serious shit.

ONE WOULD THINK that after all that bullshit, after all that pain, after everything that I had endured, and after everything that had transpired over the years, that *that* would have been enough for me to see the "big picture" and get my shit straight.

You could even go as far to say that I should have been looking at the world through a new set of eyes and that I'd never, *ever*, pick up another drug as long as I was alive on this earth. Hell, I even *believed* that for a while. I told myself– and everyone around me– that I was done, and that I was never going back down that road again. And in my heart of hearts, I felt that what I was telling everyone was the absolute truth.

However, I failed to realize three things:

1. I'm a fucking idiot.

2. I really liked getting high.

3. God hates me.

But I'm getting ahead of myself here.

First things first: I needed to get my dumb ass home.

* * *

FIFTY-FIVE MONTHS.

Between New York and Florida, I was incarcerated for fifty-five months and thirteen days. But who's counting, right? And at long last, my day had finally arrived.

Now one would think that after all that time, I'd be ecstatic with joy. That I'd be walking on cloud nine like a boy after his first blow job (receiving, not giving), or a Catholic priest when a flock of new altar boys enters his church, or Amy Winehouse after.... eh, you get the idea.

Yes, I was happy that I was getting out of prison, but that's where it stopped.

I had to walk out of prison in shoes two sizes too small, wearing clothes that a hundred-pound heavier version of me used to wear with no fucking belt. I looked like the king of the hobos after a two-week boxcar anal sex orgy.

I had to walk out of prison in my hobo king gear and stare into the eyes of the Antichrist himself: my father, Tricky.

We both stood there awkwardly for a couple of minutes just staring, sizing each other up. I hated this man, and if there wasn't 2,000 miles between me and home, trust me, I would have just started walking.

I wasn't going to blink first, so I just stood there until he did. Finally, he gave me a head nod and said:

Tricky: "Lawn Mower."

Me: "Tricky."

Tricky: "Let's go. Get in the truck."

So much for the pleasantries.

The ride to the airport was beyond awkward. We didn't speak to each other, except when I told him that he was going the wrong way. Tricky didn't seem to like that comment and mumbled something along the lines of:

Tricky: "What the fuck do you know about how to get to the airport."

So, I responded:

Me: "Well, since I worked outside clearance and for the DOT, one of my jobs was to maintain the grass and clean up garbage on the main road going to the airport. So, I've made the trip to the airport countless times in the past five months, and I'm extremely familiar with how to get there."

And of course, I couldn't help myself...

Me: "But what the fuck do I know, right?"

His glare was contemptuous.

His glare turned homicidal once he realized that I was correct and he *was* going the wrong way, and the way I told him to go was the correct way.

After an illegal U-turn, he got us on the right road to the airport. As we pulled into the parking lot, he looked at me and said:

Tricky: "Your mother's lucky she killed herself, otherwise she'd be here giving you a ride and putting up with your bullshit."

There're not many times in my life where I've been left completely speechless, but this was one of them. I could only look at him in disbelief.

He pulled up to the drop-off area, put the truck in park and handed me my ticket.

Tricky: "Have a nice flight."

I assumed that was my cue to leave, subtlety being an art that neither myself nor my father have mastered. So, I got out of the truck.

The passenger's side door was still open as he drove off.

I made a mental note to nominate Tricky for the Father of The Year award next time it comes around.

* * *

SOME PEOPLE HAVE a fear of flying.

I don't.

I've flown countless times throughout my life, both foreign and domestic. What I do have issues with are crowds and crowded places. Fairs, concerts, holiday shopping, the ball pit at Chuck E. Cheese's, etc. I have prison and multiple yard riots to thank for that. My therapist has a fancy term for it: PTSD.

Pfft, what does *he* know?

So when I walked into Orlando International Airport on the Friday of Memorial Day weekend, my anxiety hit the fucking roof. The place was packed like a porn star's ass, and I broke out in cold sweats and had trouble breathing.

After a few minutes of hyperventilating and puking in the bathroom, I cleaned myself up and got myself together; then I was ready to face the airport.

On a scale of one to ten, my anxiety was about a 115. I really thought that I was going to lose my shit standing in line. Everything seemed like absolute chaos. People moving around, not standing in a straight and orderly line. People walking wherever they wanted to, not staying to the right of the painted lines. People hugging, kissing, laughing, crying, holding hands. All the commotion and all the noise! Unless you've ever been incarcerated or institutionalized for any period of time, there's no way that you're going to understand what I'm talking about.

I didn't think that I was going to make it through the security check. I knew that I looked completely suspicious because I kept looking around for the cops like Chester the molester at Chuck E. Cheese's, and because airport security kept eyeballing me. And no, I wasn't just being paranoid. They were *staring* at me. Not all of them mind you, but enough of them to make me nervous.

I was just about to step out of line and get some fresh air when the guy in front of me decided to start a fucking conversation.

Guy: "Jesus, this airport coffee tastes horrible."

He held his cup for emphasis.

Me: "Well I'll guarantee you that it tastes a hell of a lot better than the stuff I've been drinking recently."

Guy: "Really? What the hell have you been drinking? 'Cause this tastes like shit."

Me: "Billy Brew."

Guy: "What's that? I've never heard of it."

Me: "It's the instant coffee they sell in the canteen."

Guy: "Canteen? What's that? Are you in the military or something?"

Me: "No. That's what they call the store in state prison.

Guy: "Oh, what are you, a correctional officer or something?"

Me: "No. I was the one that they watched."

Guy: "Seriously?"

Me: "Yeah."

Guy: "Wow. How long have you been out?"

Me: "What time is it?"

Guy: "Noon."

Me: "About an hour."

His eyes visibly widened.

Guy: "Wow. That's crazy. I've never met an ex-con before. What were you in for, if you don't mind me asking?"

Rule number one in prison: Mind your own fucking business.

Rule number two: Never, *ever,* ask what someone is in for.

This guy just violated two of the rules that have been a guiding force in my life for the past several years. Rules that have kept me alive on more than one occasion. This was un-fucking-acceptable to me. So, I had to fuck with him.

Me: "Manslaughter."

Guy: "Oh. Wow."

Me: "Well *technically* it was murder, but the cops screwed up the evidence chain, so they couldn't prove everything they accused me of, so all they could end up charging me with was the manslaughter 'cause of some technicality. It should have been flat-out murder, but who am I to contest the judicial system, right?"

Even though it didn't ring, the guy picked up his mobile phone, looked at the screen and said:

Guy: "Oh, shit, I've gotta take this man. Nice talking to ya."

Then turned his back to me while pretending to talk on his phone.

Suddenly I felt better. There's nothing like fucking with someone to brighten up my day.

By the time I got up to the security check point I was in a much better mood, until I got pulled out of line for a "random search."

Random my ass.

It was racial profiling. I know it.

I'm a tall, bald, white, tattooed, intimidating motherfucker.

Like I said, racial profiling, I'm telling you.

After I got through security, everything was fine. I got onto my flight without any issues and nobody from ISIS tried to blow the plane up or fly it into any buildings. I'd chalk that up as a win in my book.

* * *

HAVE you ever been to the zoo and had a monkey throw shit at you?

Neither have I.

However, I have had many days when life seems to be throwing shit.

Even though she royally dicked me over and completely abandoned me while I was in prison, Not Fuckin Gwen felt obligated to pick me up from the airport. She had always said that she would be there the day I got out no matter what, so I guess this was her way of sticking to her word. When someone's in prison it's easy to pretend they don't exist, but once they're out they're a little harder to ignore, I suppose.

I knew that Not Fucking Gwen was going to pick me up from the airport and bring me back home. During my flight I realized that I had mixed feelings about this particular situation.

One part of me acknowledged the fact that she was keeping her word about picking me up from prison and was actually thrilled to be seeing her again.

The other part of me wanted to murder her.

This part, which I'll call my "Darker self," had planned and replanned exactly how I was going to kill her, cut up her body, place her mutilated body parts in black plastic contractor garbage bags with weights in them, and discard her bits along the Erie Canal. Dexter style. This planning stage was how I occupied my time on the flight back home.

Eventually I decided that committing a serious felony offense on the same day that I got out of prison was probably a bad idea, and thus put it on the back burner. At least until after I made my initial report to parole.

Again, more personal growth.

I figured that the car ride would give us a chance to talk without a time limit or someone on the other end listening, and I'll be honest with you, I was really hoping to get laid.

Give a guy a break, okay? I'd been jerking off for over four fucking years, was tired of getting head from men and needed some vagina.

Wait. What?

Anyways...

The ride home was kind of awkward. I had a lot to say and she seemed a bit nervous, so not a whole lot was said. Some mundane chitchat filled the silence, because, had it not... well, I'm not quite sure how the ride would have gone.

We made two stops on the way to my place. The first was the greatest place ever (next to Legoland): Taco Bell.

Why Taco Bell?

Because I fucking *love* that place.

I long for a Demolition Man-type future where every restaurant is a Taco Bell. Except they won't serve all that stupid fancy shit. They'll serve the regular Taco Bell menu. With one exception: the only drink available would be Baja Blast Mountain Dew. Now *that's* a future worth living for.

And before you ask if I was concerned about the Taco Bell greatness running straight through me due to my time spent on a prison food diet, you need not worry. I had four and a half years to prepare for this moment and while I was waiting for my flight in Orlando, I had purchased a box of Pepto and a box of Imodium A-D. Which worked out well because I didn't shit myself on the ride home.

Lawn Mower wins this day!

The second stop was Walmart, which I simply couldn't face. The day had started to weigh on me, and I simply didn't have it in me to deal with Walmart people. They are a species unto themselves, and I was not ready to face them yet. So I made Not Fucking Gwen go in for me. Which in hindsight was probably a smart move; I might have been tempted to buy a hacksaw and black contractor bags.

Then we went to my place.

Can you imagine my frustration when Not Fucking Gwen told me that she had to have her IUD surgically removed the day before because it had been causing her problems, and that she couldn't have sex for two weeks?

Since we couldn't screw, we ended up talking all fucking night. And no, there were no relations of any kind. Not even a handy. I was beyond disappointed.

Things didn't stay friendly very long between Not Fucking Gwen and me. Her phone kept blowing up and she kept playing it off. After she left my house, I broke into her Facebook account and found out that she not only had a boyfriend, but that they were living together and planning on having a child. Needless to say, the next time I spoke to her, it wasn't a pleasant conversation. We didn't speak much (or at all) after that. Fool me once, blah blah blah.

* * *

GETTING my life back together was weird. I didn't really know how to act around people, and people didn't know how to act around me. It was awkward. I was living with my brother Norman, and everything I owned was stuffed into several garbage bags which were piled in Norman's living room, awaiting my return.

I had to throw out pretty much all of my old clothing. Due to my significant weight loss, I already knew that nothing would fit me. Other than my clothes, there wasn't much to go through regarding materialistic things; I had lost everything when I went to prison in Florida, and hadn't been home for all that long in New York before I went *back* to prison.

Basically, I had nothing. I was really starting from zero. I was thirty-four, I had no clothing, no job, no vehicle, and no money. The only things I had going for me were that I had a place to stay, family support, three years of parole ahead of me, and a gaggle of felonies on my record. I was pretty much the perfect catch.

* * *

AFTER A FEW DAYS of being home, I decided that I was going to try and do the right thing and reach out to my father (again).

I know, I'm a fucking idiot.

My father, being the cockmonger that he is, didn't disappoint.

Father: "Hello?"

Me: "Hey, it's Lawn Mower."

Silence.....

Me: "Um, I just wanted to give you a ring so you could have my phone number. This is it. The number that I'm calling you from."

Father: "Lawn Mower, I don't want your phone number. I don't want to talk to you and I want nothing to do with you. Why don't you do us both a favor and lose my number. I don't want you in my life and I've realized that it was a mistake coming to pick you up and I wish I never did it."

I don't know why I was surprised by his response. I should have expected it. Yet this fuckbag never ceases to amaze me.

* * *

IN PRISON you get so accustomed to constantly being around people and having so much background noise around you at all times, that it becomes part of your world. A part of the daily status quo. The total lack of noise and people at home was completely unnerving. I'd never experienced anything like that before, and I felt as if I was going to have an honest-to-God meltdown. Prison fucked me up, and I was just beginning to understand the reality of that.

And nothing can prepare you for it. No one tells you about it while you're locked up. People talk about getting home, back to their family, doing the right thing, and all that other good shit, but no one tells you how to deal with the sudden and cataclysmic change to your life. No one tells you how the faux world you just navigated and survived is meaningless, and now you've got to adapt to a whole new world on the flip of a dime.

There are so many things that have to be done in order to live/survive, it's overwhelming. Getting to parole and DSS. Getting food and clothing. Trying to find a job. Hell, just having someone smile at you or hold a door for you is nerve-racking. As soon as they do, you're trying to figure out their ulterior motive or you're looking at their hands for the shank.

Going from home to prison is one thing. Going from prison to home is much, much different. And no one can prepare you for it. Hell, I've done it before and I *still* wasn't prepared for how it would be this time.

And people wonder why there's an 85% recidivism rate.

So, what did I do about it?

Instead of talking to someone about it, I just pushed it down and acted like I was fine. I took everything that I had learned in prison, every life lesson and hard truth, every trick, tool, and skill learned via my blood, sweat, and tears, combined them all, and did absolutely nothing with them. I mean how the fuck do you tell someone that you've come home from prison even more fucked-up than you were before you went in? I know that this is a poor comparison. But I kind of understand what soldiers go through after coming back from a war or tour of somewhere very unpleasant. I guess trauma is trauma, right? Well, I let all this shit start to affect me.

And then I made some mistakes.

* * *

My first mistake was announcing my return to the world. Going on Facebook and acting like everything was kittens shitting rainbows made of sherbet, while basking in the attention from all of my "friends." You know, all the cocksuckers who never made an attempt to reach out to me or even my family to see how I was over the course of the previous four and a half fucking years, who now all of a sudden wanted to be my best friends again.

Friend 1: "Oh, I was going to write but..."

Friend 2: "OMG, life's been so crazy..."

Friend 3: "I thought about you all the time..."

Friend 4: "I'm so happy you're home."

You *all* know who you are. If you're reading this and think that I am even *remotely* talking about you, chances are, I am.

My second mistake– or maybe this is really my *first* mistake– was not reaching out to my family or people in my support network, or really anyone for that matter, and simply talking about what the fuck I was going through. I knew better, I just failed to act.

And my third mistake was #2.

I hadn't been home a month before I decided that I was ready to start looking for some sort of relationship.

Genius, right?

So, in my leisure time, which was pretty much all the time because I wasn't working yet, I decided to peruse the world of– surprise, surprise– online dating.

I mean, it's worked so well for me in the past, right?

And that's how I spent most of my time. Don't get me wrong, I was still running/working out. I had also updated my resume and was putting in applications all over town, going to outpatient, and being a good boy for parole. But I was experiencing a lot of anxiety and insomnia. I'd sleep only three to four hours a night and thus needed something to help pass my time. I was lonely and bored.

My nights were pretty much spent on the dating apps, and my days were spent doing interviews, filling out ridiculous applications and/or taking aptitude tests for jobs. One day in particular, I had to drive to the next town over to take a two-hour aptitude test for a job at McDonald's.

Just kidding. It was Burger King.

No, seriously, it was Subway.

Okay, I'll stop. We all know that the only thing you need in order to work in a fast-food place is to be able to recite your ABCs. The test was for some manufacturing plant, building rockets, sprockets, Lego men, or something similar. I really don't recall which.

As I was pulling into the parking lot and parking Norman's car, I was on the phone with my sister.

Me: "Well, I'm here."

The Sister: "Cool. What time is the test at?"

Me: "Like twenty minutes."

The Sister: "Nice. Well, good luck!"

Me: "I don't need any luck, I'm a fucking genius." (As I'm getting out of the car.)

The Sister: "Right, well good luck anyways. You coming over after?"

Silence......

The Sister: "Yello? You there?"

Me: "Uh, where's Norman?"

The Sister: "I don't know. Why?"

Me: "Because I've gotta go inside for the test and I need you to get a hold of him for me."

The Sister: "Okay..... why?"

Silence again

Me: "I, uh... just locked the keys in the car."

The Sister: "BAHAHAHAHAHAHAHAHAHAHAHA-HAHAHAHAHAHAHA. Yeah, real fucking genius material you are, broski."

It's precisely moments like this that prove my theory about God hating me.

* * *

It was also during this time that I started taking all my handwritten pages and notes for *Epic Fail* and putting them into digital format. Yes, that's right y'all, I hand-fucking-wrote the vast majority of this book. I had countless pages of notes, scribblings, stories and tales of all my merry adventures throughout my years of incarceration and life.

See, years ago I started a 4th step. For those of you living under a rock, a 4th step is the– get this– 4th step out of the Twelve Steps of NA/AA. When you read the 4th step it says: "We made a fearless and moral inventory of ourselves." Which, roughly translated, means that you write down all the fucked-up shit you've done in your life and during your addiction. You list everything you feel is wrong with you and how you've harmed yourself and others. It's basically a form of confession sans priest. That is until the 5th step comes along, and then you have to go over your 4th step with someone.

Somewhere along the line of working my 4th and thinking about my 5th step, the idea for this abortion you're reading came along. I decided that maybe I could utilize my 4th and 5th step to help not only myself, but maybe someone else as well. By turning it into a story that people who have walked in similar shoes as I have could identify with, maybe, just maybe, my story could help them decide to walk a different path. That was the premise behind *Epic Fail*.

So I wrote and wrote, and I did so in a way that most anyone who's lived a similar life would understand. I don't speak Greek. So, if someone was trying to speak to me in Greek, I wouldn't know if they were asking me where the bathroom is, or if they can fuck my dog. The same applies here. Those who haven't lived this lifestyle won't and can't understand half of what I write or my cynical, sarcastic attitude towards my history (yes, I'm referring to you L****, you fucking dickwad).

And as I've explained in the beginning of this, I find none of this humorous. I've struggled for the past twenty-five years with my addiction and have been through some *shit* (obviously). I only wanted to try and get better and possibly help someone else along the way.

This is what in "the business" they'd call *foreshadowing*. Because all this shit comes into play later, trust me.

Most of my time was spent typing all of this shit out. Editing, formatting, etc. I quickly found out that writing a book isn't fucking easy and I had a long road ahead of me in finishing it. I did a lot of work on it, then stopped. I had a digital copy on all of my computers, but as time went on, it stopped becoming a priority to me.

Now enter mistake number three: #2

I met #2 on a dating app.

Which one, you ask?

Fuck off. I'm not here to promote shit unless I'm getting paid for it.

#2 was six years my junior (born the day after The Sister, actually), separated from her husband, had three children all under the age of ten, unemployed, suffered from severe depression, was bipolar, didn't have a car, and lived in her friend's living room.

I was a recovering heroin addict, divorced, unemployed, didn't have a car, lived with my brother, and on parole.

What could *possibly* go wrong with this combination, right?

And to stay in complete Lawn Mower fashion.... there's more.

The friend she lived with was a heroin/meth junkie, as was her live-in boyfriend. The house they dwelled in was literally about to be condemned in several weeks– I've seen abandoned crack houses in the middle of the 'hood that were in better condition than that shit hole. #2 and her kids slept on a hardwood floor, and during the second week of us seeing each other, the power got disconnected for being something like four thousand dollars in arrears.

To make the situation even better, #2 had recently left her husband and was seeking a divorce. She also informed me that she was "kinda talking to" (her words, not mine) this dude Joke, who was– you're going to love this– in prison.

"Kinda talking to" was #2speak for Joke being her actual ex-boyfriend and, according to her family, Joke was "more than likely" her youngest son's biological father. Joke was also under the impression that when he got out of prison in fourteen months, that he would be paroling to #2's place so that they could be "a family again." He'd also gotten #2's name tattooed somewhere on his person in prison.

Trailer park cliché, I know.

Apparently, #2 and I had two completely different definitions of "kinda talking to."

All of this put me in a tight spot.

One thing that I promised myself in prison was that I wouldn't get involved with a chick who was in some way involved with a dude in prison. That's a situation involving a serious can of worms. Plus, I've been on the shitty side of that particular coin, and I wanted no part in being on the less shitty side. But by the time I had translated #2speak into reality, it was too late; I was smitten with her, and that promise to myself went right out the fucking window.

Going against everything I had promised myself, and knowing full well how this dude in prison was going to react, I immediately put an end to that shit. So, after getting #2 a divorce packet from the courthouse in order to help get the ball rolling with that, I gave #2 a choice:

Me or Joke.

We sat down and had a little chat one day.

Me: "You say that you want to 'build a life' with me, right?"

#2: "Absolutely."

Me: "Then Joke has to go. If we're together, then *we're* together. Not we're together while some other dude thinks that he's coming home from prison to you, and you keep stringing him along letting him believe it.

#2: "Okay."

Me: "Plus, you've got another thing coming if you think I'm going to sit here while you're getting calls from prison with this dude on the other end talking about how much he loves you and can't wait to be with you and all of that other bullshit."

#2: "Okay, not a problem. Just tell me what I need to do and I'll do it. I love you and want to spend my life with you. Not Joke."

Me: "Just tell him the truth. That you met someone and whatever you "had" is over. Then delete your phone account. Rip the Band-Aid off. Trust me, it's better this way."

#2: "Consider it done."

And just like that, I became the dude I used to despise. The guy who steals another man's girl while he's locked up and helpless to do anything about it.

What made it worse was that I knew the truth. Joke was going to lose his shit. Getting your heart broken and your dreams crushed in prison is about as much fun as shitting out a pinecone. But fuck 'em. It was done to me, so therefore I could do it to someone else. You know, karma and all that.

* * *

THE RED FLAGS were so obvious that even I saw them.

I simply thought they were for a carnival.

And then there was the lynchpin for me.

#2 took me to meet her parents. First, I met her mom and stepdad. Then, I met her father and his... whatever you want to call her. While meeting both sets of parental units, I was pulled aside and told the same thing by both of them:

Parents: "Lawn Mower, you seem like a really good guy, so I wanna give you some advice. Run. Run away as far as you can and don't look back. #2 is no good, and she's only going to drag you down with her."

My response?

About forty-five days into my relationship with #2, The Sister started to become concerned. #2 had started to refer to me as "Dad" around her kids and even had her youngest one calling me dad.

In retrospect, this should have been the mother of all red flags. Fuck the rest of them, *this* was a clear indication that I should have simply walked away, because shit was not right.

But I didn't.

And here's why.

Firstly, I longed to be a part of a family. My childhood, to put it mildly, was fucked-up, and I'd always wanted to be part of a family unit. To be needed and depended on. And I'd found that with #2 and her kids.

Secondly (oh my therapist would have a field day with this), I saw a lot of my mother in #2. The depression issues, the anxiety, the struggling, the fucked-up history, etc. And something within me believed that I might be able to find some sort of absolution or redemption; deep down I felt that had I been home and not in prison, my mother would still be alive. And since I couldn't save my mother, I was *going* to save #2.

Forget the fact that I still had a lot of work to do on myself. Forget the fact that I hadn't been out of prison two months. Forget the fact that I had pretty much zero clean time "on the streets" or that I didn't really have two fucking nickels to rub together. I, Lawn Mower, was going to become Captain-Save-A-Hoe and provide an amazing life for #2 and her children.

And that umm....

Didn't work out so well.

* * *

Two AND A HALF months into being home, I finally landed a decent job. And no, I wasn't an unemployed bum the entire time. I did have a job within my first couple of weeks being home– I'm far from lazy– but the pay was shit and it was in the food industry. Not that there's anything wrong with that, but it's simply not for me. Like how being a fluffer on a porn shoot probably isn't for you, and how being a correctional officer is generally for the kids who got beat up a lot in school and had their lunch money taken on a daily basis.

#2 and I were getting pretty serious, and now that I had a "family" to take care of, I needed a better paying job. My sponsor Jiminy kept telling me that I was "taking on too much" and "biting off more than I can chew." But as always, I figured that I was smarter than he (and everyone else) was, and I kept on adding to my plate.

I got a job with a company called CNB (cock-and-balls), and honestly, it was the best job I've ever had. I was the maintenance manager for a large construction company. It had taken me a while to figure out that "maintenance manager" was a loosely constructed term for El Jefé's bitch. But I worked by myself, made my own schedule, and answered to no one but El Jefé, the owner of the company.

El Jefé took care of me as an employee. He paid me decently and even bought a brand-new Dodge Ram for me to use/take home. He even paid for the gas. So when he called or needed something done, I made it a priority.

After several months of being run ragged by El Jefé during the day, then spending my nights, weekends, and free time with #2 and her kids, I was starting to get worn out. I barely spoke to Jiminy, and I'd gone from going to five or more meetings a week to hardly any at all.

In the recovery world, this is known as: not a good thing.

I attempted to broach the subject with #2 that I needed a day or two during the week to myself, and her response was:

#2: "Well, if we were married and living together, then you could do whatever you wanted because we'd be together all the time, so it wouldn't matter. The kids and I want to see you every day. We simply can't go a day without seeing you."

I relayed this conversation to The Sister. Her response?

The Sister: "Dude, you officially have a stage-five clinger."

And you know what?

She was fucking right.

* * *

THE WORST PART about all of this was that I didn't do anything to stand my ground. I was so blinded by my need to save #2 that I went along with all of the bullshit. Which only got worse.

Remember how I briefly mentioned that The Sister and #2 pretty much shared a birthday? Well, this *enraged* #2. #2 had already been trying to place a wedge between me and The Sister. #2 wasn't close to any of her family members and she couldn't understand how/why The Sister and I were so close. She even got mad at me because not only did I want to "buy another woman a birthday gift" (her words), but I also wanted to hang out with said woman on her birthday.

It didn't matter that said woman was my *biological sister*. It only mattered that it was another woman, and #2 was insanely jealous of this fact.

No seriously, she was beyond jealous of this issue, and it caused many hours of argument. I couldn't even make that shit up if I wanted to.

I would love to tell you that I manned the fuck up, told #2 to eat a bag of dicks, and spent time with The Sister on her birthday.

But I'd be lying.

A month and a half later, shit got worse.

This time it was *my* birthday.

#2 wanted me to spend the day with her.

The Sister wanted to have a family thing at her place (since, you know, I hadn't had a birthday at home in over five fucking years), and said that #2 was "more than welcome to come." Which was The Sisterspeak for: I don't want that crazy bitch anywhere near my fucking house.

Naturally, this caused an issue.

After some heated conversation (yes, we really fought over my birthday), it was decided that #2 and I would spend the day together alone, then go to The Sister's place for dinner and cake. Seems reasonable, right?

Wrong.

#2 was *offended* that The Sister would try to take my birthday away from her.

No bullshit.

Her exact words were something along the lines of The Sister has her own family and she needs to stop acting like my wife and leave us alone. Apparently, while I was in prison I missed the memo stating that siblings couldn't be close or celebrate birthdays or holidays together.

Never mind the fact that The Sister is pretty much the only family that I have left, or the fact that she was my *only* support while I was in prison. Never mind the fact that I'd been gone for four and a half years and had hardly spent any time with my family since I'd gotten out. #2 cared about none of this. I was her property and she was extremely territorial.

This put a *huge wedge* between The Sister and me.

And I allowed it to fucking happen.

Instead of leaving #2, or voicing my opinion, or putting my foot down, or anything to stand up for myself, I did the mature thing by bottling up my emotions, shutting down, and drinking.

Heavily.

Genius, right?

I justified it all by telling myself, *"at least you're not using dope."*

So, drinking became my thing. I started drinking whatever the store had with the highest alcohol percentage by volume. Even on days when I would go straight to #2's after work, I would stop at the store, grab a couple of cans and literally chug them on my way to see her.

Let me break that last sentence down for the slower (translation: window-licking) readers.

I was roughly six months out of prison, on parole, drinking while driving, and doing this in my brand- new company work truck. Not the best of decisions, that's for sure.

This went on for several weeks until:

A) My stomach couldn't take the massive amounts of malt liquor I was imbibing on a daily basis.

B) #2 caught on.

The rotgut I could handle for the most part. The headaches from dealing with #2 I could not. So I put down the booze and we found a solution.

Our solution?

We moved in together.

Ugh, I know, right?

It's almost like I've been here before, isn't it?

Granted there were several differences in what I went through with #2, and what I went through with Not Fucking Gwen. #2 had three kids, where Not Fucking Gwen had two. Another being that I wasn't using dope. A third being that #2 was unemployed. Which meant that all of the pressure to keep us afloat now fell solely on me.

What could *possibly* go wrong?

Well....

Corky from *Life Goes On*, high on five hits of blotter acid could see that a relapse was coming.

I, on the other hand, could not.

Now mind you, after my little drinking *endeavor*, I started going back to my meetings regularly. #2 even started going with me to some. And since I never really had an issue with drinking (more pointedly, I never told anyone about my drinking), I still considered myself "clean." I'd go to meetings acting like Mr. Sobriety, regurgitating all sorts of program stuff, while acting as if I had my shit together because I was just short of five years clean.

* * *

A FEW DAYS after my "five years clean" anniversary, there was an event taking place at the local college dealing with opiate addiction. The group hosting the event was looking for someone in recovery– specifically opiate recovery– that would be interested in speaking at said event, on stage with judges, district attorneys, cops, lawyers, EMTs and other professional-type people.

Well, guess who had two thumbs, a boatload of narcissism, was in opiate recovery, and went to speak at the event?

That's right kids, this guy.

My narcissism had a raging boner during the entire event. The whole thing was focused on "the realities of opiate/heroin addiction." So while some of the "important people" got to speak and were asked a few questions here and there, the majority of the event was focused on... you guessed it, me.

This was honestly a surprise. I didn't expect to take the event hostage, but the audience had a ton of questions, and apparently had never seen someone be so open and honest about the shit most people keep secret. It does take a bit of courage to walk into a room full of strangers and openly discuss all the skeletons you've hidden in your closet. This is why addicts are some of the most amazing people on the planet. *You* try walking into a room full of people you've never met and sharing your darkest secrets.

Go ahead, I'll wait.

Yeah, that's what I thought.

The whole event was a first for me. I'd never really spoken about my addiction/recovery with anyone who wasn't in recovery before. And I had definitely *never* sat between a lawyer and a district attorney while a judge was present without being in handcuffs before. It was a very interesting night, and I was extremely proud of myself.

A month later, I relapsed.

Naturally, it all went downhill from there.

* * *

Fucking hindsight-- it's always 20/20, isn't it?

Looking back at everything, it's fairly easy to see the *whys* and *hows* of my decline and subsequent relapse. It was a melting pot of stress, pressure, complacency, bottled up emotions/feelings, etc. I could easily spend days explaining and justifying my relapse. But that's not why I'm here.

It happened. Let's move on.

What's fucked-up about the whole thing is that even with all the warning signs (and trust me, there were quite a few), I still didn't see it coming. My sponsor Jiminy tells me that I actually *did* see it coming, but I just ignored it like I do everything else I don't want to deal with. And as much as I hate to admit it, he's probably right.

To be honest, I didn't even plan the event. I was driving home from work one day and just decided to swing by the hood and get some dope. The decision took less time than it takes to blink, and the act of finding/obtaining the dope took me about five whole minutes.

Once the dope was in hand, I drove to the nearest pharmacy, got myself a brand new pack of syringes, some Q-tips, and a bottle of water (not obvious what I was up to at all). I went out to the parking lot, got everything ready, and because I'm fucking classy, I shot up right there. And with that, I flushed five years of clean time right down the toilet.

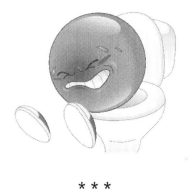

* * *

When I woke up that morning, I had no intention of getting high. Maybe somewhere subconsciously I did, but I promise you, using heroin that day definitely wasn't part of my plans. And for the record, yes, I was absolutely disgusted with and ashamed of myself immediately after I got high that day. This is something that has bothered me for a long time, and it has taken me quite a few years just to be ready, willing, and able to put it all down on paper.

Due to my decision that day– which put my addict sub-self in the driver's seat– a new path of self-destruction developed which altered the course of my life, one again. Years later, I'm still beyond pissed with myself for that decision and all that followed. Sadly, my feelings don't absolve me of my sins.

Plus, who gives a fuck about my feelings, right? You're only reading this to get a few more laughs out of my misery. Don't fret, I won't disappoint. I only wanted to sidebar to convey my true feelings, mainly because a certain cum-guzzling ADA believes that I'm incapable of remorse and that I have a total lack of emotion over my actions and who I've hurt. This couldn't be further from the truth. But he's entitled to his opinions, no matter how fucking stupid they are.

* * *

Using that day led to using the next day. This led to... oh you get the fucking picture. Before I knew it, my addict self was in control and I was in full-blown relapse mode again.

Here is probably a good time for me to break down this "addict self" stuff. This is a concept I came up with a little further down the road in life, and since most of my readers are practicing window lickers, I should probably explain myself here.

I believe that everyone– yes, that includes *you,* simple reader– has different "sub-selves" that sort of take control for a little while. A prime example of this (besides addicts and alcoholics) are those with anger issues.

I'm fairly certain that at some point in life, everyone heard someone say "I don't know what happened; I just got angry and lost control." This would be an example of the anger sub-self.

Another example would be someone who acts a tad crazily when they're jealous or envious of someone/thing. They allow their jealous sub-self to become dominant.

Basically, a sub-self is a slightly (or in some cases, extremely) different version of our "normal" self. A sub-self isn't who we are the majority of the time. Especially in the case of active addicts/alcoholics. Think of the movie *Split* (obviously not to the same extent) and you can pretty much smell what I'm stepping in here.

To keep my narcissism happy and other people off my dick for stereotyping them, I'll utilize myself as the prime example.

When I'm sober, I'm not the junkie monster I've told y'all so much about. I may be a sardonic, cynical asshole, but I'm *not* a heartless thief who would steal your firstborn child and sell its kidneys for dope. I'm not a callous monster. I'm not a ruthless animal. In fact, those who know me well say that I'm one of the best people they know (when I'm sober), and that it's hard for them to believe that I could have done half the shit I've written about.

When my addict self gets in the driver's seat, all bets are off. Once the beast has been let out of its cage, it's pandemonium. All that matters is that the beast gets fed. When this happens, it doesn't matter who I hurt or what I have to do in order to achieve my goals. My addict self is a powerful dictator who I *loathe* with every ounce of my soul, and have zero power to disobey.

But unless you've walked this path, you cannot begin to imagine the power and appeal of an opiate high, the pain and suffering that comes with withdrawal, or how truly powerful and overwhelming an addict sub-self is. Its constant whispering in your ears. Its constant presence, fighting you for control and domination of your life. It's horrible and sometimes paralyzing to live with.

This is why once someone gets clean, and the addict sub-self starts fading into the background and the true self starts gaining control again, the guilt, horror, shame, and reality of whatever was done during the relapse is almost soul-crushing. For me it is anyways. I don't know about y'all.

"Déjà vu" by Eminem covers the concept of a relapse pretty well in my opinion.

Now back to the story....

It didn't take long before I was a slave to the heroin again. One could argue that it was all over after the first hit, and they're probably right. It really doesn't matter though. The instant that needle hit my vein, deep down, I knew that I was in *big fucking trouble,* and that I was going to ride it out until the wheels came off.

And off they came.

The first bump in the road was getting caught by #2.

I'd been using multiple times a day for about a month, and was *way* beyond the point of simply stopping. It was a Wednesday morning and I was getting ready for work. My morning ritual consisted of getting up (well before #2 and the kids), letting the dogs out, getting a cup of coffee, a bowl of cereal, and getting a shot ready.

I was standing at the kitchen counter, drawing heroin into a syringe when out of nowhere I hear:

#2: "What are you doing?"

You know that feeling when your asshole puckers up and you're stuck in place?

Yup, that was me.

I couldn't think.

I couldn't speak.

I couldn't move.

I knew that I was fucked.

I also knew that I was about to have a *very* bad day.

And there was nothing I could do about it.

In that moment I perfectly understood Einstein's theory of relativity, because those brief few seconds between #2 speaking and my reaction seemed to last an eternity as my mind calculated all the possible options I had before me. And none of them were good.

In the past, I had always feared the wrath of #1. She was a vicious and vile cunt to be reckoned with when she was pissed off (or simply having a bad day). This day however, I would have gladly dealt with #1 on her worst day rather than what I felt was coming.

This was the first time that I had actually ever been in fear for my own life. The fear I felt during a riot in prison in Florida didn't even come close to my fear in this moment. Fight or flight didn't even take over. I should have run, but I couldn't. I was frozen in place. All I could do was put the syringe down on the counter, my hands down to my side, and turn around so she could see what I was doing.

This was also the first and only time in my life that I've been hit so hard that I saw stars. And mind you, I'm six foot tall and was close to 220 pounds then, while #2 was five foot three and 160ish. The one thing her father did right was teach the bitch to throw a right fucking hook. I can attest to that.

After that, she broke down crying. Ok, "crying" might be putting it mildly. #2 had a full-blown, fall-on-the-floor-in-the-middle-of-Walmart-flailing-her-arms-and-legs-snot-pouring-out-her-nose-while-crying-to-the-point-of-hysterics meltdown.

It was not a pretty sight.

Once she was able to regain a modicum of composure, the questions came. How? Why? How long has it been going on? How bad is it? Et cetera. All of which I tried to play off as if it was my first time and she had caught me before I used. She knew my answers were total bullshit, but she was in a state of denial, and was willing to believe anything rather than face the truth. Plus, I was spreading my bullshit pretty thick, and I wouldn't cough up the truth. Because as Will Smith said in *Focus,* "you die with the lie."

Somehow, I was able to calm her down and bullshit her enough so I could leave for work without a stab wound. I promised her that we would "figure it all out later" and practically ran out the door.

I couldn't get out of the house fast enough. I knew that this situation was Chernobyl just waiting to happen, I had to get my morning shot, and, most importantly, I had to get to an ATM before she figured out how I paid for the dope. Once that happened, she would demand that I turn over my debit card.

#2 had no clue that I had been spending *hundreds* of dollars on a daily basis out of my bank account. This was also the same account we used to pay our bills, and since #2 didn't work, it was also the account with all of our money.

By the time I was putting the cash I had just pulled out of the ATM into my pocket, #2 was calling me asking for the debit card. What can I say, my addict self can be clairvoyant sometimes.

When I brought her the card, I had to assure her that there wasn't any dope in my truck (which was the truth) and that I didn't have any stashed at work (which was a huge fucking lie) before I could leave again for work. During the work day I stocked up on as much dope as I could get, because I knew that my access to my own money was now nonexistent.

When I got home that night, shit got real.

To make a *very* long story short, #2 did some research while I was at work and discovered all the missing money, so she knew that I had been lying to her all day. She knew by the amount of money I had been spending that I was out of control with my using, and so, she presented me with an ultimatum: we get married, or she would call my parole officer and tell him that I've been using, which would be a one-way ticket back to prison on a violation.

Marriage?

Or prison?

Marriage....?

Or prison.....?

Al Bundy would claim that they're one in the same, and anyone who has been in a really shitty marriage and/or been to prison wouldn't argue. However, I had already been to prison twice, and I *really* didn't want to go back again. Truthfully though, I didn't want to stop using, and I knew that if my parole officer didn't get involved, I was free-ish to keep on using, as long as I could hide it from #2.

Two weeks later, #2 became the new Mrs. Lawn Mower.

Also, if you don't know who the fuck Al Bundy is, go stand in the corner because you should be a-fucking-shamed of yourself.

* * *

Now I KNOW what you're thinking here.

Actually, I don't. But I've got a fairly good idea, and honestly, I don't give a fuck. When you're ready to air all of *your* dirty little secrets to the world, then and only then can you share your stupid opinions and thoughts with me. Until then, go fuck a wood chipper.

One of the subclauses in my deal with #2 was that I "stop using." I'm using quotes here because we both knew that there was zero chance of that. Or at the very least, *I* knew. #2 knew it in her heart of hearts, but wanted to lie to herself and believe otherwise.

Obviously, I swore up and down to her that I would quit and even faked "being sick" for a few days to save face. The charade was up on that the day we got married. I was higher than a fucking kite and I was nodding out at dinner after the wedding. Of course, I denied it. But it didn't matter because in the end, #2 got what she wanted. She was Mrs. Lawn Mower.

In her convoluted mind she believed that she could somehow "save" me from my addiction. She felt that she could make me see the errors in my ways and thinking, and that by giving me what I've always wanted, a wife and family to call my own, that I would have everything that I *needed* and wouldn't turn to heroin anymore.

Poor, silly #2.

After some time, she realized how futile that all was, but to give credit where credit is due, the bitch fucking tried.

* * *

EVEN THOUGH I lived through them, I still don't fully understand how I found myself in some of the predicaments I ended up in. When I look back, I still find myself asking *how the fuck did that even happen?* Here is another fine example of such a situation:

It was a Sunday night, and I'd been using all weekend. I was already past the point of no return with my using, #2 was painfully aware of what I was doing, and the only person I was trying to hide my using from was my PO, who I had to go see the following morning. And I just fucking *knew* that he was going to give me a drug test when I saw him, but even that knowledge didn't deter me.

There I was, sitting on the couch, urine dirtier than Amy Winehouse's ashes, trying to figure a way out of the situation I had put myself in. Not reporting wasn't an option; that was an immediate one-way ticket back to prison. So I devised a plan to bring in clean piss and try to get one over on my PO.

Even though I had a plan laid out in my mind, I still lacked the material to bring said plan into play. I needed to come up with some clean urine, quickly, and my choices were extremely limited. I had enough self-respect not to ask one of the kids to pee in a cup for me. Or maybe it was because I knew they would tell #2 that I had them pee in a cup for me, and I didn't want to deal with the fallout from that. While the latter is closer to the truth, I'm sticking to the former as my reason why I didn't have one of the kids do it, because it's more mature-sounding. Plus, it's my fucking story and I'll tell it how I want to.

So there I was, sitting on the couch, high as hell, trying to come up with an idea of where the fuck I could get clean urine from when the answer to my prayers *literally* jumped into my lap.

Tundra!

The motherfucking dog!!

I did a quick Google search to see if it would even be possible to use dog urine for a drug test and found out that *yes*, it is possible, as long as it's only a dipstick screen. If it had to be sent off to a lab for any reason, then things would not work out in my favor. I knew for a fact that if I did have a urine screen the next day that it would only be a dipstick kind, so I'd be as good as gold.

After that I devised a plan on how to see this thing through: I'd take Tundra out in the morning and follow him around with a Tupperware bowl or something, wait till he lifted his leg, catch as much of that beautiful golden stream as possible, bottle that shit up, sneak it into parole, fill up the piss cup for the PO and bam! Problem solved. I smiled at Tundra, told him that he was a good boy and made sure that I gave him extra water that night before going to bed with a smile on my face.

The next morning came and I all but jumped out of bed. The sun was shining, I had my dope all ready to go for the morning shot, Tundra was pawing at me because he *really* had to go outside, and the dope man had already sent me a text letting me know that he was out and about. Life was good.

I took Tundra outside and smiled as I slid the Tupperware bowl under him to collect his urine. The chick across the street was staring at me with crazy eyes and I could only imagine what she was thinking at that moment. I just smiled at her, flipped her off, grabbed the bowl full of dog piss and led Tundra back inside the house.

After I met up with the dope man, the majority of the day was spent getting high. Sure, I took care of some actual work projects in order to appease the boss, but I had more important things to worry about. I still had to build a contraption to get the piss into parole. I knew that my PO didn't usually go into the bathroom with me, but I wasn't going to take any chances. After some minor alterations to an old pill bottle, some small air filter tubing, a couple zip ties and some duct tape, I was ready to go and on my way.

When I got to parole, we went through the normal motions, and then he pulled out the urine cup. I happily grabbed it from him and went into the bathroom. I had a slight grin on my face, not because I knew I was going to get one over on him, but because I was thinking about the shot of dope that I had waiting for me outside in my truck.

I went into the bathroom (without any company), filled up the empty cup with "my" piss, flushed the toilet for good measure, exited the room and handed my PO the urine sample with glee. It's not every day that a junkie is *happy* to be doing a drug test. My PO placed the cup on his desk, stuck in the dipstick, waited as the results came in, and as they started developing said to me:

PO: "Do you have anything you want to tell me?"

Me: "Umm, you have really pretty eyes?"

PO: "Thanks, but no. Have you been using again?"

I figured this was some sort of scare tactic used to get people to fuck themselves over when there was no need for it.

Me: "No. Absolutely not."

PO: "Are you sure?"

Hold your ground here Lawn Mower.

Me: "Yep."

PO: "Well that's interesting, because you just tested positive for opiates."

Me: "Can you say that again, because I didn't understand any of those words."

PO: "You're dirty for opiates."

Me: "There is no fucking way that that piss is dirty."

He pulled the test out and showed me for good measure.

Can you imagine my surprise when I saw the results?

Oh, come on, I bet you can.

I mean, let's break this down for a moment:

MY DOG'S URINE JUST TESTED POSITIVE FOR OPIATES!!!

Plus...

I JUST FAILED A FUCKING DRUG TEST FOR PAROLE WITH DOG PISS!!!

And...

MY DOG IS A FUCKING JUNKIE!!!

All I could see in the immediate future was jail, prison, and gang rape. For me, not my junkie dog. PO: "So, what are we going to do about this?"

Here is the point where my bullshitting skills come into play.

Me: "I honestly don't know. I'm telling you that I'm clean. And I know that you've heard this excuse countless times before, but I don't know what else I can say. I've been supervised by you for how long now? I've done everything asked of me and more. I've never been late for curfew. Never missed an appointment with you. And I've especially never given you a dirty urine before. I have no idea what the protocol is here. Is there a possibility that any of my medications can give a false positive or something?"

I knew it was a long shot but I had to try and weasel my way out of this. I had to pull every card and chance I had out of the deck. This was a life-or-death situation. I needed something to distract him for a few minutes so I could think. Plus, I didn't need him seeing me sweat. My fucking armpits were already soaked. I had to compose myself.

PO: "What medications are you currently taking?"

I rattled off every prescription that was mine in the house, whether I was currently taking them or not.

PO: "Okay, sit down for a minute, I've gotta make a call."

I'd like to say that I sat down, took a long, hard look at my life, and decided to start walking down a better path if I didn't end up going to jail. I'd like to say that at that moment, the fear of what could possibly happen to me took over, and it was the catalyst for an immense internal change. I'd like to say that a lot of things changed for me at that moment.

But I can't. If I said any of that shit, I'd be lying.

All I did while I was sitting there was try to calculate how fast I could run and get into my truck to do that final shot of dope, which was a mere eighty feet away, without getting shot by my parole officer and before he sent me to jail. All I cared about was *one last high before I said goodbye*. I didn't think about how my going back to prison would affect #2 and the kids. I didn't think about how they would survive, or if she would be able to take care of the house and bills. All I thought about was getting high, and how shitty it's going to be going through opiate withdrawal (once again) in jail.

How fucking pathetic is that?

After several minutes, my PO grunted and hung up the phone.

PO: "Okay. We've got two options here. Number one: I can send this sample to the lab, and if it comes back positive, then you're going back to prison."

Me: "Okay..."

PO: "Number two: you go home and I'll be by a couple times throughout the week for a random urine screen. If you're using again, you ain't gonna stop and you'll still be dirty. Which, at that point, you'd be going back to prison. So, what do you want to do?"

I still can't believe that he didn't hear my brain screaming *number two, number two, number two, number two!!!* Because that's all I could hear. That, plus my heart was pounding so hard in my chest that I could almost *see* my shirt move after each beat.

Of course, I wanted to jump on option number two. I would get to go home that day, get high, and keep on getting high until I got caught. Who wouldn't pick that? But I also knew that this could be a trap. Let us not forget that this is a parole officer that I was dealing with. So I sat there for a minute as if I was actually mulling both options over, then replied:

Me: "I'm good with whatever option you're most comfortable with."

He sat there staring at me for what felt like forever. This was obviously *not* the answer that he had expected. Now he seemed as if he didn't know what to do with me. It was a complete gamble on my part, based on the fact that most parole officers are lazy, and if he sent my urine to the lab, then that meant he would have to do paperwork that day. If he sent me home, then he only had the *possibility* of paperwork at a later date, but definitely not that day.

PO: "Come back Monday, and I'll be by sometime this week for a random."

Me: "Yes sir."

I all but sprinted out of the building and to my truck. I was the happiest I had been in a long time. Not because I didn't just get violated, but because I truly believed that I was going to lose the shot of dope I had waiting in my truck, and that I would have gone to jail knowing that it was just sitting there, waiting for me in the center console, and that I wouldn't have been able to get to it. Only the dope mattered. Nothing else.

I went home happy as a pig in shit and high as a kite. I told #2 about the whole incident and she was in total disbelief. First that I brought *dog piss* into parole with me and second that it was fucking dirty. I mean how the fuck do you even explain that and where the fuck is a doggy rehab?

I kept using all week long even though my PO had told me that he would be stopping by. I can't really tell you if it was the fact that I didn't care, or that I didn't believe him. All I *can* tell you is that it didn't matter. My PO was right when he said that if I was using again, that I wasn't going to stop. Either way, none of that mattered because he *never* stopped by my house during that week. The following Monday, I got urine from a buddy that I could 100% count on being clean, and I brought that into parole with me. I used it to "piss clean" for my PO, and just like that I was back to my bimonthly reporting schedule without a blemish on my record.

Lawn Mower: 1

Parole: 0

Now you may be wondering how Tundra's piss came up dirty in the first place, because I sure as shit did. For the longest time I had thought the fucker had eaten one of my bags of dope somehow, but I couldn't accept that. I was a good addict and I never lost or misplaced any of my dope, unless of course #2 found it. It didn't dawn on me until almost a year later how it happened. I put the furry asshole's piss in an old pill bottle and kept it in there all day long. Said pill bottle had once contained some prescribed pain killers, and obviously I didn't clean out the bottle well enough.

I'm a fucking idiot.

On the bright side though, Tundra didn't need to go to rehab.

* * *

After the dog piss incident, #2 decided that it was time to do something drastic. Life at home was shit; I was fucking up at work, and of course I was still using. So #2 decided to call in some reinforcements. The Sister and The Stepdad. They set up an impromptu intervention and treatment was strongly suggested. So, I went to treatment.

Well, detox actually.

We all agreed that detox was a better option than inpatient for a few different reasons. The main one being parole. We all decided that the less my parole officer knew, the better off I would be in the long run. Since I was reporting only once a month, and my parole officer rarely stopped by for a home visit, it was agreed that a short-term detox facility would be the best course of action.

I could easily take a week or two off of work without any issues, go into detox for several days, come back home and rest. After that I could go back to work while trying to get my shit back on track. This was actually a really good idea. Plus, things at work were starting to come up "missing," and I was trying to avoid that as best as I could.

So off to detox I went.

My intervention was on a Saturday morning, and I was able to get a bed at a detox facility on Monday morning. This was a good thing because I was watched like a Catholic priest in

Chuck E. Cheese's all weekend long and wasn't able to use *anything*. By the time Monday rolled around, I wasn't feeling very well at all.

The detox place was great. I was there for four days, put on Suboxone immediately, and given a script to go home with. I was also referred to a doctor who would continue my Suboxone for me. The problem with that is that I didn't want to be on Suboxone at all. I felt that I was simply jerking off with the opposite hand. Translation: substituting Suboxone for dope. Which is basically the truth. Don't get me wrong, Suboxone is an amazing drug that has helped millions of people with opiate issues. However, coming off of Suboxone is far, far worse than coming off of heroin.

I felt that being on Suboxone was simply delaying the inevitable. I wanted to be off everything, and one hundred percent clean. Or so I told myself. I spoke with my Suboxone doctor about it, and we came up with a plan to taper me off Suboxone.

Looking back, it's easy to see the writing on the wall. I was completely bullshitting myself, along with everyone else. My addict self is a cunning fucking prick, and I bought my own bullshit hook, line, and sinker.

The three and a half months I was on Suboxone during my taper were actually pretty decent. Things at both work and home were improving almost daily, it seemed. Not to mention that I felt pretty good. What I didn't realize was that this was simply the calm before the storm.

* * *

ONE GOOD THING happened during the calm.

I was at work on a Monday morning in late October when my parole officer called. Generally, this isn't a good sign, especially because I was supposed to see him later that day for my monthly report. I thought about not answering, but decided that that was probably a bad idea.

What happened next was definitely *not* expected.

Me: "Speak."

And yes, that's exactly how I answer the phone.

PO: *Clears throat.* "Lawn Mower?"

Me: "Yeah."

PO: "This is PO Wood."

No shit.

Me: "What's up?"

PO: "I've just been informed that you haven't paid a single cent towards your restitution as of yet."

Me: "Uhh.... That's correct."

PO: "And why the fuck not?"

Me: "Well, when I first reported to you, I asked you about the restitution stuff. Like how and where I make the payments and what not, and you told me that we'd discuss it later..."

PO: "Yeah..."

Me: "Well, *later* never came up again in conversation."

PO: "Seriously?"

Me: "Yep."

PO: "Unbelievable."

Shit.

Me: "Why, what's up? Am I in trouble?"

PO: "Somehow no. Also, you're off parole."

Me: "I'm sorry, I didn't understand that. Can you use smaller words please?"

PO: "Albany released you from parole early. Your sentence is now 100% complete. You don't need to report today, or again."

-Click-

I hung up the phone with him and *immediately* called Albany to verify this nonsense. Once it was verified, I called him back.

Me: "Hey sorry, we must have gotten disconnected or something."

PO: "You just called Albany to verify, didn't you?"

Me: "Yup."

PO: "Thought so."

Me: "So now what?"

PO: "Nothing. Go on with your life. Good luck."

And just like that I was done with parole and prison!

* * *

It was also during this calm that I started doing a lot of work on this book. I had a personal computer at work that I would use during lunch breaks and downtime (read: when I just wanted to fuck off). A lot of work was accomplished during these days. On the book. Not *actual* work, that's just foolish.

This fun fact comes into play shortly kids, trust me.

* * *

As I just previously stated, things at home were *improving*. That doesn't mean that the world shit rainbow skittles on us wherever we went. #2 and I had been working on our "issues" which mainly consisted of her lashing out/acting batshit crazy (yes, that's a clinical term) when she was depressed. Her main points of focus were my relapse, and her severe issue with The Sister.

The wedge between The Sister and I still existed because of #2. Yes, I'm fully aware that I allowed it to happen in the first place, so kindly fuck off. #2 felt that I communicated with The Sister way too often. Apparently texting your sibling on a regular basis isn't "normal or healthy" according to #2.

Well, one night we got into it because The Sister texted me twice in the same day, and I responded.

#2 felt that I should only be talking to The Sister once a week, and so she checked my phone on a daily basis. I felt that she was out of her fucking mind, but you know how the saying goes, "happy wife, miserable life," right? Or some shit like that. #2 was *far* from happy about my communication with The Sister, which caused her insecurity issues to go into super batshit mode (also a clinical term).

The following day I was doing some work outside when #2 threw a fucking paint can at me and then tried to introduce me to her right hook, again.

The reason for this little outburst?

One might think that she had found some hidden drugs or paraphernalia in the house.

Nope.

Another guess could be that perhaps it was a financial issue that was bothering her?

Wrong again.

Wait!

Could it be a conversation with another woman on my phone?

Not even close.

What about something to do with The Sister?

Negative.

#2 lost her shit and tried to *physically attack me* because she was scrolling through Facebook and found a post on my page from Not Fucking Gwen that was over six years old that she did not like.

I'm not fucking kidding here.

It was a dumb post over some flowers that I had bought Not Fucking Gwen with the text "I love this man and I'm prolly going to marry him," or something to that extent.

#2 lost her complete fucking mind over this.

Mind you, I hadn't even spoken to Not Fucking Gwen in years at this point. Forget the fact that six years prior I had no clue that #2 existed. It was an insult to her that I had a past with any woman, and she held complete enmity towards any woman from my past.

Seeing the post caused a short circuit in #2's brain and the situation became tumultuous. I was really trying to avoid becoming a victim of domestic violence and I knew that she needed to be snapped out of her Wolverine berserker attack before things got out of control. So I hit her with the lowest blow I could think of.

Me: "And you wonder why I relapsed. This is why, #2! What's crazy is that I made it through four years of prison, my uncle's death, and my mother's fucking suicide, all without using. Yet I couldn't even make it a fucking year with you without using! That says a lot, don't you think?!"

Have you ever seen a bipolar person snap from one extreme emotion to its opposite in the blink of an eye? It's quite a sight, trust me. #2 went from Hulk smash to uncontrollable sobbing so quickly, I felt that James McAvoy could take some tips from her. It was that impressive.

Yes, I'll admit that I felt bad after I said that shit to her. My relapse wasn't her fault. Did she contribute to my reasons behind it? Absolutely. But it wasn't her fault.

My intention wasn't to cause her harm, it was only to give her a metaphorical slap in the face to bring her to her senses. Which did work, only a little too well. When #2 hits the manic button, I can't handle it. All she does is go on and on about how worthless she is, and how everyone would just be better off without her and all that other boo-hoo, pity party, cry for help bullshit.

I have to walk away when she goes there. Suicide is a very sore subject for me, something that she's aware of. So, when she goes there, I feel as if she's doing it solely to get a rise out of me. Then, if I don't cater to her, violent #2 comes back out to play, proving that Bruce Banner isn't the only one with breathtaking anger issues.

I knew that her current emotional state wouldn't last for long and that she would quickly return to Hulk smash mode, or something equally as fun, and I didn't want to be around when that happened, so I did the responsible thing. I left her sobbing uncontrollably on the ground, said fuck it, and went to get high.

* * *

WHEN I FUCK UP, I do it really, really well. Fucking up is something that I take seriously, and it's the one thing in my life that I don't half-ass. At least that's what my track marks, I mean my track *record* shows.

I wish I could say that when I left the house that day, I had no intentions of getting high. It would be a lie if I did though. It was almost as if it had been my plan the entire time (by entire time I mean since I decided that I didn't want to be on Suboxone), and I had just been waiting for the right moment to put my subconscious plan into action.

By the time #2 realized that I was gone, it was already too late. By the time she started calling my phone, I had already begun my trip along the downward spiral of destruction.

The months that followed were *rough*.

#2 and I would go through periods of intense fighting, then peace. One day might be bad, and the next would be bliss. I had never lived such an unbalanced life before. If you knew *anything* about my childhood years, then you would understand that the previous sentence speaks *volumes*. Since you don't, you'll just have to take my word here.

As it always does, my using became a daily thing, but #2 wasn't exactly aware of that fact. She thought that I had only used the one day and that was it. She monitored the bank account hourly, and since all the money was accounted for, she felt confident that I wasn't using.

Silly #2.

What she didn't know was that I was stealing tools from work and pawning them. I had also started taking metal and selling it for scrap. You know, because both things have worked out so well for me in the past.

However, I did come up with a new trick this time around. Somehow I figured out that I could use the company credit card in a store like Lowe's or Home Depot to buy gift cards. Then I would take said gift card and sell it at a pawn shop for cash. I would make a fake receipt up for the purchase like I actually bought shit at the store, and because I thought myself smarter than everyone, I did all these purchases in four-to-five-hundred-dollar amounts, because I knew that if I got caught, five hundred dollars isn't felony level shit in New York. I pulled this scam pretty much daily for a few months.

* * *

THIS WAS ALSO around the time that #2 felt that she needed a friend. So one day she decided to let her friend Bell move in with us. Bell brought enough emotional baggage with her to put a Kardashian to shame, and #2 welcomed her into our home with open fucking arms, not once discussing it with me.

Bell is a wolf in sheep's clothing, and a fan of hers I am not. Bell is the type of person who smiles to your face, stabs you in the back when you're turned around, then helps you pull the knife back out.

I know that I am a selfish, manipulative, narcissistic prick when I'm using. But at least I have a semblance of an excuse. Bell is just a natural miserable fucking cunt who is always looking out for her own self-interest.

Bell's life was miserable, and once she moved in, she decided to bring #2 down with her because misery loves company. Since neither of them worked, they spent all day gossiping and plotting. By Bell's second week in the house, "#2" had made the decision that I should block The Sister and no longer speak to her.

This went over about as well as if Epstein tried to open his own Neverland Ranch.

Especially because every time I asked a question, Bell would answer for #2. Which royally pissed me off. When I told Bell to kindly fuck off, Bell kept going on as if she didn't hear me. Then when I told her to get the fuck out of my house since she wasn't on the lease and all, she responded with something cunty to get me fired up even more. We would then go back and forth arguing until we ended up in some sort of stalemate.

THE PROBLEM with a stalemate is that if you want to win the game, you have to play again, which was something I didn't want to do. I was far too deep into my relapse to think straight or plan Bell's destruction.

Bell spent her days trying to get back at me somehow. She knew that I was using still, but she just couldn't prove it. Finally, she got smart.

Since she couldn't prove that I was using, she did the next best thing. She convinced #2 that I should be on Vivitrol.

What is Vivitrol you ask?

Well let me tell you.

Vivitrol is a monthly injection that blocks the feelings and effects of opiates entering your body. It's a pretty serious ordeal. You have to be clean from any and all opiates for seven to fourteen days before you can get the shot. If not, you will *absolutely* go into a sudden and severe opiate withdrawal which will last for hours and require hospitalization.

If the doctor administering the shot even thinks that there's a chance that you've used in the past two weeks, they won't give it to you. The shit is no joke.

So when #2 told me that she wanted me to go on Vivitrol, I knew that I was in trouble. If I argued with her over it, then she would know that I had something to hide. If I was using behind her back, then I would have to go through a detox before getting the shot (something that I couldn't hide), proving that I had been lying and using the whole time.

Checkmate.

Bell: 1

Lawn Mower: 0

Naturally, I agreed to get the shot in order to save face, but I was desperately scrambling for a way out of it. Getting clean was *not* part of my plan.

What happened next was by far one of the *dumbest decisions* of my entire life.

And that's saying a lot.

Here's what happened:

It was a Sunday night, and the following morning I was supposed to go to the doctor's and get my first dose of Vivitrol. The tension in the house was palpable. Bell was nervous because I had shown zero signs of detoxing, which she took as a sign that I was in fact clean. This meant that I had called her bluff and was about to win the little power struggle between us in the house.

Meanwhile, I was near apoplectic because I had been using the entire time. I knew that there was no fucking way possible I could get the shot the next morning. Or the next week for that matter; my system was *loaded* with enough heroin to make Frank Lucas proud, and I was desperately trying to figure a way out of going to the doctor's the next morning.

I was lying in bed wishing that I had a way to just clean out my system. What if there was some magic pill or something that I could take that would clean my system out of opiates. And then it hit me...

(*Insert ominous music here*)

From time to time in my life, I get these amazing ideas that look *great* on paper (the dog piss incident being one of them), but fail horribly in application. The problem with these ideas is that I *always fucking fail* to realize that they are horrible ideas at their inception. It's only after they fail that I understand how horrible of an idea they were, and I question my sanity.

If you don't live in a bubble, third world country, under a rock, or this strange place they call Nebraska, then I'm willing to bet that you've heard of something called Narcan.

Those of you who have heard of it, or who've had personal experiences with it, just cringed at reading that word. Especially because you have a slight idea where I'm heading with this.

For the rest of y'all, you're as clueless as I used to be and are just along for the ride.

Narcan is a nasal spray and is used to temporarily reverse the effects of opioid medicines. It's a prescription medicine used for the treatment of a known or suspected opioid overdose emergency with signs of breathing problems and severe sleepiness or not being able to respond

Narcan is a lifesaving tool that can revive someone who is overdosing from opiates. It rips all the opiates off of the opiate receptors in the brain and throws the person into *instant* withdrawal. It's not a pretty sight. The person usually becomes belligerent and/or violent once revived because they just went from high as fuck into horrible fucking withdrawal. YouTube the shit, it's fucking bananas.

Most opiate users have a thing or two of Narcan lying around. It's kind of a given these days. They give the shit out for free at most pharmacies. Plus, Narcan is given out to anyone/everyone who's leaving jail, prison, treatment, or most birthday parties, like some sort of participation trophy.

The brilliant idea that I came up with was: if Narcan can clean someone's system of opiates and bring them back from the brink of death during an overdose, then it would *definitely* clean my system out– and if I'm not overdosing, what's the worst that can happen?

If you've ever been "hit" with Narcan, then you already know how truly terrible this idea is. The rest of you are in the dark, as I was, because I had zero experience with Narcan.

All that was about to change.

An opiate/heroin detox is slow, painful and lasts for days because the opiates in your system are breaking down while slowly being removed from the receptors in your brain. The vomiting, the sweats, the chills, the pain, the shitting your-self and the wanting to put a bullet through your skull are all part of your body's reaction to being without opiates after becoming dependent on them. I'm not trying to beat a dead horse here, but opiate detox is fucking hell.

Narcan encompasses all of that (and more) within minutes of being used, and lasts a few hours. Narcan brings you from the brink of death to being alert and wide awake– like a shot of adrenalin straight to the heart, Pulp Fiction style– with *violent* force. When you regain consciousness, you're in complete detox. There's no gradual build up. It's like hitting a brick fucking wall at 90 mph.

Sounds fun, right?

Well, I can assure you that it's *not*.

And as I found out the *very* hard way that night, Narcan is ONLY supposed to be used in the case of an overdose. It's for emergency use only. It's not meant for ANY. OTHER. PURPOSE.

But hey, nothing ventured, nothing gained, eh?

Here is my Narcan timeline:

6:00 p.m. - used the last of my dope.

8:00 p.m. - used the Narcan.

8:05 p.m. - felt fine.

8:10 p.m. - started feeling a little strange.

8:15 p.m. - started feeling a little ill.

8:17 p.m. - started sweating, went to lie down in bed.

8:19 p.m. - started feeling worse.

8:22 p.m. - started getting worried.

8:24 p.m. - the world as I knew it ceased to exist and all hell broke loose.

It started with a slight, whole-body spasm/convulsion thing.

I stretched.

I yawned.

I convulsed.

Then I launched myself out of bed and raced for the bathroom. The toilet was to the immediate left as I entered the bathroom. Yet from some reason beyond my comprehension, I felt it necessary to go to the *other* side of the bathroom to turn on the light. Don't ask me why I did this, because I still have no fucking clue. Apparently, I felt that I needed the light on to puke.

Well, I didn't make it.

I entered the bathroom, and made it half a step towards the light switch when I started projectile vomiting all over the bathroom in a way that would have made William Friedkin (director of *The Exorcist*) envious.

I hit the walls, the shower, the medicine cabinet, the sink, and even the fucking ceiling somehow. I literally hit everything in the bathroom *except* the fucking toilet.

This was round one.

There was a brief– and by brief, I mean three seconds– lull where I was able to catch my breath, hit my knees, find the toilet, and proceed to vomit out my entire intestinal tract.

This was round two. This lasted about ninety seconds, which in vomit time, is a *very* long fucking time.

Meanwhile, I was starting to realize that my perception of the world had altered. Everything seemed to be in some sort of strange, spiraling, multidimensional tunnel vision. Think watching *Doctor Strange* on some serious mushrooms.

Round three consisted of even more vomiting, trying to get a grip on reality, and having #2 scream at me. I'm pretty sure she was screaming:

#2: "What the fuck is wrong with you?!"

But all I could hear was:

#2: "Mmm mmm mmm mmm?!?!?!?!"

Like Kenny on South Park.

Round four was painful. The multidimensional tunnel vision thing was in full effect, I was drenched in sweat, my stomach was in knots, my abs were killing me due to all the clenching and unclenching, my head was pounding, I was still convulsing, #2 was still screaming at me, and then I started puking out of my ass as well.

Ugh, fine!

I fucking shit myself. Okay? As much as I hate to admit it, at thirty-six years old, I was still shitting myself.

All the while. Bell was standing in the corner watching the (literal) shitshow unfold with a smug, cunty smile on her face. To be honest, I would have been too, had the roles been reversed.

After I shit myself, a sort of transitional period occurred. The vomiting stopped. The multidimensional tunnel vision stopped. The Kenny language stopped, and I had a moment to catch my breath and wipe my face.

Then something different happened.

Life went into slow motion.

I felt like I got hit with Hot Rod's "I will slow the time" gun from *Transformers: The Last Knight*.

Moving took great effort.

Thinking took greater effort.

I recall #2 asking:

#2: "Whhhhhhaaaaaaaattttt iiiiiiiiiiiiiiissssssssssssss ggggg-goooooooooiiiiiiiiinnnnnnggggggg oooooooooonnnnnnnnnnn?"

And me replying:

Me: "IIIIIIII uuuuusssssseeeeeddddddd nnnnnnnaaaaaaar-rrrrrcccccccaaaannnnnnnnnnn....."

Then darkness. I'm pretty sure #2 punched me, but to this day she adamantly denies it.

Shortly after, I came to and was flopping around on the floor like a fish out of water. It wasn't like a seizure. It was more like I thought I was on fire and decided to "stop, drop, and roll."

It was during this not-seizure that I noticed a lot of boots around me. And a strange voice.

Voice: "Lawn Mower?"

Me: "God?"

Voice: "No, I'm not God. My name is Andy and I'm an EMT. Your wife called 911. I'm here with the police to make sure that you're okay."

For some reason, no matter how fucked-up you are, the phrase "the police are here" usually has a pretty sobering effect on people.

Myself included.

My not-seizure fully stopped, and I was back to a quasi-normal state.

Not God Andy: "What happened, man?"

And in a state of utter shock and defeat, I broke down like Chunk in front of the Fratellis and told Not God Andy the truth. Not God Andy

Well.... *almost.*

Me: "I'm a heroin addict and I've been hiding my using from my wife. I'm supposed to get the Vivitrol shot in the morning, but I know I can't because I haven't stopped using, so I thought that I could Narcan myself and clean my system out enough so that I could get the shot."

You know that saying "the truth will set you free"?

It's complete bullshit.

In the background I could hear #2 freaking out, while all the cops were mumbling something about how stupid I was and doughnuts. Only Not-God-Andy– by far the most professional person in the room– remained impassive.

Not God Andy: So, you used Narcan on yourself, and you weren't overdosing?"

Me: "Yes and no."

Not God Andy: "Do you have any idea how dangerous that is?"

I looked towards the bathroom.

Me: "I have a pretty good idea, now."

Not God Andy: "And how are you feeling?"

Me: "Can I borrow a gun from one of those cops?"

Not God Andy: "No."

Me: "Well, then I guess I feel like Debbie after she did Dallas."

Not God Andy: "Excuse me?"

Me: "Really fucked."

Silence.

In my state of mind, that joke was fucking epic. But apparently everyone's a fucking critic.

Not-God-Andy coughed.

Not God Andy: "Do you think you can stand so that I can check your vitals?'

Me: "That depends."

Not God Andy: "On what?"

Me: "If a set of handcuffs follows."

Not God Andy: "Why would you say that?"

Me: "Because it looks like one PP in here."

Not God Andy: "As far as I know, you're not in trouble. The officers were just responding to the call. It's common for them to respond to a distress call."

Me: "Lucky me."

I was able to stand with the help of Not-God-Andy. He checked my vitals and was a bit concerned with my heartbeat, considering that it was close to breaking my ribcage. Not-God-Andy suggested that I go to the emergency room, and I acquiesced. The way I figured it, a trip to the emergency room meant that I still had a few hours to live before #2 killed me.

In the ambulance Not God Andy told me how utterly stupid I was for doing what I did, and I have to agree with him. Then he added:

Not God Andy: "On the other hand, Narcan is only for 4 mg of Naloxone. Vivitrol is 380 mg. Imagine what *that* would have done to you."

He let me think on that for the rest of the ride.

* * *

WHEN I THINK of hospitals and ERs, one word comes to mind: antipathy (ooh, someone's being grandiloquent).

And for good reason.

Nine times out of ten, when I go to the ER, I'm treated with enmity. Healthcare professionals (except for Not-God-Andy) take one look at me, then my file, then look down their holier-than-thou noses at me. It's very frustrating.

Yes, I'm a fucking heroin addict.

Yes, I've fucked up a few times.

Yes, I just Narcaned myself when it wasn't warranted.

I fucking get it.

But still, it's like what the fuck.

If you're an addict or in recovery, then you know what I'm talking about.

If you're not, consider yourself lucky.

The nurses in the ER that night were oh-so-judgmental, and had nothing but great things to say about me when they thought I was sleeping, which made for an even better night. Then #2 arrived, and added so much fun to the fiesta.

After speaking to the doctor and receiving pretty much the same speech that Not-God-Andy gave me, I was released.

I was in fear for my life on the ride home. Not because of what #2 was saying, but because of what she *wasn't* saying. She didn't say a word.

Not a single fucking word.

In fact, she didn't speak to me for several days.

Which made me nervous. Very nervous.

But she didn't kill me (obviously) and she basically left me alone.

So, I did the only reasonable thing I could think of.

I just kept getting high.

THINGS CAME to a major head shortly after New Year's. Late one Thursday night, El Jefé sent me a text saying that he needed to see me *first thing* in the morning.

I knew what that meant.

I was fucked.

I hardly slept that night, and had no idea what the fuck I was going to say when I saw El Jefé in the morning. I left the house for work a little earlier than normal and copped some dope, so I could be high as fuck when I went to see him.

Our meeting went as I expected it would.

Me: "Morning boss, you wanted to..."

El Jefé: "Sit down and shut the fuck up, Lawn Mower."

Shit.....

As I sat down, he threw a file at me that was about two-and-a-half-inches thick.

I had a pretty good idea what was in that file.

El Jefé: "What in the *fuck* is all that?"

By this point in my life, I'd experienced situations like this a time or two, and I knew better than to say anything that could be incriminating. Especially because we weren't the only people in the room. El Jefé had one of his top guys, Little John, in the office with us.

His role would be known as a "witness" in Legalspeak.

So, I said nothing.

El Jefé: "Yeah, that's what I thought."

More silence.

El Jefé: "I can't believe you'd do this to me, Lawn Mower. You're a great employee. What happened?"

Again, more silence.

And it's not because I didn't have anything to say. Believe me, I did. I felt like a giant piece of shit for stealing from the guy, but I knew what was coming next and I was trying to minimize the damage to myself because I wasn't exactly sure how much he knew about.

El Jefé: "Well, I think this goes without saying, but I'll say it anyways: you're fired. Give me your set of keys and whatever credit cards you have, and get the fuck out of my building."

Wait, what?

No cops?

I gingerly took his keys and cards out of my pocket, looking around for the cops. I couldn't see any, so I got up, put everything on his desk, and started to walk out.

Just before I got to his office door, I stopped, turned around, and against my better judgement, spoke.

Me: "El Jefé, I..... I'm sorry."

He just looked at me with complete disappointment and nodded his head.

Then, naturally, I decided to push my luck.

Me: "Umm, can I get my personal effects from the warehouse, sir?"

The coffee mug missed my head by *millimeters*.

I WALKED out of his office deflated and on edge. I was expecting the cops to be around the next corner.

They weren't.

Then, I expected them to be outside waiting for me.

They weren't.

I couldn't fucking believe it!

This guy had me dead to rights. He knew that I'd been stealing from him, and he just let me walk out the door. No cops, no nothing.

I was flabbergasted.

I also took this as a sign that it was time to get my life straightened out, and that perhaps I could do it *without* going to prison for once.

I WAS DREADING GOING HOME, but during my walk home, I came up with a pretty decent excuse as to why I was no longer employed. I was able to drum up some waterworks for good effect, and I told #2 that El Jefé had let me go because he found out about the Narcan incident, knew that I had been using, and felt that I was a "liability" for his company.

A pretty fucking plausible reason if I do say so myself.

#2 seemed to buy it and after a long talk, was surprisingly understanding about the whole thing. I admitted to #2 that I had still been using, and that I was going to go to an inpatient rehab to get myself straightened out.

And that's exactly what I did.

Lawn Mower

NOW IT ONLY TOOK ME thirty plus years, but I finally made it to rehab. Yes, we all know that I should have been placed in some sort of really long-fucking-term facility before my shenanigans in Florida, but that's not how life– or the judicial system– works.

Unless you're me. If you're someone else, then you would have been placed in some sort of luxurious resort like they show on intervention. If you're me, you go directly to prison. You don't even get jail time, unless you're waiting to be sentenced.

Like I told you before, I'm a special type of asshole.

Over the years, I have cried, begged, pleaded with judges and district attorneys to put me into a program. I have offered my services in both oral sex, anal sex, vaginal sex, nose hole sex, and earlobe sex, and still nothing. I have even offered to toss a few salads, yet every time, I get my ass sent to prison.

It seemed as if nothing I could do or say would get me the help that I needed.

Until I started doing it for myself.

Somewhere down the line, I realized that no one was going to go out of their way to get me help. No one was going to do the legwork for me. I was on my fucking own.

I was tired of all the bullshit in my life. I was *beyond* tired of fighting with #2. I hated myself. I hated getting up every morning and being sick. I hated trying to scam someone in order to get money to get high. I knew that it was only a matter of time before I really fucked up and ended up right back in prison.

So, I made a few calls.

And guess what??!!!

I had to fucking wait.

APPARENTLY THERE WAS no shortage of junkies, and every place that I called had a long fucking waiting list. Which really pissed me off. I mean, how the fuck is someone supposed go get help if they have to wait *weeks* in order to receive said help? Someone could fucking die while waiting for a bed to open up.

But who cares, they're only junkies, right?

After going off on more than one rant with more than one facility, I finally got smart, put my name on the waiting list, and sat around with my thumbs up my ass until someone called me.

It's just like waiting for the dope man to call. Only it's not the dope man. It's the anti-dope man. But the process is still the same. You sit for hours staring at your phone, trying to will it to ring so that you can go and get well. Same process, different people, places, and things.

My wife didn't even believe me that I was going.

I went to rehab on a Wednesday. The Monday before, I had to go to the emergency room because I was experiencing extreme chest pains. I woke up in the morning and thought that I was going to die. I couldn't move my entire right side and it hurt to breathe. I was scared shitless. #2 told me it was because I was going through detox. I told her to shut the fuck up because she didn't know what the fuck she was talking about.

So I went to the ER and sat there *all fucking day long,* and had about twelve different tests done on me. The doctor had no clue what was going on with me, but my wife accompanied me and took it upon herself to inform the staff that I was going through withdrawals (again). After that, they treated me like a two-dollar crack whore. Which is par for the course with hospital staff and me.

Now I've *never* gone to the hospital in order to seek out drugs. I know a lot of junkies that have and still do to this very day. I'm not one of them. When I go to the ER, something is seriously wrong with me. One time I went because I was withdrawing so badly from dope that I was hallucinating. Other than that, it's all been for a legitimate reason. I made the mistake of telling them one day (many moons ago when I had a lot of clean time under my belt) that I was a recovering heroin addict, and ever since then, I've been a redheaded stepchild to those fuckers.

During my long stay in the emergency room, a few things happened. The first thing was that the dope man called me and told me that he had some absolute *fire*, which is Addicts-peak for *some good fucking dope* The next thing that happened was I started scheming how I could get some cash together so I could go get some dope. And the third thing that happened was that a rehab facility had called me back and told me that they would have a bed open for me Wednesday morning!

All I had to do was make it through the rest of Monday, all day Tuesday, and all night Tuesday, then I would be on my way to getting better!

Well anyone who's ever been dope sick or knows someone who's gone through that shit knows that Monday afternoon to Wednesday morning is a long fucking time. Plus, I already had the dope man calling me, so I knew that I was going to have to pull some bullshit either that night or first thing Tuesday morning.

Then the idea came to me.

Since I had already been ripping off El Jefé, why stop now?

So, I came up with a plan.

I called one of the supply houses that I used to deal with when I worked for CNB and asked about a few tools. None of them were in stock except for one: a $975.00 demolition saw. $975 was less than $1000, which meant that in terms of the New York state penal law, this equated to a misde-meanor theft.

When you start thinking of your actions in terms of if it's a felony or a misdemeanor, you have some serious shit going on in your life and should probably seek help. I can only say this now because it's in hindsight. When I devised the plan however, I thought of myself as a fucking genius.

My plan was simple. Tell #2 that I had a side job to go do and leave first thing in the morning. I'd go right to the supply house and charge the saw to El Jefé's account. Then I'd go straight to the pawn shop, get some cash, meet up with the dope man, and enjoy my last day of freedom before I jumped back on the wagon.

By the time I got home I was so excited for Tuesday that all I wanted to do was go to sleep and get the shit rolling. I tried taking a few sleeping pills and some ZzzQuill. That didn't work. Then I took about 100 mg of melatonin. Didn't work. So just like any other night going through detox, my ass was up all fucking night long tossing and turning. I fucking hate heroin.

When Tuesday morning came, I was ready to fucking go. And aside from a few minor issues, my plan was a success. By noon I was feeling great. I hadn't a care in the world. I had dope, I wasn't sick, and I was happy. Not even a blow job would have made me any happier. I had my girl, and her name was Heroin.

#2 started calling me shortly thereafter, giving me a bunch of shit. She wanted to know where I was, when I was coming home, and blah blah blah. Then she uttered the four words that I always hated hearing from her mouth.

#2: "We need to talk."

I DON'T KNOW about anyone else, but I really hate those four fucking words. Especially when #2 said them, because I just *knew* that some bullshit was absolutely going to ensue.

And of course, it did.

While I was out on my little adventure, #2 took it upon herself to call the rehab that I was going to the following day. You see, #2 had some trust issues with me due to my relapse and recent behavior, and didn't believe that I was actually going to go into treatment. So when she called the facility to verify that I was actually going and they said:

Rehab: "We can neither confirm nor deny that information."

#2 lost her shit.

What #2 failed to realize was that no medical releases had been signed yet with the facility, so even though I was a prospective new patient, under the HIPPA laws, they could not give her any information. Wife or not, she was entitled to shit. And that didn't sit well with her at all.

#2 and I went round and round fighting about the next day. She didn't believe me when I said that I was going, nor did she believe that I wanted to get clean. She'd heard all my lies and bullshit before and was done with it. So I told her that she could eat her words, along with a bag of dicks on Wednesday after she dropped me off.

That comment went over well.

The next morning we got up, got ready, and left for rehab. #2 was still kind of apprehensive and thought I was still pulling her chain. We drove for about five minutes and then I pulled into the parking lot of a gas station.

#2: "I fucking *knew* it!! You're not going, are you?!!"

Me: "Yes dear, I *am* going. My stomach is in knots right now and I have to take a shit."

#2: "Oh."

Me: "Yep."

Bitch.

What #2 didn't know was that I didn't have to take a shit. I had four bags of dope in my sock and a rig waiting to be set up. She was up my ass the entire time before we left, so I wasn't able to get things ready. I wasn't going to rehab sober. I had no idea when or even *if* I was going to get anything to help with the withdrawals. Self-medicating was my mission.

I went into the bathroom, got my stuff ready and got high. No bullshit. Usually, I just got not-sick. But on this day, I got *high*. That was discouraging. I hadn't been high in a long time. By this point, the only reason I was using so much was so that I didn't get dope sick. I wanted to turn around and go home and get higher, but I couldn't. #2 would lose her shit. Plus, I was out of dope.

So, I got back in the car and drove the hour and a half to rehab.

Luckily for me, #2 slept pretty much the entire way, so I was left to myself and my thoughts. Which was fine by me. For the week or so prior to me going to rehab, all #2 and I did was fight. And fight. And fight.

#2 has what most would call "anger issues." She gets violent and has a wicked tongue. I'd be lying on the floor in the fetal position going through severe withdrawals, and she would decide that that particular moment was the correct one to start getting into all of our shit. Trying to solve all of our issues and problems and demanding answers from me about how I'm going to fix everything, and about what exactly my plans were. I tried to tell her that I couldn't even count to thirty if my life depended on it right then and there, but she didn't care.

When she didn't like what I had to say she would kick, punch and break things, then tell me how much of a fucking scumbag junkie I was, and how I'd ruined her life. She would proceed to tell me what a piece of shit I was, and how she wished that she never met me. Then she would compare me to my mother and tell me how I was *exactly* like her.

#2 knew full well that being compared to my mother was the worst thing you could do to me. I would strive to not be thrown into that boat with her. And here was #2, my "person," the one who was supposed to be there for me no matter what, completely tearing me down with her words, when I was at the lowest and weakest point in my life.

It may be hard to believe from how I carry myself, but I'd rather be punched in the face and have my ribs broken than have someone cut me down with their words. That sticks and stones shit doesn't apply to me. Words cut deep with me. Especially words from a loved one that are intended to cut the jugular. I can put on a pretty tough exterior, but that shit kills me every fucking time.

And she knew that.

Long story short, I enjoyed the peace and quiet of the drive. Had I been dope sick, I would have been a fucking wreck. But since I was high, everything was kosher.

Arriving at rehab was interesting.

The facility was located on the same property as a prison. There was nothing but barbed wire fencing for miles, it seemed. The whole area was owned by the state. When I pulled into the gates, I could see inmates walking around and doing inmate shit. It was a bit unnerving considering that I should have still been on parole, and only by stroking God off a few times, I was somehow released early for "good behavior."

That shit still cracks me up. How I got off parole early will always be a mystery to me. I was fucking around so much and committing so many felonies it was insane.

Even #2 said that she felt weird driving through the place.

And I was going to be fucking stuck there for a month.

Awesome.

While I was waiting to be seen and admitted, I decided to send an e-mail to El Jefé. I felt obligated to inform him of what I was doing. I knew that he was pissed at me, but I really liked the guy and I wanted him to know that I was finally getting the help that I needed, and that I was trying to do the right thing. By the time I sent the e-mail, they were calling me into the admissions office. I said goodbye to #2, and started my adventure in rehab.

* * *

MY STAY in rehab was mainly uneventful. Since I wasn't court or probation/parole ordered to be there, I basically made my own rules. Staff couldn't dictate or control me as they could with some of the other patients. This pissed them off because I was my normal asshole self, turned up to about an eleven on the dial.

I was there for a total of twenty-two days, went through the detox period with the help of a low dose of Suboxone, and then started on a course of Revia, because I didn't want to be on Suboxone any longer than I absolutely had to.

Two things of note happened while I was in rehab.

The first being that #2 decided to go through a stack of my old letters from when I was in prison. Don't ask me why. They were in a box in the basement with some old Christmas decorations and what not. After reading some of these letters that I had saved, she called the rehab and told them there was an emergency at home and that she needed to speak to me. Staff immediately got me on the phone.

Me: "What's wrong?"

#2: "So are you going to leave me for Alex?"

Me: "Excuse me?"

#2: "I read all of her fucking letters that you saved. Seems you two were pretty close. You're a piece of shit, you know that? I can't believe you."

Me: "This is a joke, right?"

#2: "DO I SOUND LIKE I'M FUCKING JOKING?"

Me: "Let me make sure I've got this right. You're mad because of some letters a girl wrote me *five fucking years ago*, while I was in prison?"

#2: "YES!!!"

Me: "First thing, this is not the time or the place for this conversation. Secondly, do you have any idea how foolish this conversation is? You're legitimately mad because a girl was writing to me while I was in prison."

#2: "And you kept her letters!!"

Me: "I kept *every* letter written to me. It's what you do in prison. I also have letters from my mother, and my grand-mother, and my sponsor. They're all in some box in the.... Did you seriously go through my boxes in the basement?"

#2: "Yes."

Me: "Wow, okay. Well, we can talk about this when I get home, but I don't understand why you're mad. Those letters are over five years old, and I haven't spoken to her since. That was at a time when I didn't even know you existed, and you were still with your kids' father for fuck's sake. I don't even know why I have to explain all of this, but I am. And we can discuss it when I'm out of here.

#2: "OKAY. Fine. I'm sorry. Love you, bye."

This was the point when I really started disliking #2. Who the fuck gets mad over something like that?

The second noteworthy thing that happened was that El Jefé had called my phone while I was in treatment. He had received my e-mail and was checking up on me. I wasn't home (obviously) so #2 had answered my phone and talked to him.

#2 said that the conversation went really well, and that El Jefé told her that even though I betrayed him, he still wanted me to work for him, and told her to have me call him once I was home and ready to go back to work.

Lawn Mower

When #2 told me about her conversation with El Jefé, I was beyond ecstatic. A giant sense of relief washed over me. I was relieved because if El Jefé wanted me to come back to work, then the cops weren't involved and I wasn't going to jail. For the first time in my life, I was going to catch a break and not go to jail for the bullshit I did to get high.

As soon as I got off the phone with #2, I immediately started working on a plan to pay El Jefé back and to get my life back on track. I was tired of the way I had been living, and it was beyond time to start doing something differently.

I left rehab about a week later, fully detoxed from heroin, on Revia, and ready to face the world. I had a decent plan in place, and I was beyond excited to put it into action. I felt that I had been given a gift from El Jefé. This would be the first time that I'd ever put myself into treatment, and didn't have to detox in a jail cell. By not being in jail, I had the opportunity to put my life back together and fix all the things I had damaged along the way.

#2 picked me up and the ride home was slightly awkward. She did a lot of talking during the ride, and I did a lot of noncommittal grunting. My plan to leave was still in place, it was just the details of the execution that I was slightly hung up on.

#2 on the other hand, had quite a few of her own plans about "our future together." Honestly, they weren't half bad, other than the fact that I wanted absolutely *nothing* to do with them/her. There was definitely a new barrier between us, and that was fine by me. I had already made the decision to leave her, I just needed some time before I could make that move.

Then she filled me in on everything that had happened while I was away.

First, she told me that she had thrown all my old letters away, which *really* pissed me off. I had letters from my mother in that pile that were irreplaceable. Then, she told me that her father had somehow broken my brand new 75" LCD TV with a can of Monster. She was extremely vague on the details, which didn't really matter because the damage had been done, and I already knew that her father was not going to make it right.

Then #2 informed me that her friend Penny (and her three fucking kids) needed a place to stay "for a few days," and that #2 told Penny that they could stay at our house.

Penny and her children staying at my house (without me being consulted first) really pissed me off. *Especially* because PJ used to *hate* Penny due to the fact that just a few short years ago, #2's husband was cheating on her *with Penny!!* I could already see the bullshit headed my way.

Losing the letters hurt my heart.

Losing the TV hurt my *soul*.

The reason I was so upset at losing the TV is because no possession of mine has ever completed me the way that TV did. Not only was it an amazing television, it was also a once-in-a-lifetime deal. Nothing made me happier than waking up on the weekend and watching the Liverpool football club in perfect 1080p HD amazingness. And that trailer park piece of week-old hobo semen trash took it all away from me. This is a trespass that can *never* be forgiven.

The memory of losing that TV, even years later, still brings a tear to my eye.

WE ARRIVED home to a quiet house. #2 was smart enough to ensure that all the extra house guests weren't around on my arrival home. We had a decent dinner with the kids, and just hung out. #2 had some grand ideas about us and our future and how to make it better, while I had a different plan, which I was going to set into motion the following morning.

We had a nice "family" dinner (all the unwanted house guests were gone for a few days) and spent the night just hanging out without any drama. Before I went to bed, I sent a text to El Jefé letting him know that I was home and to see if we could meet up for coffee or something sometime in the next few days. Obviously, he and I had a lot to talk about, and I was excited to get back to work.

The next morning, I woke up early, ready to set my plan into motion.

I discovered that life had *different* plans already in motion for me.

There are three certainties in life:

1. Death

2. Taxes

3. The sound of a cop knock.

At 7:30 a.m, this occurred:

BANG

BANG

BANG

#2: "Who the fuck is banging on the door like that?!"

Me: (*sighing*) "The cops."

#2: "How the hell do you know that?"

Me: "Just trust me. I've been down this road before."

#2: "Ok, then why the hell are they here?"

Me: "Because I'm about to get arrested."

#2 got up and answered the door. And I knew that I had been caught off guard *again*. This was confirmed when the cops at the door told #2 that they had a warrant for my arrest, and that they knew that I was inside the house.

So much for me catching a break and not going to jail, eh?

Now, some of you clairvoyant pricks out there might be thinking, "I *so* saw this coming." Well, I didn't. So go fuck a duck or gargle dog semen or something.

Strangely, I wasn't really mad at El Jefé per se. I did steal from the guy. I was more hurt from his clever deception in making me believe I wasn't going to jail over this shit. Ironic, isn't it?

And since it was so early in the morning, I was able to get processed by the cops and brought to arraignment first thing that morning.

Lucky me, right?

I also discovered that I wasn't as smart as I thought I was. Remember me telling you how I only made purchases in small, non-felonious amounts?

Yeah.... apparently since they were done using the same account, they could all just be added together to make one big felony charge.

Stupid Lawn Mower.

* * *

DUE TO THE fact that I live in a small town, not much crime goes on here. So, there were only two people being arraigned that morning in court. Me and some other dude. The other dude didn't think that he was going to be released because he was already on probation. I knew that he was fucked and that the judge was going to remand him to jail, but I decided not to share this information with him. It would have taken all the fun out of the surprise when it happened.

His shitshow of an arraignment gave me hope that I was going to be released that morning.

After all the important court-type people got done speaking, the judge started asking the dude a few questions.

Judge: "Are you currently on parole or probation, Mr. Guy?"

Mr. Guy: "No, sir."

Oh, shit. This dude just straight out lied to the judge!

Judge: "Ok, good."

Then the judge started flipping through some of the dude's paperwork speaking Legalspeak, until...

Judge: "Wait a minute Mr. Guy, it says here that you are currently on probation in Balls County."

Mr. Guy: "Oh. Yeah. Uh, sorry judge. I forgot."

You forgot?!?!

Judge: "I see...."

A brief pause.

Judge: "Well then, in that case, I'm going to..."

Remand the fucking shit out of you for lying straight to my face.

Judge: "Release you on your own recognizance and strongly suggest that you call your probation officer immediately and inform him or her of this situation."

WHAT THE FUCK?!

This dude just got a new charge, while on probation, then lied straight to the judge's face, and *got caught in his lie*, and he's getting let go? Well then, I'm *definitely* getting released.

It only made sense, right?

Wrong.

See, I'm what's known as a "second time felony offender." Which is Legalspeak for someone with more than one felony conviction on their record within the past ten years. A category I clearly fell into.

Due to this, a city court judge has zero authority to release or set bail for the accused, and thus said person must be remanded to the county jail until they can be seen by a county court judge.

And that's how less than twenty-four hours out of rehab, I was going to jail.

Pretty much par for the course in my life.

* * *

Going to jail fucking sucks. It's one thing if you're out physically committing a crime or two and get caught in the act– when you're out doing dirt, there's always that thought in the back of your mind that you're going to get caught and go to jail.

But when you're completely blindsided by it, well, that's something different. That's like getting ass-raped by a donkey with *two* dicks. Or, is it a horse of a different color? I don't know. It's one of those stupid sayings.

Either way, it still fucking sucks.

Although, on the plus side, this was the first time *ever* that I wasn't going to jail strung out on dope. So I didn't have to worry about getting dope sick or detoxing in a goddamn cell.

How's that for some glass-half-full shit?

* * *

A FEW HOURS into my stay, I was taken to go see "pre-trial." For the uninitiated, that sounds scary, but it's not. Pre-trial is Legalspeak for pre-trial release. Basically, it's a background interview to see if you would be eligible for an ankle bracelet, or to be RORed (released on own recognizance). Which *never* applies to me, so I almost didn't go.

Almost.

The interview was your basic bullshit. Name, rank, serial number. Criminal history, substance abuse history, etc. And for some reason, the chick that was doing my interview got all excited when I mentioned my opiate addiction, and the fact that I committed my crimes due to my drug-seeking behavior.

Once we got on this particular topic, she started taking some pretty serious notes. I found this rather unsettling, and I told her as much. Then she explained.

Apparently, my county had recently started (as in the week prior) a new program called, get this, Opiate Court (OC). Opiate Court is a voluntary program for addicts who have hit rock bottom and are facing criminal charges for opioid related activity. The mission of the opiate recovery court is to provide a court-managed drug treatment and monitoring program that addresses rehabilitation in the form of medication and counseling for opioid-dependent participants as an alternative to traditional case processing.

She explained that Opiate Court is held five days a week; each person reports to court and speaks with the judge to explain how they're doing in treatment or if they're having any issues. The goal of the program is to get them out of jail, into a MAT (Medically Assisted Treatment) program, which is basically suboxone or methadone, and get them stable. The premise is that if they do well in OC, then once they finish the program, it should be a segue into a drug court program.

Well, guess who has two thumbs and was a perfect candidate for OC?

That's right kids!

This guy.

All I had to do was go see the county judge the next day and let him know that I wanted to participate in the program. Then I would go see the judge that ran the OC program, plead my case to him, and if accepted.... *I'd be released from jail!*

This type of shit simply doesn't happen to me. Normally I would be arrested, sit in jail, then go to prison. So naturally, I was a bit excited about this possibility. All I had to do was one silly little weekend in jail, and I could go home. I could do that shit standing on my fucking head.

* * *

I WENT to court and everything went off without a hitch.

Sort of.

All the necessary important people agreed that I would be a great candidate for the program. Even douche canoe L**** said that I was a great fit for the program (our issues didn't develop until later on down the road).

The guidelines for the program were simple: report to court daily, go to treatment, and stay clean. It was the fine print however, that caused some issues. This was discovered once the supervisor from the treatment provider started speaking.

Hambone was the treatment provider for the program. They offered two different types of treatment: Suboxone or Methadone. *Only.* They weren't able to provide patients either Vivitrol or Revia. And since the program was still in its infancy stage, there was zero wiggle room on this point. This caused a problem for me.

Let me explain:

I was already on Revia.

I wasn't at risk of being sick or of going into opiate detox.

I had zero need/want for Suboxone or Methadone.

In fact, at this stage in the game for me, taking either of those medications would've actually been a step *backwards* for me.

This caused some debate in the courtroom.

Supervisor: "In order to participate in our program, you have to be taking either Suboxone or Methadone."

Judge: "And in order to participate in the Opiate Court program, you have to be participating in Hambone's program."

Me: "Can't I do simple outpatient?"

Supervisor: "No."

Judge: "No."

Me: "So... you're forcing me to take medication that I don't want or need. Isn't that, I don't know... illegal?"

Hambone: "We can't force you to take any medication that you don't want to take."

Me: "But I can't do your program without taking Suboxone or Methadone."

Supervisor: "Correct."

Me: "Uh-huh."

Judge: "This is a voluntary program. It's your choice whether you want to participate in it or not."

Me: "Let me make sure that I understand this correctly. My choices are A) go sit in jail and fight my case from there, or B) sign up for the program and take meds that I don't want *or* need, basically taking a giant step backwards. But I'd be out of jail, right?"

An uncomfortable silence fell over the courtroom as they decided how to tap dance out of the little corner I just painted them into. Clearly there were still a few glitches in the Matrix that needed to be ironed out, and I had just discovered one of them.

The joys of growing pains, right?

Even L**** kept his cock hole shut and took a sudden interest in his legal pad while he let the judge handle this little issue.

You don't become an ADA by jumping on grenades. You become an ADA by jumping on cocks. Right L****?

The judge knew that he was on a slippery slope here, and he worded his response carefully.

Judge: "This program has a strict set of guidelines that we have to follow. You are free to decide if you would like to participate in it or not. No one is forcing you to do anything. Everyone here agrees that you are a great candidate for this program, and given your substance abuse history, I personally feel that you could benefit greatly from it. You are of course free to decline our offer and return to jail and address your case from there. But, if I may offer some advice, I believe that the outcome of your case would be considerably more in your favor if you took part in this program."

Me: "May I have a moment to speak with my attorney?"

Judge: "Of course."

Me: (*pulling my lawyer to the side*) "He just avoided answering my question, didn't he?"

Lawyer: "Yup."

Me: "So take the drugs and go home, or go to jail then?"

Lawyer: "Basically."

Me: "Am I the first addict in history who's having trouble deciding if I wanna go home and take drugs or go to jail?"

Lawyer: "I'm inclined to believe that yes, yes you are."

Me: "What can I say, I'm special."

Lawyer: "Apparently."

Me: (*turning back to the judge*) "If I agree to this, I'll go home today?"

Judge: (*smiling like a cat about to eat its prey*) "You'll be out of jail and at Hambone before noon."

Me: "Where's the knife?"

Judge: "Excuse me?"

Me: "I've gotta sign this thing in blood, right?"

Judge: "Ink will be fine."

So I signed my deal with the devil, and as promised, I was out of jail and at my appointment with Hambone before noon.

* * *

SINCE I WAS FREE, once I got to my appointment with Hambone, I decided to push the envelope a little further. I told the counselor that I was having second thoughts about taking the Suboxone, and that I wanted to speak to a supervisor, who just so happened to be in the courtroom that morning.

We went back and forth for a bit until he finally got frustrated with me and said:

Supervisor: "Look, we can't force you to do anything. But if you decide to refuse the treatment, then I will have to call the judge and let him know that you're refusing the program. Most likely he'll send you back to jail."

Seriously, how does one even argue with that?

Exactly. You can't.

Unless you want to go to jail.

The lesson of the day? When someone tells you that they can't make you do something, you have to read between the lines, because what they're really saying is that they've got you by the balls and you're fucked.

Call me a pussy, but I acquiesced.

Then I went to see the doctor.

Once all the preliminaries were out of the way, the doctor said:

Doctor: "After we wait a week to make sure the Revia is out of your system, I'm going to start you on twenty-four milligrams of Suboxone a day."

Me: "Excuse me?"

Doctor: "Considering your history, I feel that twenty-four milligrams is an appropriate dosage for you."

And here we go...

Seriously, treatment doctors *must* get some sort of kickbacks from the pharmaceutical companies. Twenty-four milligrams is a ridiculous dosage for someone to start taking, especially for someone who was thirty days clean. Eight milligrams would have been excessive.

As kindly as I could, I explained to the doctor that I would not be taking the twenty-four milligrams, but that I would be taking two milligrams a day. Which he didn't understand. The doctor assumed that I was like all the other people in the program and would want to get the maximum dosage that I could. I was proving to be the exception to the rule *"that's what addicts do."*

The doctor didn't know how to handle me, so he got the supervisor involved. But this time I knew that I had *them* by the balls. The guidelines said that in order to be in their program, I had to be taking either Suboxone or Methadone. However, the guidelines did not say how *much* of the shit I had to take.

And this was our compromise.

I did feel as if I was taking a step backwards in my recovery by going back on Suboxone, but I wanted to be out of jail more than I cared about said step.

WHAT HAPPENED over the course of the ninety days that followed could fill the contents of an entire book. I'm not going to bore you with those details because they aren't very relevant, so I'll give you the very abridged version.

I left #2.

Okay, perhaps that's a bit too abridged. So, how about just the basics...

#2 and I started arguing often.

On top of my legal issues, I was unemployed and we had zero income. The financial situation became a major issue.

Bell was still filling #2's head with a lot of bullshit, causing untold problems.

#2 and Bell started doing a lot of cocaine.

Our other houseguests were overwhelming. Plus, Penny was trouble with a capital HIV.

The stress at home started to wear me thin.

I had hit my breaking point.

Finally, #2 and I got into a *huge* screaming match over $1.50, and no, I'm not kidding. One dollar and fifty cents.

During this screaming match, #2 became extremely violent and attacked me, leaving some serious marks on my face. This left me with no choice but to file an incident report with the cops.

Being a documented heroin addict is one thing.

But being a documented domestic violence victim is where I draw the fucking line.

You can scroll through the pages of the domestic violence history book and find Tina Turner, Nicole Brown Simpson, Rihanna, and now me, Lawn Mower.

Do you know what the worst part is?

All the domestic violence and battered women jokes are *completely ruined* for me! Take, for example:

What do you say to a woman with two black eyes?

Nothing you haven't told her twice already!

Or:

What does a woman do when she comes home from the domestic violence shelter?

The dishes, if she knows what's good for her!

They're all ruined! Thanks for that, #2.

The domestic violence incident was the stone that sank the ship for me. After that shit, I left.

* * *

SINCE I WAS TRYING to take control of my life, I decided to cover my ass a little.

Years ago, I learned a valuable lesson after I was "blind-sided" by the cops showing up looking for me. I started checking the county sheriff's website on a daily basis to see if I should be worried or not. When you're out doing dirt, one should always be prepared for the worst.

So, when my lawyer informed me that because I also pulled my little credit card scheme in Balls County, an arrest might be coming out of that county as well. Apparently, if you do the same crime, in the same store, but in a different county, a whole new charge can ensue. Who knew? Anyways, once he told me that, I made the decision to try and nip it in the bud.

How did I attempt this feat?

Well, first I started making some phone calls and came across the name of the cop investigating the case.

Then, I decided to give him a call.

Lawn Mower

It seemed the logical move at the time.

Donald Duck: "This is Investigator Donald Duck."

Me: "Hello Investigator Duck. My name is Lawn Mower, and I understand that you're the guy in charge of a case that involves me, and, umm, I was wondering when you would be coming to arrest me?'

Donald Duck: (*coughs*) "Excuse me?"

Me: "I know this is a bit unusual. See, I was arrested here in Truffle Butter County back in January, and I've been told by my lawyer that a charge that's directly related to this case will be coming from Balls County. Right now, I'm out on pre-trial release, I'm going to treatment and participating in the Opioid Court program. Are you familiar with the program?"

Donald Duck: "I am."

Me: "Excellent. Well, it's a brand new program here, and I'm doing well in it. I'm trying to take care of my shit, and not run away from the problems that I've caused. I know that a charge will be coming from our county, and I'd really like to avoid having a warrant just pop up. So, if we could like, meet up somewhere and you could arrest me, that would be swell."

Donald Duck: "Umm..."

Me: "This way I can get everything taken care of now, with a very limited disruption in my treatment. Plus, I could avoid having that warrant screwing up everything that I'm currently working so hard to achieve."

Donald Duck: "You know, I've been in law enforcement for over twenty years, and this is the first time anything like this has ever happened. I've never actually spoken to someone who was actually *looking* to get arrested. Generally, this isn't how this thing works. You do know that, right?"

Me: "Oh yeah. I'm painfully aware of how the process normally works."

Donald Duck: "I've had people turn themselves into me when they knew that they had a warrant out for their arrest, but this... I haven't even *looked* at the file yet. And the only reason I know what case you're talking about, is because I was handed the file *this morning*."

Me: "So, no meeting up then?"

Donald Duck: "Listen, how about this... Give me your phone number and some time to do my job. If it turns out that I will be making an arrest in the case, and that you will be the person arrested, then I'll reach out to you before issuing a warrant. Sound fair?"

Me: "Seriously?"

Donald Duck: "Yeah, seriously. You appear to be trying to take care of your shit, and if you're out there doing the right thing by being in treatment and in that program, I'll do my best not to screw that up for you."

Me: "Wow. Thank you."

Donald Duck: "No problem. But if the time does come and you try to fuck me..."

Me: "Understood."

Donald Duck: "Good. Now, give me your number, and I'll be in touch."

So, I gave the dude my number and went about my business.

The following day I went to Opiate Court and informed all the important and necessary people about my chat with Donald Duck and was actually commended for trying to be proactive. Which I guess I was. Even though at the time I didn't look at it that way. I simply saw it as me trying to avoid getting fucked.

I LET a friend read this part of the story, and their response was:

Friend: "Dude, what you did was the exact definition of 'proactive.'"

Me: "No it wasn't. I was just covering my ass."

Friend: "Dude, seriously. Merriam-Webster's Collegiate Dictionary 11th edition defines proactive as: 'Acting in anticipation of future problems, needs, or changes.'"

Me: "Well, Lawn Mower defines proactive as: 'Trying to avoid getting fucked.'"

Friend: "Did you seriously just refer to yourself in the third person?"

Me: "Lawn Mower says to eat a bag of dicks."

* * *

Leaving #2 was the best thing I could have done for myself. Our relationship had turned extremely tumultuous, and I couldn't see us getting back to amicable without an act of sweet baby Jesus.

Once I left, I moved in with a friend and I was able to focus on finishing up Opiate Court, getting into drug court, and starting divorce proceedings.

Even though I had new felony charges and a bad name in the community, I was still able to land a halfway decent job at a local gym doing maintenance work. This was a good thing. Mainly because I needed money. Also because it helped me feel like my life was slowly making a turn for the better. Opiate Court was going great, and I was a few weeks away from signing my drug court contract, which meant that I wasn't going to prison. I also was approved for a grant so I could take a course to become a CRPA (Certified Recovery Peer Advocate).

Things were good.

Then life handed me another "gift."

#3.

In the beginning of this book, after the multiple warnings, and after the description of me waking up in the ICU, I briefly discussed how I may or may not have liberated a large amount of cocaine and dashed off to Florida. What I *didn't* discuss was how exactly I had gotten to that point.

Well, one could argue that I started down that path with #3's assistance.

Let me explain.

#3 and I dated just after high school and we were quickly enamored of each other. As a matter of fact, I took #3's virginity. The only downside to our relationship was her cunty sister Anathema, and the fact that #3 was going to be going to college in South Dakota in the fall.

Anathema and I did *not* get along at all. Mainly because she is a racist cunt, and I'm an asshole. Anathema had her own issues to deal with, so I ignored her often, and luckily, even though she opposed my relationship with her sister (because I'm white and #3 isn't), #3 and I stayed together. We even planned on sticking it out together while she was in college.

As you can imagine, that didn't work out too well.

About a month into her first semester of college, #3 broke up with me, and I didn't take it too well at all. That night I dropped twenty-five hits of blotter acid, and tripped balls for close to three days. What followed was utter ridiculousness.

During this stage of my life, I was basically a garbage can. I had yet to discover opiates, so I did anything and everything I could get my hands on, and in copious amounts. Anything to ease the pain of the hole in my soul. The same thing Anathema did with fellatio.

The garbage can shitshow went on for a couple of years until it became a good idea for me to leave town. So, while I'm not directly blaming #3 for my actions, her actions definitely helped get the ball rolling.

Back to the future twenty years and we find ourselves talking about #3 once again.

Through a series of strange events (which is Mowerspeak for: none of your fucking business), #3 and I crossed paths once again, and after that happened, any stray thoughts about #2 and I getting back together went right out the window. The shitshow that had been my life with #2 was no more, and my life was *finally* changing for the better.

That notion was short-lived.

One day in mid-May, I received a call from my lawyer. I had been waiting and waiting to sign the paperwork for drug court, so when I saw his number pop up on my screen, I became very excited.

My excitement lasted about as long as it did when I lost my virginity. Two seconds.

Me: "Hey Lawyer."

Lawyer: "I've got some bad news, Lawn Mower."

No dinner and dancing.

No drinks and small talk.

No foreplay.

Straight to the fucking, with no need for postcoital cuddling.

Me: "I'm listening...."

Lawyer: "Drug court is off the table and the DA wants prison time."

It's amazing how life can turn on a dime. One minute things are fine. The next– BAM– the universe throws a sucker punch.

And even though I've grown accustomed to the words "you're going to prison," they still sting when I hear them.

Me: "Okay.... What the fuck happened?"

Lawyer: (*clearing his throat*) "Well, the DA thinks you're an asshole."

Me: "That's not exactly breaking news, Lawyer."

Lawyer: "I can't argue that. So, tell me about this book of yours."

Now, I'd never mentioned *anything* to Lawyer about my book. I'd barely spoken about it to anyone, so Lawyer's comment was a bit disturbing.

Me: "In the immortal words of the Virgin Mary, come again?"

Lawyer: "The DA has a copy of your book. As do I. As does the judge. As does pretty much everyone in the legal community in three counties. L**** is calling your book a 'manifesto' and after reading it, has decided to rescind his offer of drug court. He wants you to go to prison."

Me: "Wait, can he even do that?!"

Lawyer: "He can do what he wants. Drug court isn't a mandatory thing. It's an alternative to incarceration. And no, before you ask, I don't think we can do anything about it.

L**** called me and said, and I quote, 'Your client has a sick and demented mental psyche, is seriously troubled and I do not want him at-large in the community. The only thing he deserves is the three hots and a cot he'll get in state prison.'"

Me: "Seriously?"

Lawyer: "Yes, seriously. Even *I'm* having trouble believing that you said some of this shit. I mean, 'I'd gladly gargle a judge's balls in order to get a better deal,' you seriously wrote that?"

Me: "That's taken out of context. No one wants to go to prison, and most people would do anything to *not* go to prison. It's a figure of speech, for fuck's sake."

Lawyer: "Well, that may be so. However, that figure of speech– amongst many others– is the reason why you're going to be sent to prison, and why you won't be going into drug court."

And that, my friends, is how my book got me sent to prison.

So much for the First Amendment.

Or the fact that I was following the advice of every self-help group in existence.

Or that I was trying to help not only myself, but others as well.

L**** got his fucking panties in a wad over something I said about a situation that had nothing to do with my case what-so-fucking-ever, something that had transpired in a Florida courtroom well over a decade ago.

None of that shit mattered.

I spent the rest of the conversation explaining myself and the concept of the book to my lawyer with the hopes that if I could convince him of my goals, then perhaps he could do some lawyer magic and change bitch-tits L****'s mind on the subject.

It was a long conversation.

I got off the phone with my lawyer, called #3 to tell her what had happened, and cried like a little bitch.

I DID everything in my power to try and fight the DA. There was no way I was simply going to let L**** fuck me without a fight. So, I rallied the troops. And by troops, I mean anyone and everyone who would listen to my story and who might be able to do something to help.

I spoke to every judge who was involved in my case. I spoke to the counselor at Hambone, the people from the county who gave me the CRPA grant, miscellaneous people in the legal community, a chick from the State Justice Department who was affiliated with the Opiate Court program, the drug court people, the ACLU, FBI, CIA, NA, AA, and even the NAACP. Although, for some reason they wouldn't give me the time of day.

Weird.

No stone was left unturned in this endeavor. I wasn't just fighting the going-to-prison thing. I mean, I didn't *want* to go there, but over the years I had grown accustomed to being incarcerated. What I was fighting for was the fact that I was being punished for trying to better myself, for trying to fight my addiction and personal demons while trying to help others as well.

Now, are some of the things I say in here offensive to others? Probably. Get over it. What ever happened to sticks and stones? The world has gone fucking soft. Now, offending someone is apparently beyond detrimental to their physical well-being and we must all walk on eggshells all day, every day in perpetual fear that we might offend someone with our words and/or actions.

Fucking pussies.

L**** was far from impressed with my "Save Lawn Mower" campaign. I knew this because when he graced Opiate Court with his presence, he wouldn't even look at me. Also because my lawyer told me so.

My lawyer also informed me that whatever I was doing was working.

Lawyer: "Listen, keep it up. You've got L**** dodging bullets. He's *pissed.*"

Me: "Really?"

Lawyer: "Yeah. He's got a meeting set up with me and his boss about you."

Me: "Can I come?"

Lawyer: "Do you want to go to prison?"

Me: "Not particularly."

Lawyer: "Then no, you can't come."

Me: "Fair enough."

Lawyer: "Then just sit back, stay out of trouble, and let me do my thing."

* * *

In a rare move on my part, I listened to my lawyer and did just that. Besides, I knew that I had already done everything I possibly could. All I could do was stay on course and not fuck up.

During this time, #3 picked up a DWI charge. This should have sent up a few red flags for me, and actually it did, but I have a documented history of ignoring red flags. Which is exactly what I did in this case. To make matters worse, if her DWI somehow got brought up by The Sister or Jiminy, I would refer to it as "her DWI from before" that hadn't been resolved in court yet.

Yes, the foolishness of this is beyond apparent to me now. The fucked-up thing is that it was apparent to me *then* as well. I just chose to ignore that fact.

#3's DWI also caused quite a few issues with her baby daddy, Ginger.

There aren't many things/people in this world that I hate: L****, Beavis, guacamole, and the fact that the McRib isn't available year-round, just to name a few. Ginger is also on this list. Mainly because he is a giant man-baby cunt. He's a pussy who picks fights with women because he believes that he intimidates them, and then he runs and hides behind his girlfriend Ginger Cunt. This is because she has his balls in a jar.

I could go on for *hundreds* of pages detailing the skeletons in Ginger's closet, but I don't want to waste any more time than I already have on the bitch. Just know that I hate him to the depths of my soul. He's a pussy, and he knows it.

I will say this however:

Ginger, please give me a reason to exploit your skeletons to the world. And we *both* know that you have plenty of shit hidden in your closet. I would like nothing more than to tell you and the world all about yourself, so please, *please* give me a reason to do it.

I hope that you read this book, grow a spine, and finally stop hiding behind Ginger Cunt. If that ever happens, I have four words for you:

Come.

At.

Lawn Mower

Me.

Bro.

Ginger Cunt, this also applies to you. You ugly, vile, cum-guzzling, two-dollar crack whore.

Lawn Mower, taking the call-out game to a whole new level!

* * *

I STARTED STAYING WITH #3 quite often, and pretty much moved in.

An addict and an alcoholic both in early recovery living together– what could *possibly* go wrong, right?

While things were progressing between #3 and I, I heard back from my lawyer and was informed that he had worked his magic. L**** had agreed to let me into drug court, under the condition that I sign a ridiculous contract stating that if I fucked drug court up, I would be going to prison for a long, *long* time. Once the contract was signed (which I was more than willing to do), I could transition from Opiate Court into drug court, and avoid prison.

All I had to do was wait for the contract to be prepared. Which for some reason was taking longer than it normally should.

While all of this was going on, I was helping #3 along with her DWI case. It was still in its infancy, and even though it wasn't a felony, she was still a nervous wreck over it. Given my expertise in the criminal justice system, I was trying to give her the best guidance and support that I could.

My guidance and support could only go so far. #3 was quite neurotic most of the time, and didn't listen to half the stuff I told her. She foolishly believed that her public defender was working hard for her, and was staying on top of her case 24/7. This couldn't have been further from the truth.

#3 felt that she should be in contact with her lawyer on a daily basis, with minute-by-minute updates. I tried explaining to her that she should expect to go weeks without hearing from her lawyer, and this was a concept that she just couldn't grasp.

What can I say, some lessons need to be learned the hard way.

Dᴜʀɪɴɢ ᴍʏ ᴏғғ time from explaining the legal system and how slow the wheels of justice truly move, I began cutting my losses, by which I mean I started working on my divorce from #2.

All and all, things were moving along smoothly.

Until they weren't.

Once again, it all started with a phone call.

Me: "Hello?"

Donald Duck: "Lawn Mower? This is State Trooper Donald Duck. Remember me?"

Fuck......

Me: "Yeah."

Donald Duck: "Sorry it has taken me so long to get back to you; I've been swamped."

Me: "No problem. How can I help you?"

Donald Duck: "Well, I just wanted to reach out and let you know that I'm ready to arrest you now."

Well, isn't that just fucking swell.

Me: "Is that so?"

Donald Duck: "Yes. Considering the whole situation, and taking into account the fact that *you* reached out to *me* regarding the matter, I will do you the courtesy of letting you turn yourself in to me. If you still want to proceed like that. Then when you come in, I'm going to process you and send you off with an appearance ticket."

Me: "What?"

Donald Duck: "I'm not going to take you to jail. We'll take care of the processing here, photograph, fingerprints, et cetera, then send you on your way with an appearance ticket for court. As long as you show up to court, there won't be any problems."

Getting arrested is never a good thing. But when you get arrested and don't go directly to jail– mind you, this is pre bail reform days– well, it just makes things all that much easier. Since an appearance ticket was part of the package, I set up an appointment to meet with Donald Duck, to get arrested.

When I hung up the phone with the investigator, I realized that while most people pencil in lunches and meetings on their calendar, I was now in the business of scheduling my arrests.

The day of my arrest, things started to make sense.

While Donald Duck was true to his word, I found out that other people were sneaky little cunts.

And for the record, I didn't trust what Duck told me he was going to do. My stepfather was a cop, so knowing that cops lie is like knowing that Herpes isn't a Greek god. Basic common knowledge type shit.

I had left my phone in my car on the off chance that Duck was blowing smoke up my ass. This was because if I did get sent to jail, I wasn't going to provide the jail staff the opportunity to "misplace" my property, like they have a tendency to do.

Everything went smoothly at the trooper barracks. I walked in. Got arrested/processed. I walked out with an appearance ticket. Easy peasy.

By the time I got to my car in the parking lot, my phone was already ringing. It was my lawyer.

Odd.....

Me: "Talk to me, Goose."

Lawyer: "Lawn Mower, I've got bad news."

Me: "I'm starting to believe that you have no concept of what the term 'good news' actually is."

Lawyer: "No, I do. You're just a magnet for shit."

Can't argue that.

Me: "So?"

Lawyer: "Drug court is off the table. Again."

Me: "For what?!"

Lawyer: "L**** says that the Balls DA wants prison time, so there's no point in letting you into drug court."

Me: "The Balls DA wants state time? Lawyer, I *literally* just walked out of the trooper barracks. The fucking ink on my fingerprint card isn't even dry yet. There's no fucking way...."

Oh shit.

Lawyer: "Yeah, I know. For what it's worth, I'm sorry Lawn Mower."

At that moment, the picture became clear.

L**** had *zero* intentions of letting me into drug court in the first place. He knew all along that there would be a charge from Balls County. He was simply biding his time. This was a calculated move.

I'm well aware of how slow the wheels of justice move. The Balls County DA didn't even know my fucking name yet, so there was no possible fucking way that he had a sentencing recommendation for me. I hadn't even been arraigned!

Lawn Mower

L**** fucked me.

The drug court contract taking forever to be put together was L**** stalling so that I wouldn't be participating in the program when this charge came about. The reason for this was, had I been participating in the drug court program prior to this arrest, and since *the new charge* was an extension of the original charge (and not something completely different), not to mention that all of the restitution issues would be handled by my county and not Balls County, then Balls County would have to either dismiss the charge altogether contingent upon my completion of drug court, or simply transfer the case to my county. Meaning no one could send me to prison unless I fucked up the drug court program.

But since I wasn't *in* drug court yet, then both counties could do whatever the fuck they wanted with me.

L****, you're a sneaky little cunt.

I've spent countless nights wide-awake thinking about this.

They say that insanity is repeating the same thing over and over again, expecting different results.

Apply that logic to this situation: got in trouble in Florida, didn't get a program and got sent to prison. Came home and relapsed. Got in trouble in New York, didn't get a (needed) program, got sent to prison (again). Came home and relapsed (again). Got in trouble in New York (again)....

Is anyone else seeing a pattern here?

'Cause I sure the fuck am.

Now, this is me just spit balling here, but perhaps prison isn't the end-all, be-all answer to everything. Perhaps some sort of treatment for those who have a clear issue with drug dependency might be a bit more beneficial.

Now I'm not saying that there shouldn't be consequences for one's actions. All I'm saying is simply sending them away to prison isn't a solution to the problem. It's tossing the problem in the basement and forgetting about it, while simultaneously letting it become someone else's problem.

And I can personally attest to how utterly ridiculous state prison programs truly are. They might look great on paper, but in application... epic fail.

Trust me on this.

Once the fact set in that I was going back to prison, I gave up and said fuck it.

Yeah, I relapsed.

Again.

It didn't happen right away, but it did happen. And it wasn't a random thing, it was planned. What wasn't planned was everything that followed. It never is.

* * *

THE FIRST TIME I USED, I overdosed.

I dropped #3 off at an appointment, went and got some dope, drove to a pharmacy, got some rigs, and shot up right in the parking lot, because I'm fucking classy.

I remember feeling all warm and fuzzy, like I was about to hug God.

Then nothing.

Next thing I know, I'm on the ground, surrounded by legs, boots, and strange voices.

Talk about déjà vu.

They brought me to the hospital, hooked me up to all sorts of IVs and did doctor shit. They were surprised that I wasn't a belligerent asshole, because most everyone who wakes up after being Narcaned is. This is generally because they're in instant withdrawal. Even you, my sheltered reader, would be homicidal if you experienced that shit. But since this was my first time using, I wasn't in any sort of withdrawal.

The moment I got to the ER, I was trying to leave. I was already extremely late in picking up #3 and she was blowing up my phone. I didn't want to tell her the truth, and I had no plausible excuse as to why I was late. It took me a good twenty minutes to get out of that hospital. Since I wasn't in any sort of trouble, I was free to leave. And even though I looked and felt like absolute shit, the doctors couldn't stop me. So I left AMA. Which is Medicalspeak for against medical advice.

By the time I picked up #3, she was livid.

Picture Joan Crawford finding the wire hanger in the closet, multiplied by a hundred.

When #3 saw how I looked, she calmed down a bit. Andrea Bocelli could have seen that something was wrong with me. Even so, she was still *pissed*.

And then came the questions.

Of course I tried lying to hide my actions, but when the truth finally came out, she was furious, yet supportive. She asked me why, and all I could muster was that I didn't want to go back to prison. I couldn't handle it and I wanted to take the coward's way out. We talked about it for a few hours and she promised me that everything would be okay, and for some foolish reason I believed her.

The conversation went so well that I decided to omit one small detail.

I still had dope.

I never got searched before I went to the hospital, so I still had the rest of the dope I had bought.

And instead of getting rid of it, I stashed it.

Stupid, I know.

It definitely came back to bite me in the ass, almost instantly.

THE FOLLOWING DAY WENT WELL. #3 and I hung out, then went to a recovery meeting later in the evening. At the meeting I discussed what had happened the night before, and got a lot of support from the people there. It was nice to get some of that stuff out– my fears about going back to prison, the whole situation and how it frustrated me to no end.

When we got home my phone was blowing up with texts of support from the people at the meeting, and it made me feel really good. Knowing that I had support helped. Not enough to make me throw out my dope mind you, but it still helped.

#3 and I were home for about thirty minutes, and we were hungry, so I got up to make dinner. One minute I was grabbing stuff out of the fridge, and the next I was on the floor getting CPR from a distraught #3.

What the fuck, right?

As I was coming to, I noticed two paramedics rushing into the room.

Again, what the fuck, right?

Here's what happened: I went into cardiac arrest. I had stressed my body the fuck out, and my heart told me to fuck off. I fell to the floor and stopped breathing. #3 called 911 and gave me CPR for seven minutes until the paramedics arrived.

Seven. Fucking. Minutes.

That's a lot of CPR. I still have the scar on my chest from the skin that was rubbed away during that time.

#3, along with everyone else, thought that I had overdosed again. To make matters worse, while I was being taken to the emergency room to get checked out, #3 had found the dope that I had stashed, which prompted her to call The Sister. #3 gave her the rundown on everything that had transpired over the past couple of days, which caused all sorts of chaos.

The Sister also believed that I had overdosed, and after hearing the things I had entrusted to #3, she believed that I had done it *on purpose*. The Sister took it upon herself to call the emergency room I was in and inform them of said belief.

I was unaware of any of this until it was time for me to be discharged from the emergency room.

The doctor entered the room with four very large men. The largest of the four had a hospital gown in his hands.

Godzilla: "Hey Lawn Mower, the doctor here has your discharge papers for the ER. Once you're done siging them, I'll need you to put this on."

He showed me the gown.

Me: "Why would I put that on when I'm going home?"

Godzilla: "Because you're not going home."

Me: "Pardon?"

Godzilla: "You're being discharged from the emergency room, but you're not being released from the hospital."

I didn't immediately respond to that because I was waiting for the punchline. When I didn't speak, Godzilla continued.

Godzilla: "You're being discharged from the emergency room, but you're being released into our care."

Me: "I hate to break it to you, but I'm tone deaf and I'm not gay."

Godzilla: "What?"

Me: "I can't join your boy band. Listen, it's been a tough couple of days and I just want to go home."

Godzilla: "We're not a boy band, we're with CPEP."

Me: "What's that, an a capella group or something?"

Godzilla: "No, CPEP is a Comprehensive Psychiatric Emergency Program."

Me: "Then you're *definitely* in the wrong room, 'cause I'm not crazy."

Godzilla: "What about suicidal?"

Me: "Only in the morning..." I made a show of looking at my watch, "...and since it's 10 p.m., you're a few hours early. So kindly fuck off so I can go home."

I made a move to get out of bed, and Godzilla took a step forward.

Godzilla: "Look, we've received a call from a concerned family member who thinks that your actions tonight were an attempt to hurt yourself. We have to take that seriously. You'll have to come with us."

Me: "And if I don't?"

Godzilla: (*sighing*) "Then we'll make you."

Me: "You and what army?"

Godzilla actually paused and looked behind him as if the other three titans had left the room. When he saw they were still there, he turned back to me.

Godzilla: "Seriously?"

Me: "I'll tell you what, I'm feeling generous tonight. So, if you answer two questions for me, I'll go with you peacefully. If not, then you'll have to earn your pay tonight."

Godzilla: "Okay, sure."

Me: "Who called?"

Godzilla: "I can't tell you that."

Me: "Fine. Don't say anything if it was my sister."

Silence.

Me: "How long do I have to stay?"

Godzilla: "Until you see the doctor. After that it's up to him. He could let you go immediately, or keep you for up to seventy-two hours."

Me: "And when will I see the good doctor?"

Godzilla: "That's three questions."

Me: "You never *answered* my first question."

Godzilla: "Fair enough. Sometime in the next couple of hours."

Me: "Fine. Let's go."

Godzilla: "Seriously?"

Me: "Yeah, why not? Besides, it would be embarrassing for you to have to tell your boss that one dude kicked all four of your asses."

Even the doctor laughed at that.

* * *

I MET with the doctor around 4 a.m., which didn't impress me. I don't deal with crazy well, and I was in Crazyville ground zero. Plus, I was already pissed off about having to be there in the first place. When the doctor and I finally talked, I did my best to keep my cool.

I explained the situation to him the best I could. Prison, drug court, etc. and then I gave him a little family history. I told him that The Sister was simply overreacting. I also explained that Narcan wasn't used to revive me, and that if I actually *had* tried to overdose or hurt myself, then Narcan would have been absolutely necessary.

When the doctor asked me about what happened the previous night, I told him that it was a moment of weakness. That the pressure of having to go back to prison had gotten to me and that I went to my crutch, heroin. He asked me about me telling #3 that I wanted to take the coward's way out, and I asked him if *he* would be okay with knowing that he was going to prison. He admitted that no, he wouldn't be. I explained to him that it was a figure of speech. I had no intentions of hurting myself or anyone else, and that this whole situation was a giant misunderstanding.

I'm not sure that he completely believed me, but it *was* plausible. So, we made a deal.

Doctor: "How about this. Since your sister is the one with the concerns here, and since she knows you and the family history better than I do, why don't you talk to her. If she thinks that it's okay for you to go home, then I'll sign off on it."

Me: "What time is it?"

Doctor: "A quarter after five in the morning."

Me: "I'm sure she's up. Can I have a phone?"

All I needed to do was get The Sister to tell the doctor that it was cool for me to go home and I could leave! Piece of cake. It was a simple matter of life and death. As long as she acquiesced, she would live. If not (and I had to stay in Crazyville for seventy-two hours), I'd fucking kill her.

She answered on the third ring.

The Sister: "Hello?"

Me: "Hiya."

The Sister: "Umm.... It's five in the morning."

Me: "Well it's nice to know that you're still a master of the obvious."

The Sister: "No, I mean why are you calling me?"

Me: "No, you mean *how* am I calling you, and why am I not drooling on myself in some sort of Thorazine stupor in the loony bin right now."

The Sister: "Uh..."

Me: "Right. Well here's the thing, little sister, I've been talking to Dr. Finch here."

The Sister: "That's seriously not his name, is it?"

Only my sister could get a *Running with Scissors* reference at five in the morning.

Me: "Sadly no. Anyways, the doctor here and I have been talking, and I've explained to him that you simply jumped to a conclusion with your 'my brother tried to hurt himself' line of thought, and I explained a little of the family history to him. And the doctor said that since you know me so well, that if you think it's okay for me to go home, then he will let me go."

The Sister: "And if I don't tell him that?"

Me: "Then I'd have to stay here. In a close observation 'mental health unit.' For a minimum of seventy-two hours"

The Sister: "Don't you think that might be a good idea?"

Have you ever wished for the ability to jump through a phone and murder someone?

Me: "CPEP. Mental health unit. Crazy people who bark at the moon and eat their own shit."

The Sister: "Yeah I know, but I'm worried about you."

Me: "Duly noted."

The Sister: "So maybe it's not such a bad idea."

Me: "For at least seventy-two hours."

The Sister: "Then what?"

Me: "You mean what happens after they realize I don't belong here and let me go?"

The Sister: "Yeah."

The doctor was listening, so I had to be subtle, which really isn't my strong suit.

Me: "Remember Dorothy's?"

Everyone in my hometown remembers Dorothy's. It was a local liquor store that burned to the ground three days after I came home from prison the first time. The Sister and I always joked about how it was an omen that such a local landmark had burned immediately following my return home.

And even though my sister isn't the sharpest tool in the shed at times, she could read between the lines.

Tell the doctor that it's okay for me to go home, or I'll burn your fucking house down.

A complete bluff.

Maybe.

The Sister: "Let me talk to the doctor."

An hour later I was walking out the door.

* * *

IF I HAD a dollar for every lie I've ever told that was believed, I'd probably never have to work again.

Simultaneously, if I had a dollar for every truth I've told that wasn't believed, I'd probably never have to work again either.

That's the rub about being an addict. It's not all about the drugs. It's about the actions. The deceits. The lies. The manipulations.

It was difficult for most people to accept that I didn't use that night. But I didn't, so y'all can suck a cock.

The problem was that I had drugs in my system from the first incident, and due to my history, people have a very hard time believing what I was saying. Even knowing Narcan wasn't used on the second night, most everyone still didn't believe me. The doctors agreed with me that had it been an overdose, it would have been "next to impossible" to revive me without the use of Narcan.

And still, I wasn't believed.

And again, y'all can suck a cock.

Anathema is at the top of that list.

Anathema is a professional bottom-feeder. She hasn't had a job in well over fifteen years. She lives in the hood with her bottom-feeding boyfriend Nooner, living off the system, while Nooner makes a living off the books, selling drugs. Mainly heroin.

Anathema is a "recovering" (this is a very loose use of the word) heroin addict who had lost and/or given up custody of not one, not two, not three, but all *seven* of her children due to her drug use and inability to function like an adult.

And let's not forget that Nooner is the biological father of at least three of those children, and has stood by his girl as they *both* abandoned/lost their children. Allow me to describe the scenario of the last abandonment: Anathema literally went into the hospital to give birth, didn't provide her name to staff, popped out the child, and then walked out of the hospital, leaving her newborn baby behind for someone else to take care of.

This was the person running the Anti-Lawn Mower bandwagon, who caused countless issues between #3 and myself.

I've never hit a woman in my life, but for Anathema, I'd make a serious fucking exception.

It's not that Anathema didn't have a decent argument against me. Plus, she was also just trying to protect her sister,

I get that. However, the whole stones-and-glass-house thing comes into play here. Even more so because how do you give someone advice like "you need to get away from that fucking junkie" when you yourself live with an active addict who sells heroin for a living? And let's not forget the fact that she was most likely using during this time as well.

Sadly, her advice was pretty solid. Over my years of use and abuse, I've generally become desensitized to many things. Especially my actions. Now, that does *not* mean that the things I've done don't bother or upset me, it's that their sting(s) are...... muted.

Now, what happened next will haunt me until the day I die; simultaneously, I will forever have gratitude for it.

Intrigued?

Good.

Because I'm about to piss *a lot* of people off with my next sentence.

I turned #3 into a junkie.

AND NO, you didn't read that wrong up above. I am grateful for it.

What the fuck Lawn Mower, L**** was right about you! You are fucking sick and demented!!

Well, you can take your opinion and go fuck a duck with L****.

Also, you've yet to hear me out on this. I'm not saying that turning *anyone* into a junkie is a good thing here. So before you try to burn my house down while I sleep or something, just hear me out, okay?

As SCARY AS THEY WERE, my two flatlining experiences didn't put the brakes on my using. Oh, they put it on hold for a few weeks, but soon enough, I was right back at it.

My overdose happened in August.

My divorce from #2 was finalized in September, which was right around the time things went south. #3 caught me getting high one day. She'd been watching me closely and knew something was up. She set a trap for me, and I fell right into it. Instead of losing her shit over it, curiosity got the better of her because she couldn't understand why I kept going back to the drugs time and time again. She felt that she *needed* to try it so she could have a better understanding of what was so appealing about it to me so that she could help me get clean.

And in a moment of weakness and vulnerability, I let her try heroin.

She was hooked instantly.

#3 already had an addictive personality. To make matters worse, alcoholics seem to easily fall into opiate abuse after they stop drinking. Something about both substances being depressants. Now, none of this actually matters. What does matter is that she started using heroin, and it was my fault.

Oh, how I can already hear your comments: Hypocrite. Beavis. Scumbag.

None of which I can argue with.

Even so, go fuck yourselves.

#3 and I quickly spiraled out of control. Within a *very* short period of time, we were using *hundreds* of bags, almost daily. #3 and I both lost our jobs, and she had her car repossessed. Our days/nights revolved around using.

Heroin had taken over our lives.

We were dealing with her family court issues, my court issues, our severe money issues (which involved rent as well as dope), and we had even discussed getting married.

We were completely out of control.

We just couldn't see it.

OK, perhaps *refused* to see it is a bit more accurate, but I'm not here to argue semantics.

And then....

I got arrested.

Twice.

The first time, I was given another appearance ticket.

After my arrest, #3 and I decided that we should get clean. Or at least that we should *try* to get clean. With that in mind, I was able to find us some Suboxone, and we gave it the "old college try."

It didn't turn out well.

There's a large group of people who will argue that being on MAT (Medically Assisted Treatment) doesn't mean that you're clean. I myself have argued that you're simply jerking off with the opposite hand. I've also begged for Suboxone while going through detox. So yeah, I tend to vacillate on the subject depending on my mood.

What I won't argue is that the shit works. If you're on Suboxone, you have zero desire or need to use. Even if you tried to get high, you'd fail due to the opiate blocker in it. If you're completely dope sick and take Suboxone, within a half hour you'll start to feel *much* better. Within an hour, the sickness is gone and you'll be feeling "normal" again. Which is really all you want.

There is, however, one little... issue.

Suboxone contains Buprenorphine and Naltrexone.

Naltrexone is also the active ingredient in Narcan.

What this means is that if you take Suboxone when you're dope sick, it's fucking magical. The flip side is that if you take Suboxone too soon, it's complete fucking hell. There's actually a medical term for it– precipitated withdrawal– but complete fucking hell is far more accurate.

This is a lesson I learned the very hard way.

One weekend, #3 and I decided that we were going to get clean. We had a lot of Suboxone between us, and figured that since we got high together, then we could get clean together. All we had to do was tough it out for a day or so.

Fuck!

Okay, I'm lying. We were broke as fuck and didn't have a choice. We were going through fifty to eighty bags of heroin a day, and our income source had run dry. I'd love to tell you what that was exactly, but I can't. There's this wonderful thing called the *statute of limitations*, and as of this writing, it has yet to expire. Sorry.

We were about twenty-four hours into our detox when #3 started feeling ill. Even though I wasn't feeling too bad at all, for some reason I got it in my fucking head that enough time had passed and that I would be okay to take a strip.

Boy was I fucking wrong.

While pharmaceutical companies recommend that you wait at least a *minimum* of twenty-four hours between your last use and your first dose of Suboxone, the general rule of thumb is that you wait until you start feeling *really* shitty before you take it. Twenty-four hours is a fairly safe bet, but how you're feeling is the best determination. The shitty feeling is your body's way of saying, *"Hey asshole, it's time for some more dope, or things are going to get bad around here."*

Naloxone violently rips all the opiates from the opiate receptors in your brain in an extremely painful way, and the Buprenorphine puts up a "shield" to protect the receptors from any more opiates attaching to them. But I've already explained this to you.

What I'm trying to say here is that taking Suboxone too early fucking sucks. It's not quite as bad as getting hit with Narcan, but it's still pretty fucking bad.

Twenty minutes after taking the Suboxone, I knew that I was in *big* trouble.

The sweating.

The shivering.

The irritability.

The runny nose.

The restless legs.

And of course, the shit.

Shit isn't being used here as a blanket term for everything that ensued. I mean shit in the literal sense.

Liquefied. Fucking. Bowels.

It was not pretty.

I couldn't even get out of bed without shitting myself. It was bad. I had to throw out almost every pair of boxers I had the following day.

The precipitated withdrawal lasted for *hours.*

And there was nothing I could do but ride it the fuck out. What made things worse was that #3 was already sick as fuck and could have taken a Suboxone with no problem. Seeing my reaction scared the shit out of her, so she went on being sick. This made me feel even worse than I already did, which I didn't think was possible.

Instead of doing the "smart" thing and going through the entire detox (we were already two days into it), the *moment* I realized that my bowels were completely evacuated of all possible excrement, I grabbed twenty Suboxone, ran out of the house, and traded them for some dope.

Yes, people will accept Suboxone as payment for dope. Ironic, isn't it? I know a dude who sells both dope and Suboxone, and according to him, people ask for Suboxone almost as often as they ask for dope, if not more.

On this day I learned a very painful and important lesson.

Taking Suboxone too soon is a *very bad fucking idea.*

We didn't try to get clean together again.

The second time I was arrested– on my fucking birthday, no less– I left home to pull a scam to get some dope, and got caught while pulling said scam. I was immediately arrested, and this time I was *not* let go.

* * *

Now THIS PART doesn't have much relevance to the story at hand, but it's my fucking story and I'll write what I want, where I want.

I've already been sent to prison over this fucking thing, so why not, right?

Anyways, this is perhaps one of my most favorite Ginger moments.

We were at family court one day dealing with more of Ginger's bullshit. #3 and I were standing in the hallway waiting for court to start, minding our business. We knew that Ginger was planning on using the entire hearing to bitch about me and my history and how horrible of a human being I am, and why #3 shouldn't be allowed to have their son. Mind you, this was before my relapses and turning #3 into a junkie.

None of what Ginger was going to bring up had anything to do with why they were actually there that particular day. He had filed his motion *months* before #3 and I had even started talking again. His hard-on for me was him just trying to drag me through the mud, while making himself look like father of the year.

That pissed me off.

Well, misery loves company, does it not?

As we were standing there paying absolutely no fucking mind to them, Ginger, Ginger Cunt, Ginger's mother and their lawyer all came strolling down the hallway as if they owned the fucking place. Ginger, being Ginger, was staring at us in an attempt to be intimidating. Apparently, he believes that because he is tall, bald, and has a beard and tattoos, people are supposed to be intimidated by him or something.

I guess that works for him.

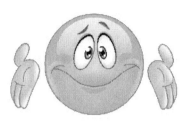

Well, since his awesome man powers don't have an effect on me, I decided to intimidate him myself by blowing him a kiss.

What can I say, maturity is my middle name.

And that's when this big, rough, tough, tattooed, bearded bitch, broke down and *literally* cried to his mom.

Ginger: "Mom!!" (*insert foot-pounding temper tantrum here*) "-He just blew a kiss at me!"

I shit you not. This actually happened. I cannot make this stuff up.

It was like seeing Mike Tyson, the hulk of an iron monster that he was back in the day, then hearing him speak for the first time.

You couldn't help but fucking laugh.

Only, I wasn't the only one who laughed.

The entire *hallway* had heard him, and was laughing at him.

Family court folk. My kind of people.

The whole thing became even funnier when Ginger's face (which was covered in a ginger beard) became as red as a ripe fucking tomato.

People were laughing so hard that they were having trouble breathing.

A grown man throwing an infant-like tantrum in the middle of a court hallway.

I couldn't have planned it better had I tried.

Lawn Mower, impromptu genius.

Oh, and to add insult to injury, I just happened to know that Ginger had a warrant out for his arrest for some stupid shit. As the law-abiding citizen that I am, I duly informed the uniformed officers in the building that Ginger was a wanted man, and was in fact currently present in their building.

Hey, I was just doing my part as a concerned citizen.

Like I said, that didn't have much relevance to the story. I just wanted to add another *fuck you* into the story for Ginger.

* * *

GETTING ARRESTED on your birthday is a whole different type of suck. Every time you speak to someone new during the jail intake process, you have to provide them with your info (name, rank, serial number, etc.) and when they realize that it's your birthday, and you've been arrested, they make some obvious comment about it being a shitty way to spend your birthday. Or something to that extent.

Well, no shit, Sherlock.

They've definitely mastered the obvious.

I bet that their uncanny deduction abilities are equally impressive on Thanksgiving, Christmas, and New Year's.

Once the intake process was finished, I was escorted to my cell, which I was not looking forward to. Not because I was in jail, but because I was acutely aware that a severe and painful detox was heading my way. I was also worried about #3.

Prior to being arrested, I had spent the previous weeks ensuring that #3 and I didn't get dope sick. Without me around, #3 had pretty much no idea how to fend for herself in that arena. I knew what was coming next and what to expect. She, on the other hand, did not. And I was apoplectic with anxiety as to how she was going to react.

There was a little dope still at the house which I knew should last her a couple of days. After that though..... and that's what worried me the most. I didn't know the lengths to which she might go in order to not be sick.

Translation: I was worried about her whoring herself out to some dope boy in the hood.

Did I have bigger fish to fry than worrying about my girlfriend sucking dick for heroin?

Yes.

A new felony charge, especially with all the other bullshit over my head was *not* a good thing. Yet I was more concerned for #3 than I was for myself.

I don't know if that was selfless or retarded. I'll let you decide.

* * *

THE FOLLOWING MORNING, #3 came to see me in jail. She was rather chipper/spritely, while I wasn't feeling too well at all. She filled me in on all the details of what she'd been up to. She was able to get my car before it went to impound, she had contacted my doctor to let her know that I was in jail, and my doctor was working on getting me a Suboxone script sent over to the jail. #3 was also going to have a long chat with her sister and "come clean" about what we had been up to. Even though I wasn't very thrilled about that, I could see the logic in it.

Nooner (Anathema's boyfriend/baby daddy) sold dope. #3 was hoping that he would be able to "help her out" so she wouldn't get sick. There was also talk about Anathema and Nooner possibly coming to stay with her for a while so she wouldn't be alone.

I knew this to be total bullshit. She just wanted Nooner around so she could get dope, but I didn't voice that opinion.

THEN SHE SURPRISED me with something I didn't expect. She said that we were getting married.

Really Lawn Mower?

Yes, really.

So fuck off.

#3 told me that she was one hundred percent standing by me during this, and that I wasn't going to be alone in prison. She was going to be my wife before my sentencing, and we would make it through this no matter what.

Who was I to argue with a woman with a plan?

* * *

I HAD to spend my first few days in "detox," which meant that I was locked in a cell twenty-four hours a day to wallow in my pain and misery. It was really awesome. My detox only lasted three days because between my doctor, The Sister, and #3, they were able to get my Suboxone script sent to the jail and administered to me. Which the staff was *not* happy about.

I was given a twenty-eight-day script and told by staff that once that ran out they would be tapering me down so that I wouldn't be on any meds when I went to prison. This meant no full detox for me. Thank you, sweet baby Jesus!

Once I was out of detox I was sent to population, where I could walk around, watch TV, use the phones, etc. I immediately called #3, and she told me that not only did we have a court date in less than thirty days to be married, but her talk with Anathema went "really well." I knew this last part to be complete bullshit. #3 had this horrible tendency to seriously sugarcoat shit when she didn't need to.

It doesn't take a genius to figure out that if an immediate family member comes to you and says, "Oh, by the way, even though I've stopped drinking, I just wanted to let you know that my boyfriend (who's currently sitting in jail) let me try heroin and we started using together. I'm completely hooked on it, and I can't go to rehab because my baby daddy will use that to destroy me in court and take my child away from me. I have no job, no money, no means to provide for myself, and I was hoping that you and your drug-dealing boyfriend could help me out."

Even though I knew that this had to have taken Anathema's hatred for me to an entirely new dimension, I would have *loved* to have been a fly on the wall for that conversation.

* * *

I BELIEVE that I've mentioned a time or two about the power of hindsight. Having that bird's-eye view of the past helps one gain insight and perspective. That's how I know that the two months I spent in jail were life-changing for me. New truths were discovered. New perspectives were gained. Something new began.

This isn't because I was on a program unit in population. Fuck no. Ninety-nine percent of incarceration programs are useless. They look great on paper, yet fall breathtakingly short of producing the final product. This isn't a biased opinion either. It's a simple fact. Just look at the recidivism rates of the New York State prison system and you'll see the truth in my words.

The first couple of weeks in jail went by fine. #3 was coming to see me, I wasn't dope sick, and #3 told me that she was tapering off the dope and going to see a Suboxone doctor. She was going to start taking Suboxone right after we got married. She planned it this way so that neither of us would be "sick" for our wedding day.

It was a great plan. In theory.

Three days before the wedding, I found out that the medical staff had lied to me. They would *not* be tapering me off of my Suboxone. Once the last dose was gone, that's all she wrote, so prepare yourself for a shitstorm because you're about to enter Sucksville. After hearing this, I immediately filed a grievance against the medical staff.

This did not make them happy.

The day before I was to be married, I went to the nurse's station to get my *final* dose of Suboxone. I usually took it at about one in the afternoon, which was fine because I was going to be married around nine the following morning. I usually don't start feeling sick from Suboxone withdrawal until at least twenty-four hours have passed, so I would be well within the "safe zone" for my wedding.

When I approached the nurse, I was informed that she had "left my medication upstairs" and that she would bring it down to me shortly.

Three hours later when she returned to my unit and I saw her face, I *knew* something was wrong.

Nurse: "I don't have your meds."

I could only stare at her.

Nurse: "Did you hear me?"

Me: "Who, me?"

Nurse: "Yes, you."

Me: "I heard you, I just figured that you were speaking to the guy behind me or something."

Nurse: "There's no one behind you."

I turned around and looked for good measure.

Me: "So I see."

A pause.

Then....

Me: "So, you've gotta go back upstairs to get it or something, right?"

Nurse: "No."

Me: "Pardon?"

Nurse: "I can't go back upstairs to get it."

Me: "Right now you mean."

Nurse: "At all, I mean."

Me: "Clearly, I'm missing something here. My last dose is supposed to be today."

Nurse: "Yes, I know. But I can't give it to you."

Me: "And why the fuck not?"

Nurse: "Because we can't find it."

Me: "I'm sorry, can you say that again please. Perhaps with smaller words?"

Nurse: "We lost your medication."

Me: "You *lost* my Suboxone?'

Nurse: "Yes."

Me: "Let me make sure I'm understanding this here. You– not the personal *you*, but the collective *you*– a group of licensed medical professionals, have *lost* a strip of Suboxone. A Schedule III narcotic. Inside of a maximum-security correctional holding facility. A place where the medication is probably more secure and counted than we..." (*pointing at the other inmates around me*) "...are. Is that what you're telling me?"

Nurse: "Yes."

Me: "Well then, how about a suggestion? Since I'm not the only one in this jail taking Suboxone, why don't you go upstairs and just grab one from storage or wherever they're stored and give me one of those?"

Nurse: "It's not that simple."

Me: "It's not that simple? Inside that cart you have hundreds of different medication pill packs for hundreds of different inmates, and if you need a pill for one inmate, you could take it from the pack designated for another inmate. I see you do it all the time. So, what's the problem here?"

Nurse: "Yeah, but those aren't controlled substances."

Me: "Oh. So, you can't rob Peter to pay Paul when dealing with controlled substances, but you can simply *lose* them instead?"

She declined to answer this question.

Me: "So now what?"

Nurse: "I don't know, but I have to go."

Me: "You do know that I'm getting married tomorrow morning, and if I don't get my Suboxone, I'm going to be a fucking *wreck* in the morning, right?"

This is the point when she broke eye contact with me and looked a bit sheepish.

Nurse: "No. I didn't know you were getting married tomorrow. I'm sorry."

And that's when it hit me.

They didn't "lose" my Suboxone.

This was retaliation for filing that grievance against them.

This was their way of saying, "you shouldn't have fucked with us, asshole."

These fine, licensed medical *professionals* were purposefully withholding my medication because they knew that I was getting married, and they knew exactly what was going to happen to me without it. They fucking *wanted* me to be sick as fuck at my wedding.

Kids, we have just discovered a new level of discrimination. An addict in jail seeking medical attention. And here I thought that the emergency room staff was bad.

Me: "I need to speak to your supervisor. Immediately."

Nurse: "Sure."

Yeah, that didn't happen.

What *did* happen was about fifteen minutes later I was told to pack my shit because I was being moved to a different location.

Lawn Mower

Where was I being moved to?

I was brought downstairs and thrown into a cell on the detox floor.

It was a very long night.

Detoxing from heroin is bad.

Detoxing from Suboxone (in my opinion) is far, far worse.

My dosage of Suboxone was helping me get over a fifty to eighty bag daily habit of heroin. Going cold turkey from Suboxone– which is *far* from recommended by doctors– opened up the floodgates for a painful and severe detox.

IT WAS ABSOLUTE HELL.

At some point during the night, the nurse came to check on me and gave me some detox meds (mostly Imodium and Tylenol). When she came to my cell, I was curled up in the fetal position, on the cold floor next to my toilet. I was covered in vomit, snot pouring out of my nose, sweating, yet shivering, I was in incredible pain, and yes, I had shit myself.

Calling me a hot fucking mess would be generous.

The nurse asked me if I wanted any detox meds, and I told her yes. She told me that I needed to get up off the floor to get them. I told her that I couldn't. She told me that if I didn't get off the floor then I wouldn't get any meds. I attempted to get up, and failed. The nurse slammed the cell door and moved on, leaving me to suffer.

I'm pretty sure her last name was Ratched.

* * *

As the minutes passed– each passing moment feeling like its own eternity– and as my descent into hell continued, I knew that there was no way that I'd be able to get up and make it to court for my wedding in the morning.

So desperate, alone, in pain, and beyond sick, I did the only thing I could think of.

I prayed.

Cliché, I know.

Now I know what y'all are thinking *oh here we fucking go.*

No, I'm not going all God Squad on everyone.

I'm what I'd call a spiritual person. Do I believe in God?

Sure. Just not the capital G one.

I believe in gods (plural and lower case).

I don't believe that *any* religion has it correct, so I take aspects from each that I like, and leave all the other bullshit behind.

See, where some call their God Christ, I call mine The Old Guy, or Old Fucker, Pain In My Ass, etc. I just can't get with the Christ thing. Sorry there Jesus, you were a swell guy I'm sure, but all that virgin-born, son of God, water into wine stuff, I don't buy into it. And while I don't pray to you for forgiveness– or whatever it is Christians pray for– I do like your basic philosophy of "don't be a dick" (obviously I'm paraphrasing here), even though I have tremendous trouble following it. So, you should feel special, Jesus. I like your style, guy. Just can't get behind all the bullshit surrounding your story.

Christians who just read that:

Hey, you fuckers were warned.

Anyways, so yeah, I prayed.

Not one of those 'please get me out of this' type prayers, just a simple 'please don't let me shit my pants at my wedding' type prayer.

And then something happened. About an hour before I was supposed to head out, I started to feel better. Not great, mind you, just *better*. I felt good enough to get up off the floor and get myself cleaned up. Which I was grateful for.

I don't give a fuck what you call it— placebo, coincidence, divine intervention, etc.– but whatever came over me lasted long enough for me to get to and through my wedding without looking/feeling like a hobo's asshole after being anally raped to death. Which by all rights, forty-five hours into a Suboxone detox, I should have.

It wasn't until about twenty minutes after returning to my cell that I started feeling shitty again. The next couple of days were an absolute shitshow, which is a story for another time. Just know that if I could have put a bullet through my skull during those couple of days, I would have, gladly.

After I was done with detox, I was moved back to population. Once I was back in population, I was able to use the phone again, which was good. My main focuses were getting #3 off the dope, and getting out of jail.

Lawn Mower, wait. Out of jail? What about going to prison?

Oh, I was definitely going to prison, but this was just when the New York State bail reform act was going into effect, and guess who was an eligible candidate?

As long as everything went to plan, I would be able to get out of jail for about a week before I was due to be sentenced. I had a lot of shit I had to take care of before I went to prison, so the timing couldn't have been better. Thanks, Cuomo!

The first time I was able to speak to #3, she told me that she was off the dope and using Suboxone, which made me very happy to hear. I knew that she was very hesitant/worried about taking Suboxone, (especially after what she saw me go through when I took it too early), but she knew it was either that, or stay on the dope. With #3 on Suboxone, it was one less thing to have to worry about, and to be completely honest, it gave me a sense of relief. I've never regretted anything more in my life than allowing her to walk down the path of heroin use. Yes, she made her own decision to use, but I allowed it to happen. I could have easily said no. I could have been more assertive, and had I been, there's a high probability that she *never* would have tried it.

Also, in my heart of hearts, I knew the real reason why I didn't stop her. I didn't want to stop using, and I wanted a using buddy so I didn't have to hide what I was doing. A completely disgusting and selfish act, I see that now. But back then, I didn't.

Because of that decision, #3 ended up not only getting hooked on heroin, but she also lost her job and her car, and got severely behind on the rent and bills. She had missed multiple appointments for family court, and she'd also been very late both picking up and dropping off her kid to Ginger, which caused countless issues.

Like I said, no matter what *her* decision was, I still felt responsible for everything that transpired and blamed myself.

* * *

ONE MORNING IN EARLY JANUARY, I was called to court. I didn't have any upcoming court dates for over a week, so I knew that something good was about to happen. And happen it did. The bail reform act was in full effect, and I was released from jail! I couldn't have been happier. Even though I was still being sentenced to prison in less than a week, I would be able to go home and prepare– something I'd never been afforded the opportunity to do before.

I was finally released from jail around seven at night. I hopped on the last bus I could, and worked my way home. I could hardly contain my excitement during the ride. I had so much nervous energy it wasn't even funny. Being released from jail, getting to see #3, being able to sleep in my own bed and not on a steel cot. You know, the little things.

As I was walking up to our apartment door, I kept on thinking about how things were finally starting to work out in my favor for once. Yes, I was still going to prison. Yes, I still had a lot of time to do, but I was with someone who supported me one hundred percent, and even married me while I was in jail to prove this point. She had also gotten herself off the dope and was on Suboxone, which was no small feat.

I was still guilt-ridden about all that had happened, and I wasn't sure what I could do to make up for that. I knew that I had a price to pay for my actions, I just didn't know what the price was, but I soon found out. Guilt doesn't absolve us from our sins. Life generally demands a greater price to be paid for our actions. Most people call this Karma, and sometimes, Karma can be a bitch.

#3 had no idea that I was getting out of jail, and the look on her face when she answered the door spoke volumes. Fear, worry, and anxiety were written all over her face, and for the life of me I couldn't understand why.

Then I entered the apartment.

It was a fucking mess.

She was a mess.

Anathema and Nooner had a mattress laid out in the living room, which meant that they were staying there.

And there were bags of dope everywhere.

#3 was still using.

She had lied to me.

As I walked through the apartment, I noticed some things. Or, more pointedly, a lack of things. Mainly my stuff. My TV, my computers, my PS4, my tools. Everything was gone. Before she even spoke, I knew what had happened. She had sold all of my stuff for dope.

I was devastated.

I was furious,

I couldn't fucking believe it.

I immediately walked out the door to get some fresh air, and #3 followed me. At first, she thought that I had escaped and was pleading with me to turn myself in before I got into any more trouble. I could only laugh at her ridiculousness. She didn't find this funny.

While I was pacing the parking lot, I noticed something else. Or, once again, a lack of something else. My car. The bitch had sold my fucking car!

I couldn't believe it. I had trusted her, and she had been lying to me. She never came to see me while I was in jail because I would have immediately known she'd still been using. She had pawned all of my shit, and bought dope with it. She put the dope before me.

And that's when I saw it.

The reflection of myself.

I finally saw what other people have been seeing in me all these years. Every time I did something wrong, or got into trouble, or stole, or lied, or anything else that had to do with my drug use. I saw it.

It crippled me.

It broke me to my core.

It destroyed me.

It shattered everything I believed in.

What I saw in #3 was the junkie. The thief, the liar, the manipulator. The Addict.

I saw it all.

And I fucking *hated* what I saw.

I felt the pain that my family has felt. The sorrow. The sympathy. The anger. I felt it all. It was as if a Pandora's box of emotions had exploded within me. It was paralyzing.

This singular, unexpected moment changed my life forever. This was *the* moment. I was done with heroin and drugs. Ironic, isn't it? My trip along the downward spiral of addiction had started because of #3, and now that trip was going in a different direction. All because of her as well.

Almost poetic, is it not?

THE FUCKED-UP thing about it was that I wasn't mad at #3. Was I upset? You better fucking believe it. All my shit was gone. Sadly, I also understood. I've been there. I know what it's like to be sick and desperate. Willing to do anything for some heroin. Shit, I was a few days away from being sent to prison for my actions due to said desperation.

After I got over the initial shock of everything– which I will admit, took me a minute– #3 and I sat down for a long chat. Anathema tried to muscle her way into the conversation, and I politely informed her that if she attempted to step foot into the room, then the following morning, I would inform each and every alphabet agency looking for her of her current whereabouts.

Petty?

Yes.

But fuck that cunt and the horse she rode in on.

A "chat" is a generous term for our conversation. It was more of a "this is how it's going to be" conversation. I told her that she was going to the appointment that she had set up with the Suboxone doctor, and I didn't care if I had to commit a new felony to do it, I was going to make sure that she had enough money for the appointment and the Suboxone. I told her that she would be on Suboxone before I left for sentencing, or I wasn't going. Simple as that.

She fought me on a few points but eventually gave in, because she knew that I was right and that she had to get off the dope.

Before we went to bed, I noticed that there were a few bags of dope and some syringes on the nightstand next to the bed, and I made sure that she slept on the opposite side of the bed, away from the dope. As I lay in bed that night, I couldn't help but laugh at the irony of the situation. During my first few nights in jail, I would have punched my grandmother in the face for some dope. Now, I would punch my grandmother in the face to keep myself *away* from the dope.

Funny how that shit works.

The next morning, I went for a walk to clear my head. A lot needed to be done in a short amount of time, and I had no idea how I was going to pull it off. First, I needed money. Money so I could get #3 to her appointment, and then her script filled. I also needed money so I could go to prison with something and not starve to death.

While I was in county jail, I had nothing, and it sucked. I would eat the leftover slop off of the meal trays about to be thrown in the trash because I had nothing, and a jail meal wouldn't satisfy a five-year-old child. It was both embarrassing and humbling. I hated myself more and more each day. It was horrible.

I knew that if she didn't get help, that it was only a matter of time before #3 went down a bad road and wound up in jail. I wasn't sure about the lengths she was willing to go to in order to get high, but if selling my stuff was any indication, then I had a pretty good idea. I had created a monster, and this was one problem that I had to fix. Even if I had to commit a new felony to get enough money so #3 could have a fighting chance before I left for prison, I would. That's how serious I was about this.

While I was walking around the neighborhood, I decided to grab a coffee and take a seat at the bus stop. I just wanted to sit and think. The area we lived in was pretty populated, and people were coming and going from the bus stop all the time. But at this hour of the morning, it was empty. Sitting on the bench and thinking my thoughts, I was actually planning a new crime in my head. Not to *get* dope, but to get someone *off* dope (again, irony). I was willing to go that far if I had to, and I didn't really see that many options ahead of me.

Until I looked down.

On the ground, between my feet, was a gold chain.

I don't know how I missed it when I walked up to the bench and sat down, but there it was. Clear as day. And it was real. Twenty-four karat gold!

I saw the necklace for what it was. A gift. A sign from the gods that I wasn't supposed to go out and commit a new crime. So I picked up that gift, put it in my pocket, and walked home with a smile on my face.

Later on that day I went to the pawn shop and got five hundred dollars for that fucking chain! Whoever lost it must have been *pissed*.

Sorry for your luck.

The money I got from the chain allowed me to take care of everything I needed to and more. I was able to get #3 to her appointment, get her script filled, leave her with money, and I still had some left over to take to prison. Definitely chalked that up to a win in my book.

* * *

My last night of freedom was difficult. I don't know what is a more surreal feeling: being in prison and knowing that you're going home the next day, or being home and knowing that you're going to prison the next day. They both carry their own flavor of stress and anxiety, that's for certain.

Even though leaving that morning was difficult, I did it with a sense of safety and security. I had prepared the best I could. #3 wasn't using dope, and she had enough Suboxone to last her until her next appointment. Her insurance would be active by then, so that was one less thing to worry about. I had some money to fall back on while I got settled in prison, and I wasn't going into the situation alone like I had before. I had someone on my team that supported me and understood me better than most.

I walked out the door with a definite strength, which I needed. I knew that what lay ahead of me would be difficult. Had I known exactly *how* difficult it was going to be, there's no fucking way I would have gone willingly.

#3 DIDN'T GO to my sentencing, but I wasn't alone. Jiminy picked me up and we had breakfast together, plus, The Sister was in the courtroom with me for moral support. I half expected to see El Jefé there, but he must have been busy getting a prostate exam. However, he did send a "company representative."

When I saw my old co-worker, I smiled and gave her a friendly head nod to say: "Hey, I know I fucked up and spat in the face of a really good guy and caused a bunch of headaches, and while we could have handled this out of court and not pursued the charges I'm being sent to prison for, there's no hard feelings."

The ex-co-worker looked at me with complete contempt, as if I was a piece of shit she had just stepped in.

Bitch.

So, I decided to be the bigger person in the situation.

And by being the bigger person I mean that I made direct eye contact with her, stuck my tongue out, and flipped her the bird.

How I've mastered the art of maturity astonishes even me.

Sitting in the courtroom and waiting for your name to be called is like looking down the barrel of a loaded shotgun. You know nothing good is about to happen, and you do a mental check to make sure you're wearing clean underwear.

The only one who seemed to be chipper that day was L****. Personally, I believe that he masturbates over his case files at night while snorting cocaine (picture Ron Jeremy in the Sin Bin scene in *The Boondock Saints* and you'll have a proper mental image). Especially over the cases, such as mine, where he really fucks someone over. If I'm correct in my hypothesis, then the night before he rubbed a good one out. Which would explain his extremely chipper mood.

My sentencing went fine, until the end, when I was given a chance to speak. I made an honest and heartfelt speech about taking responsibility for all I've done and my remorse for my actions, and all that crap. I don't mean that what I was saying was crap, I was being fully honest and open. I just mean that it fell on deaf ears. Neither the court nor L**** gave a flying fuck about how bad I felt, or about my substance abuse history.

During my speech, I even requested the Shock incarceration program (I'll explain later), which L**** *vehemently* opposed. I mean, why would you want to send a drug addict to a strict and disciplined drug treatment program? That would only make sense. When it was his turn to speak, L**** flipped out his well-thumbed copy of my "manifesto" and then proceeded to tell the judge how I was *manipulating the system* by *claiming* that I was a drug addict. He then went on to quote my "gargling a judge's balls" quote several times, to emphasize that I would do/say anything to get a lesser sentence.

It was during L****'s rant that I realized once again, God wasted a perfectly good asshole by putting teeth in someone's mouth.

I mean, seriously. He'd already won. Why add insult to injury? The big bad felon was going to prison for three to six years. He had already taken away my chance at drug court. Now he was making it clear to the court that "the people" opposed any sort of treatment programs for me while I was in prison. Again, why would you want to send a drug addict to a treatment program that might actually do some good? Plus, the fucking prick sent a copy of something that I wished to be anonymous to pretty much everyone in two counties.

Why twist the knife any deeper?

Clearly it's because he's a self-serving, goat-fucking, cock-gobbling, shit-eating, cum-licking, narcissistic piece of shit who breastfed until he was thirty-two. Isn't that right, L****?

Then– just to spite me, I believe– I had to wait for the next guy to get sentenced before I could be brought to jail. This fucking guy, who also had L**** as his ADA, pled guilty to vehicular manslaughter (most likely while under the influence) and received *ten weekends in jail* for his crime.

Ten fucking weekends.

Twenty fucking days in jail.

For ***killing*** someone.

Somebody lost their life due to this dude's negligence, and he only had to spend a few *weekends* in jail.

Meanwhile, me, someone who suffers from a deadly and debilitating disease, someone who the world recognizes as having a diagnosed mental disease and disability, borrowed (I say borrowed because I have to pay it back) some money without permission, and I get sentenced to three to six fucking *years* in prison.

On what fucking planet does that make sense?

Obviously, it's on the planet where the guy gargled L****'s balls, or maybe sold him some coke, in order to get a better deal.

And that pretty much sums up the New York State judicial system. It's not who you know, it's who you blow.

Right L****?

Y'all question why I hate this man.

As a small consolation prize, shortly after I was sentenced, L**** ran into my stepdad and told him how it was nothing personal– sending me to prison– and how he was just doing his job, blah blah blah. He said he wishes me the best of luck (bullshit). He also promised my stepdad that out of respect for him, he wouldn't go out of his way to keep me in prison. Whatever *that* fucking meant.

* * *

I had a few days to sit and think before my sentencing in Balls County. My main focal point wasn't in what lay ahead of me, but about this book, *Epic Fail*. I was at a point where I didn't know what to do with my life, and even if I did, I didn't know when I would be able to do it. Three to six years is a long time, and shit changes. And as Jiminy has reminded me *countless* times, my mouth always seems to get me into trouble.

Perhaps it was time for me to try something different? I knew that I was built this way for a reason, but maybe that reason wasn't for writing? I'd already taken a few serious hits because of things I'd said or put on paper; maybe it was time to start learning from those things.

Maybe it was time to let this foolish idea go?

Thinking hurts my head sometimes, and I'm also a horrible decision-maker. Usually, it's because I make the *wrong* decision. I think I've established this fact by now. I knew I needed some guidance, and since it had worked for me before, I decided to try it again. I prayed a simple prayer and asked for some advice. But not subtle advice, I don't get subtle.

A few days later I went to court for sentencing, an event I've grown accustomed to during the course of my criminal career. It's always the same shit. Legal stuff. A few words. A chance for me to speak. A final statement of things. A chance for the ADA to speak again if they wish, then the judge brings down his/her wrath.

I gave another honest and heartfelt speech taking responsibility for my actions, and expressing remorse for them (again). Standard shit.

Then the Judge asked the ADA if he had anything to add before he commenced sentencing.

ADA: "As a matter of fact, I *do* Your Honor."

Great....

Then he took out a file, opened it, and pulled out a copy of my "manifesto."

Motherfucker.

I turned to my lawyer.

Me: "Are you fucking kidding me?"

Lawyer: "Shhh."

Me: "Did you just shush me? This has *nothing* to do with this case."

Lawyer: "I know. Listen and shut up."

Listen and shut up?

I was about to cuss out my lawyer in a manner that would make a sailor blush until I heard the ADA speak.

ADA: "Your Honor, I have here a copy of a novella written by the defendant..."

Novella?

"...and I would like to state for the record that I completely disagree with its assessment by ADA L****. I've had an opportunity to read it in its entirety, and while a bit raunchy, I think that it's obvious that the defendant is a quite talented, articulate, and gifted writer. I understand what the defendant is trying to accomplish by writing this, and I hope that he continues to pursue his quest. I believe that Lawn Mower has the ability to reach and help many people through his writing, and I would like nothing more than for him to finish his sentence, put this behind him, and move forward with his novella."

Judge: "I couldn't agree more. This isn't the first time you've been in front of me, Lawn Mower, nor is it the first time that I've been impressed with something that you've written. You're extremely smart and very articulate. I hope that you can put this behind you. Because if you can, you have a very bright future ahead of you."

What in the actual fuck, right?

I didn't know what to say. I was waiting for Ashton Kutcher to pop out with the *Punk'd* crew or something. I don't know what I was expecting that day, but it *definitely* wasn't that.

As I was being escorted back to my cell after sentencing, I couldn't help but smile.

I might not understand subtle.

But I understood *that*.

Ask, and ye shall be touched.

Or something to that effect.

* * *

A FEW DAYS LATER, I was sent to prison.

I arrived at Elmira Correctional Facility on January 13th. Which was, interestingly enough, six years to the fucking day from when I was brought there the first time.

Weird, right?

Since I'd already been dealt this particular brand of bullshit, I knew what to expect walking in. The sights, the smells, the screaming, the yelling, the balls of fire, the pounding on the bars, the catcalls, all of it.

It's much less overwhelming the second time around, I promise you.

Or maybe I'm simply desensitized to all of it.

I went through the intake process, was able to make my intake phone call (to let my family know where I was) and brought to my cell relatively quickly.

After that, the fun began.

* * *

PRISON IS DIFFICULT.

Mainly because of the people.

Convicts and inmates are cunts. And yes, there's a *big* difference between the two.

In reception, you're only afforded an opportunity to use a phone three times a week. This is on the days when you go to the gym for rec. During this time, you have to decide whether you want to use the phone, shower, or shave, because... well, it's prison, and politics come into play.

In the gym there are sixteen phones on the wall. Which seems like a lot. But when fifty to eighty dudes are trying to use those sixteen phones, problems arise. Even with the COs "keeping order," it's a shitshow. A bag of chips or a pack of smokes still goes a long way in prison.

It's very difficult to have any sort of conversation when you get about six minutes at a time to talk on the phone, maybe twice a week. A thirty-minute phone call could take a month to get through in reception. This put a serious strain on my relationship with #3. It also caused me an ungodly amount of stress. Some things were going on at home, and I was helpless to do anything about it.

Instead of the phone, I would write pages upon pages to #3, almost on a daily basis. I would beg her on the phone to just put her thoughts on paper so we could "talk" in the only way we could, but she never replied. She wasn't working or doing much with her time, so it was very frustrating for me.

The lack of communication started to take its toll.

Then COVID hit.

When that happened, they shut the entire prison down. Guys in reception were locked in their cells twenty-four hours a day. I didn't leave my cell for three months. It was the most painful experience of my life.

I would write *countless* letters home, to which I would get no reply. She was supposed to be standing by me through this (that's why she wanted to marry me, wasn't it?), and I was getting nothing from her. Not even a fucking postcard.

What made matters worse, was that DOCCS approved me to go to Shock.

The Shock Incarceration program is a six-month discipline and treatment-oriented activity. Eligible incarcerated individuals, both men and women, are provided the opportunity to develop life skills which have proven to be important for success in society. The program includes rigorous physical activity, work, intensive regimentation and discipline, instruction in military bearing, courtesy, drills, physical exercise, network community living skills, a structured work program, intensified substance abuse and alcohol counseling, and structured educational programming to the high school equivalency level. Quote, New York State Department of Corrections and Community Supervision.

Note the six-month part.

Once you complete the program, you can go home. Now, instead of having to do three years, all I had to do was complete a six-month program.

Getting there was the problem.

All prison movement was shut down. No one was being transferred anywhere. And no one had any idea how long we would be sitting there for.

I went a bit mad.

Lawn Mower

Being locked in a cell twenty-four hours a day is tough. Add to that not having any contact with your "family," on top of starving, and shit gets real.

I walked into prison with some cash. Since I had restitution to pay, the prison took my money and applied it to what I owed. So instead of being able to get commissary, I got to sit in my cell and watch rapists, murderers, and Catholic priests stuff their fat faces, while I contemplated how a cockroach would taste with some toothpaste or ramen noodle seasoning on it.

It was a very humbling time for me.

And then there was #3 and the phone.

Once COVID struck and everything in the state got shut down, we were allotted specific times to use the phone. We were given a phone schedule a week in advance so that we could let our family know when we would be able to call. I gave #3 this schedule each and every week that I received it, and she *rarely* answered when I called.

If the roles were reversed and I knew that someone important to me would be calling at a certain time, and that time was the *only* time I'd be able to speak with them, I would be waiting with the fucking phone in hand. Furthermore, if said person had previously expressed how important that phone call was to them, then I'd make *double* sure that I didn't miss their call.

But that's just me.

#3 however, is quite different. She's a Gemini. Translation: she's extremely lackadaisical. Personally, I think Gemini is just a synonym for bipolar, but what do I know. When I finally *did* get a hold of her, she would say things like...

#3: "Oh, I forgot."

#3: "Sorry, I fell asleep."

#3: "I was watching a movie."

#3: "I was in the shower."

Shit like that.

Do you have any idea how shitty it feels to be in a prison, waiting for days for the chance to use a phone? Knowing that you'll only have a few precious minutes to talk when you get to make your call? Knowing that the person you're calling is absolutely aware of the day and time you will be calling... and then they don't answer? And when they do answer, they give you some ridiculously bullshit excuse as to why they didn't answer before?

It fucking sucks.

On the rare occasion that I was able to get through to her, she proceeded to inform me about how hard it was on the outside, and all the bad shit she had going on in her life, all of which I could do fuck all about. Then by the time she started telling me that she'd been "rethinking our relationship," my phone time would be up, and I'd be brought back to my cell to stare at the walls for a week before I could make another call.

This went on for months.

Not knowing if I'd have contact with her that week.

Not knowing if I did get in touch with her, if it would be good or bad.

And when it was bad, it was *really* bad.

The head games were the worst.

One call she'd tell me how she "can't do this anymore," and then the next (a week later) she would say things like "I know you'll be home in six months after you get to Shock, but I don't care if I have to wait six years for you, I'm not going anywhere."

We always seemed to be in a state of fluctuating chaos.

Most days, I didn't know if I was coming or going.

Then, Ginger started playing fuck-fuck games with their son: denying #3 her parenting time, claiming COVID concerns for one reason or another. #3 went months without seeing her son, and I felt responsible. Had she had her shit together, or had I been there, things might have been different.

Add this to the guilt I felt for leading her down the path of heroin addiction in the first place, and allowing my imagination to run wild, well... things started getting bad for me in that cell.

I had thought that seeing my reflection in #3 before I left for prison was painful.

I knew nothing of pain until I spent those months in that cell.

Being approved for a program that would get me home six months, but having no idea how long I was going to be locked in that cell before I could start it didn't help.

Begging for some sort of communication from #3 and receiving hardly any didn't help.

Starving in that cell while watching rapists stuff their fat fucking faces didn't help.

Having nothing to read didn't help.

Having no form of social interaction with anyone, short of screaming out of my cell door to the dude a few cells down didn't help.

And with the guilt and shame of my actions weighing down on me, my psyche broke.

I became a broken man in that cell. Deflated and defeated.

I saw no light at the end of the tunnel.

I saw no future for me.

I saw nothing.

I even tried to take the coward's way out, but quickly discovered that hanging yourself in a cell is *a lot* harder than it sounds, and that I was too much of a coward to do even that.

I was so broken, I didn't even have it in me to end my life.

So I endured the pain and let the floodgates of pain and emotion entomb me.

I started writing on my walls.

Poetry.

Song lyrics.

Ramblings.

I covered every square inch of the walls that I could reach.

It's all I could do to keep myself sane.

Then, finally, in late May, the day came when all the dudes approved for Shock were being shipped out on a special draft.

In the words of Ricky Bobby: *Thank you dead sweet baby Jesus!*

* * *

I COULD EASILY WRITE an entire book on how fucked-up Shock truly is (and probably will at some point later on in life), but for the sake of *this* book, I won't. You're just going to get the highlights. But keep in mind, *I'm merely scratching the surface here.*

And before I get started on my experience in the Shock program, you should probably go and YouTube the New York State Shock Incarceration Program so you can have a better understanding of what I'm going to discuss here.

* * *

IN 2020, there were two Shock facilities left in New York State. There used to be four, but ole Uncle Andy Cuomo decided to shut down two of them for some reason.

Since there were only two facilities left, you had a fifty-fifty chance of where you were going. Lakeview (Hell) or Moriah (Camp Cupcake). Under normal circumstances, everyone that goes to Shock goes to Lakeview first because Lakeview is Shock reception. Once you arrive there, the Shock gods apply some sort of magical Shock algorithm and figure out if you are going to go to Moriah, or stay at Lakeview.

No one wants to stay at Lakeview. There are countless stories floating around DOCCS about Lakeview. How they beat you, how they treat you, and the horrible shit that they do to you there. The worst part about it is that you don't know what's true. You hear the same stories over and over again, and you start to believe them.

2020 was anything but normal due to Covid, and when they packed up all the assholes going to Shock, it wasn't for one destination, but two! One bus for Lakeview, and the other for Moriah. When I got packed up with the Moriah group, I was beyond relieved. I took it as a sign of nothing but good things to come for me. Not so much for the assholes going to Lakeview.

It was a long ride from Elmira to Moriah, but it was nice. Moriah is up in the Adirondack Mountains, closer to Vermont than anything else actually, and the views as we drove were gorgeous. Plus, there wasn't a lot of tension during the ride. Usually you're crammed on a bus like sardines, with a bunch of miserable fucks who really don't want to be going wherever it is they're being taken to.

But not us.

We were the jolliest bunch of assholes this side of the Mississippi. We were out of our cells and on our way to start our six-month journey home.

When we arrived at Moriah, all that changed.

All the smiles and jokes stopped once the DIs (Drill Instructors) started screaming at us. Picture getting off the bus at a military boot camp, and you've got a general idea of what we experienced. Except we were convicts, and we weren't being trained on how to defend our country.

On my first day at Moriah, I learned some important lessons:

1. The first and last words out of my mouth for the next six months would be "sir."

2. You're not allowed to look at staff when speaking to them, *at all.* You have to look at some spot above their head or to the side of them while speaking to them. Do you have any idea how fucking hard it is not to look someone in the eye when you're speaking to them?

3. I would have to speak in the third person. I had to refer to myself as "this inmate"; I couldn't say: me, my, I, etc.

4. Split bids would be going to the board around month four.

Let me translate that last one for you, because when I first heard it, I had a hard time understanding what it meant as well.

All that bullshit I had heard about everyone who completes Shock gets to go home was just that, *bullshit*. If you were serving a "split bid" (as I was), then sometime during the fourth month of the program, your paperwork goes in front of the parole board commissioners and they decide if you get to go home or not once you complete the program. Meanwhile, the asshole next to you serving a "flat bid" was *guaranteed* to go home, as long as they completed the program.

We were *flat-out told* by staff that how we did in the program had *absolutely zero bearing* on the parole board's decision. You could be the best and brightest of your platoon, score all the highest marks, stand out above all the rest, and it would mean jack shit to the parole board. All they look at is your criminal history, and the information surrounding your current case. They ask for no recommendation from staff, as they do not care. It's a numbers game, plain and simple.

This was all explained to us on day one, which made me realize that not only is Shock a fucked-up place, but it didn't matter what happened in the program. It meant fuck-all to the people making decisions. So much for positive programming, right?

* * *

THE FIRST WEEK of Shock wasn't too difficult because we were quarantined due to Covid bullshit. My first day of *actual* Shock however, was difficult.

At 5:30 a.m., eight DIs came running into the squad bay blowing whistles, flipping beds, and banging on garbage cans, all while screaming at us. It was rather shocking, excuse the pun. Then we had fifteen minutes to get dressed, shave, use the toilet, brush our teeth and make our racks (military style) before we went out for PT (physical training).

PT was exhausting. For the few months prior to Shock, I was locked in a cell pretty much twenty-four hours a day, seven days a week due to Covid, so I was *severely* out of shape. During PT I was selected as a temporary squad leader (obviously because the DI realized how awesome I was), and after an hour and a half of calisthenics, running, and other insanity, I got to lead my platoon into the mess hall.

My first time in the mess hall was very overwhelming, and I took more food than I knew what to do with. In the mess hall, you can take all the food you want, but you have to finish *every bit of it* in eight minutes. If you don't, bad things happen, which I learned the hard way.

When the DI told us that our eight minutes were up, I still had a hearty portion of food on my plate. My platoon was excused and went to wait for me outside, while I had to find the nearest wall and do a wall sit while finishing my meal.

A wall sit is where you place your back flat against a wall, with your feet shoulder-width apart. Then you bend your knees until your thighs are parallel to the floor, as if you're sitting in a chair.

I had to stay in that position until I finished my food. By the time I was done my legs felt like Jell-O.

After I finished, I had to sprint outside to regroup with my platoon, my mouth still full of food like a fucking chipmunk.

And of course, my DI was there waiting for me.

DI T1000: "Lawn Mower! So nice of you to join us!"

Me: (*mumbling*) "Sir yes sir."

DI T1000: "Still eating I see."

Me: (*between bites*) "Sir yes sir."

DI T1000: "Whatcha have?"

Me: "Sir?"

DI T1000: "What. Did. You. Eat?"

Me: "Sir, this inmate had-"

DI T1000: "No, no, no. I don't want you to tell me what you had, I want to see what you had."

Me: "Sir... this inmate doesn't understand, sir."

DI T1000: "No? Well then, let me explain. And since you clearly have a problem with simple fucking instructions, I'm going to make myself crystal clear so you can understand."

Ut-oh.

DI T1000: "I want you to side-straddle-hop until you puke it all up."

Side-straddle-hop is Shockspeak for a jumping jack.

Me: "Sir yes sir."

DI T1000: "Begin."

Fuck my life...

435

And so, I did.

My platoon, as well as the other platoons stood there and watched while I side-straddle-hopped until I puked.

486 was the magical number.

At 486, it all came out. Just like Lardass in *Stand By Me*.

One would think that after I puked up my meal, the DI would be happy. But no, he wasn't. He was pissed at me for making a mess and made me clean it all up. By rolling around in it. He made me roll around in my own vomit until it was cleaned up off of the ground.

So let me recap the morning for you.

I was beyond exhausted and overwhelmed. I was covered in my own vomit. And I was ready to die of embarrassment. Oh, and I lost my squad leader position.

I felt that it was going to be a *very long* six months.

And it turns out I was right.

THE FIRST TWO weeks in Shock are known as "Zero Weeks." They're called Zero Weeks because during that time, you're nothing. You're at zero, and they (the staff) are weeding out the weak among the group.

Zero Weeks are designed to see if they can break you. And they definitely give it their all. The philosophy behind Shock is "we're going to break you down, so we can build you back up." Which is a bullshit way of allowing them to fuck with you in unimaginable ways. Since Shock isn't a mandatory program, and it's something that you sign up for, you're giving Shock staff the ability to do whatever the fuck they want to you. Plus, it's still prison. Let's not forget that part.

During Zero Weeks, you don't get to use the phone, at all. They allow zero contact with the outside world. Even during the normal part of the program, you only get to make one ten-minute phone call every other week. The idea being to focus on the program and what it's trying to teach you, rather than focusing on what's going on in the outside world.

From 5:30 a.m. to 9:30 p.m., you're on your feet and actively doing *something*. Whether it's polishing your boots, hemming/sewing your clothes, working, learning the Shock rules, philosophies, and standards, or PTing. There is very little downtime. In fact, some days the only time you're allowed to sit down is during the eight minutes you get for chow. And that's even questionable. There were plenty of meals where I had to stand facing the wall as I ate, for a violation of some stupid rule or another.

On the last day of Zero Weeks, you have to do this thing called the Knucklehead drill. For about four hours, you and your platoon are put through the ringer. You have to prove that you've learned all the exercises properly, and that you can do them. Then there are countless stretches, and a ridiculous amount of stupid shit that you have to have memorized, verbatim, or else you'll pay dearly.

One of the things that you must have memorized is the Shock Philosophy, which states: *"Shock is a positive environment for human development in a caring community where members can help themselves and each other. Staff and participants work together to establish and maintain positive, growth-filled environments within prison. Community members focus on behavioral change and confront attitudes which are destructive to members and the life of the program. A place to set goals and to practice behaviors which lead to successful living. A disciplined lifestyle bringing a process for examining attitudes and values for learning to deal with stress. A chance to change, to confront mistakes and accept responsibility for our lives."*

That's just one example of something they give you to memorize. And you are literally given less than twenty-four hours to have it memorized. During the Knucklehead drill, you could be in the middle of some excruciating exercise, where you're close to puking, and a DI will demand that you recite the philosophy. If you're unable to, well, things tend to get physical. Staff claims that if you can make it through the drill, then you can make it through Shock. Which I found to be utter bullshit. I've witnessed dudes get through the drill, and not last another week in the normal program. Once the actual program starts, you quickly realize that the physical stuff is the easiest part. It's all the extra mental stuff they do to you that makes the program beyond difficult.

ONCE THE KNUCKLEHEAD WAS COMPLETED, we were finally a platoon and could start the actual program the following day. The remainder of the day was spent resting up, and preparing for what lay ahead. We were also allowed to make a phone call. I called #3, and the conversation was good for about ninety seconds. Then it started going sideways.

Me: "So how is everything at home?"

#3: "Oh, not bad. Ginger's being a dick as usual, and Peter's been sick." (Peter's her son.)

Me: "Ugh, that sucks, I'm sorry."

#3: "Yeah, it's okay. My friend had to give us a ride the other day to Peter's doctor appointment."

Me: "That's cool. Was everything okay?"

#3: "Yeah. He was given an antibiotic, so we went to pick it up, then we picked up my friend's daughter and went to the lake for some ice cream and skipped some rocks while the sun was setting. It was really nice."

Me: "Uh-huh. Who's this friend exactly?"

#3: "Huh? Oh, it's just my friend Charlie."

Me: "Charlie. The dude you used to work with, the one who was always trying to take you out?"

#3: "Yeah..."

Me: "Let me make sure I heard this correctly. While I'm sitting in prison, getting mentally and physically abused in unimaginable ways, you're out doing date shit, that *we've* done, with Charlie. A dude who's been trying to get with you for years."

#3: "It's not like that."

Me: "Then what's it like?"

Silence.

Me: "Next thing you're going to tell me is that you're sleeping with this dude."

More silence.

Me: "You've got to be fuc-"

DI: "Time's up! Get off the phone!"

Me: "I gotta go. I love you."

#3: "Okay. Later."

Click.

Later...?

That's how my first call home went. What's really fucked-up about it was, as far as she knew, I was five-and-a-half months from coming home, and she's out doing God knows what with this dude.

Needless to say, I wasn't very impressed with #3. I was even less impressed with her when she didn't answer my call over the weekend.

Pretty awesome, right?

To add insult to injury, a few days later, I found out the hard way that the Shock staff absolutely listens to our phone calls. It was during one of our morning PT sessions when about halfway through, the DI (Henry) called me out in front of everyone.

DI Henry: "Lawn Mower! Report."

Fuck me...

Me: "Sir yes sir."

I fell out of formation and ran up to the front of the PT area where the DIs stood and everyone could see me.

DI Henry: "Lawn Mower, how's it going?"

Me: "Sir good sir."

DI Henry: "Excellent. And how is everything at home?"

This can't be good...

Me: "Sir fine sir."

DI Henry: "Outstanding! And how's Charlie?"

Me: "Sir Charlie sir?"

DI Henry: "You know, Charlie. The guy banging your wife."

Things got progressively worse after that.

DI Henry continued to humiliate me by making me lead the *entire facility* in an exercise where I had to call a cadence of "Please Charlie fuck my wife." And everyone responded by saying "Charlie, Charlie, fuck his wife."

This lasted for a full twenty minutes.

I'm sure you can imagine how awesome it was.

This is just one example of the shit they do to you in Shock.

* * *

WHEN I FIRST GOT TO Moriah, I did all my initial parole stuff with my ORC. She had all of my case paperwork and I had specifically asked her if there was any mention of a book, novella, manifesto or otherwise in any of it. She went through everything in front of me and said that she didn't see anything. Nor could I. Had anything been in the paperwork, I feel that I would have noticed it.

Fast forward a few weeks.

One night while I was taking the trash out, I ran into DI Henry and his gay lover. The moment I saw them I knew there was going to be an issue, but I was hoping that perhaps I'd be able to do what I needed to do, get past them and back without incident.

I was wrong.

As I was walking back to my unit, the prick stopped me.

DI Henry: "Lawn Mower! We were just talking about you."

Great.

I had already learned not to engage the prick as best as I could. I had also learned that "Sir yes sir" is usually the best answer to everything. So that's what I said.

Me: "Sir yes sir."

DI Henry: "Don't you wanna know what we were talking about?"

Me: "Sir no sir."

DI Henry: "Really? If people were talking about me, I'd wanna know what they were saying."

That's because you're an insecure little man and a closet homosexual.

Me: "Sir yes sir."

DI Henry: "Let me ask you a question...."

No, I will not have sex with you.

"...If I said you were in trouble with the law and most likely going to prison, what would you do?"

What the fuck...

Me: "Sir, this inmate doesn't understand, sir."

DI Henry: "No?"

Me: "Sir no sir."

DI Henry: "Let me rephrase it then..."

He paused and started tapping his finger on his lip as if he was thinking dees thoughts, like one plus one equals two, right?

DI Henry: "Aha! I've got it! If you were in trouble and about to go to prison, would you gladly gargle the judge's balls to try and get a better deal?"

Oh, dear God no.

He turned to his lover.

DI Henry: "It seems we've got ourselves our own Mark Twain here. Lawn Mower fancies himself a writer. Don't cha Lawn Mower?"

Fuck me...

Me: "Sir no sir."

DI Henry: "Huh. I must be confusing you with another inmate with that tattoo on your head who's been to prison in both New York and Florida. Strange. Okay then, you're dismissed. Get the fuck out of my face."

The implications of what that cum dumpster just said to me were immense. The fucker just quoted my book, which meant that A) it was at Moriah, or B) someone at Moriah had access to it. Neither option was very good.

The next day when I saw my ORC, I accused her of being a liar in the nicest way possible.

Me: "You lied to me."

Master of the art of subtlety, I am.

ORC: "Shit..."

Me: "Shit?"

ORC: "It's not that simple."

Me: "How is it 'not that simple'? I asked you if my book was mentioned anywhere in my paperwork and you told me that it wasn't. Now I've got DIs quoting the thing to my face."

ORC: "What?! Who?"

Me: "Negative. I'm not opening *that* door."

ORC: "Ugh, okay. Listen... I promise you that when you first asked me about it, *nothing* about a book was mentioned *anywhere.*"

Me: "But."

ORC: "But then, I had to prepare your parole board report. And in order to do so, I had to contact the DA, your lawyer, and the judge to notify them that you were up for parole. They then have the option to do nothing, or to write a letter for or against your release."

Fuck....

Me: "And let me guess, the DA responded."

ORC: "Yeah, you could say that. The DA wrote a pretty biased letter opposing your release. He also attached a copy of your book with it for the parole board to review."

So much for not going out of his way to fuck me over or keep me in prison, eh?

Me: "Great. And who has access to it?"

ORC: "Only guidance staff. And parole."

Me: "Parole is going to see it?"

ORC: "Yeah..."

Me: "Awesome. So, if only *guidance* has access to it, then why is a *drill instructor* quoting it to me?"

ORC: "Another ORC must have told them about it."

Me: "Well this sucks."

ORC: "I'm sorry Lawn Mower. For what it's worth, I think what you wrote is great and that the DA is way out of line."

Me: "Thanks. Is that something you can put in my parole board report as well?"

ORC: "I'm sorry, but no. If I could, I would."

Have I mentioned that this particular ORC was a recovering heroin addict and ex-con who had also been through Shock before? At the very least, her comment meant that my target audience was being reached.

* * *

THE FACT that the parole board would be getting a very rough copy of this book caused me a bit of alarm. Like a chick who agrees to do a "specialty film" only to find out on the day of the shoot that she's about to literally get fucked by a horse.

And it's not that I regretted anything that I'd written. It was my life/story and I'd earned the fucking right to tell it the way I wanted to. What concerned me was that "normal" people don't really understand what addicts or convicts have been through and they definitely don't get our particular brand of humor. L**** is a prime example of this. When you speak the language, you get it. When you don't, you find it offensive. Offensive isn't how I wanted to portray myself to the parole board.

So much for that, I guess.

A few days later, someone in my platoon got busted with a shank. In regular prison, this is an everyday thing. In Shock, especially Moriah, this is a once-in-a-decade, state-of-emergency, lock-the-jail-down type occurrence.

The dude who had it was a known gang member who was in prison for a gun charge. He was also an epic douche canoe, so we weren't really surprised when he got caught with it. Staff, however, shit kittens that shit bricks.

Naturally, the guy denied all knowledge of it and claimed sabotage. As he should. He was four months away from going home and just got caught with something that could literally *add* more time to his sentence. Claiming ignorance is exactly what anyone would do.

Apparently, the dude was a good actor (translation: he cried like a little bitch long enough to make a few staff members believe him), so they started to do some investigating.

And guess who the first person of interest was?

That's right, Dick Tracy.

Staff pretty much singled me out for some shit that I had nothing to do with, because I had "prior prison experience" which apparently means that I was the only one capable of making a shank. My eight-year-old niece knows how to make a fucking shank. But that was irrelevant to them.

This singling-me-out thing led other staff members to believe that I had something to do with it. In retaliation, they put me through hell by throwing buckets of ice-cold water on me to wake me up in the morning and ostracizing me from my platoon.

One day they even made me stand at attention, back straight, hands down at my sides, heels together with my feet pointed at a forty-five-degree angle, while I held my ID up to a light pole. With the tip of my nose. I did this for about three and a half hours.

Then, of course, staff always had some sort of fucked-up comment to say like:

Staff: "Be careful boys. If Lawn Mower doesn't like you, he knows how to get rid of you."

Staff: "One down, how many more to go, Lawn Mower?"

Staff: "Check your lockers, boys, Lawn Mower is in the room."

Staff: "Don't forget guys, his wife is out banging Charlie, so Lawn Mower might take it out on you."

This shit made for some really swell days.

The situation eventually died out because the cocksucker finally admitted that the shank was his, but the damage had already been done. My platoon disliked me and staff hated me because I was a "manipulative prick who thought himself smarter than everyone else," thanks to L****, his letter, and my book.

It made my days at Moriah really awesome.

* * *

About two weeks later, things got even worse.

I was having a great conversation with #3 on the phone one Sunday. We were actually laughing and joking, and I was telling her about the shank incident.

Me: "Irregardless of what they thought..."

#3: "That's not a word."

Me: "What isn't?"

#3: "Irregardless."

Me: "Yes, it is."

#3: "No, it isn't Lawn Mower."

Me: "I was once sodomized by a dictionary. I assure you it's a word."

#3: "Ugh. I know that you know a lot of big, fancy words, but 'irregardless' isn't one".

Me: "Google it if you...."

DI: "Time's up! Hang up the phone!"

Me: "Ugh. Gotta go. Love you."

#3: "I love you too!"

Me: "Hey, who's cooking Thanksgiving dinner?"

#3: "Definitely you. Love you! Bye!!!"

-click-

It was a great conversation, and for once I was happier than a priest in a playground after getting off the phone. I was even happier later that day when I was flipping through the dictionary and on page 662 of the Merriam-Webster's Collegiate Dictionary 11th Edition I found:

Irregardless\ adv [prob. Blend of irrespective and regardless] … Its fairly widespread use in speech called it to the attention of usage commentators as early as 1927. The most frequently repeated remark about it is that "there is no such word." There is such a word, however. It is still used primarily in speech, although it can be found from time to time in edited prose. Its reputation has not risen over the years, and it is still a long way from general acceptance.

So, what did I do?

Why the mature thing, of course.

I cut the fucking word out of the dictionary and wrote a letter to #3 with the word taped to the top page, silly.

I couldn't miss such an opportunity to exude my greatness and prove myself right (once again). I even wrote a little sentence that said *"technically this is destruction of state property, but I won't tell if you don't."* Just for kicks. Then I dropped the letter in the mail the following day, anxious for my next phone call so I could gloat.

The following day I got pulled out of work and brought to my ORC's office, which I knew couldn't be good. Of course, I thought the worst and assumed someone had died.

ORC: "Hi Lawn Mower. I've got some bad news for you."

Me: "Who died?"

ORC: "Died? No one died. But I do have a couple of things that you need to sign."

Me: "Sign?"

ORC: "Yeah. The first one is for a ticket..."

A ticket is Prisonspeak for a misbehavior report. I think that's pretty self-explanatory.

ORC: "...You, umm, did some damage to a dictionary."

No fucking way...

ORC: "The second is a negative correspondence letter."

Me: "What the hell is that?"

ORC: "Well, your wife called me this morning and said that she doesn't want you to be able to contact her anymore."

Me: "Excuse me? I just spoke to her yesterday and every thing was fine."

ORC: "I know, I listened to your phone call, and quite frankly, I don't understand it myself. All I know is that she told me that she doesn't want you to be able to contact her anymore. So, I took her number off of your call list and put a mail block on her name and address."

Me: "Wow."

ORC: "Also, she told me that she's seeking a divorce and hopes that you two can remain friends."

So much for *"I'd wait ten years for you if I had to,"* eh?

This is why I recall that phone call so well. It was the last time I spoke to #3 while I was in prison. She gave me no warning. No indication. No nothing. Then she pulled the most passive-aggressive stunt in history. Completely abandoning me in prison while simultaneously shattering my hopes and dreams.

I know how to pick 'em, don't I?

Anyways...

Is anyone wondering how in the fuck they knew about the dictionary?

Well let me explain.

I have extremely bad timing.

The morning I put the letter in the mailbox was the same morning that she called the facility. Then three things happened in sequence.

1. My ORC entered the no-contact bullshit into the computer system.

2. The mailroom people went to process the outgoing mail. Since Covid was crazy at that time, DOCCS was supplying us with five free letters a week, so we could keep in contact with our families during the epidemic. The people in the mailroom were Nazis and documented every single piece of mail entering and leaving the facility.

3. When they tried to process my letter, the negative contact thing popped up on their computer. Since the letter couldn't be sent out, it was considered "return to sender," and all return mail must be opened and inspected by staff.

Imagine their surprise when they found not only the evidence of my crime, but also my written confession directly under said evidence.

My little stunt cost me $55.00 and a couple of bruised ribs.

$50.00 for the ticket, and $5.00 for the processing fee.

The ribs happened at the ticket hearing when I was (obviously) found guilty of said offense. Just before the hearing was over, I was asked if I had any questions.

Me: "Sir can this inmate keep it sir?"

Hearing Officer: "Keep what?"

Me: "Sir the dictionary sir."

Hearing Officer: "The dictionary?"

Me: "Sir yes. If this inmate has to pay for a new one, then this inmate would like to keep the damaged one sir."

I found this to be a reasonable request.

The officer standing behind me, however, didn't.

Officially, I got dizzy and stumbled during my hearing.

I really don't recall that part. What I do recall is getting punched in the ribs by the asshole standing behind me.

But who am I to call a correctional officer a liar?

So JUST TO RECAP WHAT's gone on so far:

I found out parole would be getting a copy of my book and a very biased letter from L****. I was accused of planting a weapon and almost got kicked out of the program. I learned that irregardless is a $55.00 word, and I found out that my wife was leaving me and wanted a divorce.

I also discovered another fine example of how utterly ridiculous the New York State prison system is.

Here is said example:

Years ago, some *genius*– and I hope you picked up on my sarcasm there– came up with something called the "COMPAS RISK ASSESSMENT," which is defined as: "**A case management and decision support tool developed and owned by Northpointe (now Equivant) used by U.S. courts (and prisons) to assess the likelihood of a defendant becoming a recidivist**."

Basically, it's a packet with a bunch of information about you and your criminal history. The assessment is prepared for you by your ORC and presented to the parole board as a "tool" they can use in determining whether to release you or not. If you have really low scores (which is good) they can completely ignore the assessment and still deny you parole for a plethora of other reasons. If you have really high scores (which is bad), then the board can utilize that information and deny you parole.

The board refers to the assessment as a "tool," and it is completely at the board's discretion whether to utilize that tool or not. A fact that is total bullshit.

On the front page of the assessment is a little bar graph that shows how the individual scored in all the different areas. When I received the COMPAS that was prepared for my Shock parole board, I noticed some serious discrepancies.

I want to first note that the scores in the assessment range between 1-10.

The first discrepancy was that I had a *medium* score of 5 for "absconding," which is Legalspeak for running from the cops or parole/probation, not showing up for court, etc.

The second was that I had a *low* score of 5 for "risk of felony violence."

Apparently 5 is an ambiguous score.

I'd also like to add that I've never run from (or failed to report to) parole, probation, the cops, or the court in my life.

I've also never been convicted of a violent crime in my life.

So how both of these areas had a score of five was quite beyond me.

And this isn't even my point.

When I asked my ORC about my scores, she gave me a vague answer about how she has nothing to do with the scores and how they "calculate themselves."

Uh-huh.

Now, to add insult to injury, enter Joey.

Joey, like me, was on his third prison bid, and knew that every checkmark against him mattered. After seeing how messed up my COMPAS was, he decided to go through his more carefully. Upon investigating, Joey found some interesting things in his assessment.

On page two of his assessment, it stated that a few years prior, Joey absconded from parole and went to Florida, where he is suspected of *several* bank robberies.

Just so we're clear here, while on parole, Joey decided to say "fuck you parole" and left the state without permission from his parole officer. He lived in Florida for close to two years, while New York state parole had a warrant out for his arrest for violation of parole. Joey continued to live in Florida, *knowing* that he was wanted in New York.

This is fucking *definition* absconding.

Guess what his COMPAS assessment had for his score under absconding.

Did you guess 9?

Perhaps 8 or 10?

WRONG!

It was a fucking 1. The lowest possible score.

Both Joey and I asked our ORC (same person) about this, because we were confused. She responded that she "didn't know" and that she had "no control over the scores."

Please tell me that I'm not the only one who sees something wrong with this.

Joey has a clear and documented history of absconding while on parole, and he scored a 1.

I have no documented history of absconding for *anything*, and I scored a 5.

On what fucking planet.....

One would think that something like this (a mistake on a document that has a direct and severe impact on one's life) would be addressed and corrected.

But no.

Once it's there, it's there.

According to the ORC.

And this is just one *more* example of how fucked-up and ass-backward New York State Corrections is. People's lives are at stake here. Not just ours (criminals), but yours (society's) as well, and the correctional system doesn't give a flying fuck.

That was my July.

* * *

#3'S LITTLE STUNT HURT. It wasn't because of *what* she did– I'm no stranger to being dropped like prom night panties while in prison– it was *how* she did it that fucking irked me. Plus, there wasn't a fucking thing I could do about it until I got out of prison, which pissed me off even more.

Thankfully, the DIs didn't give me too much shit over the situation, or let anyone else for that matter. They chalked it up to program integrity and bullshit like that, but the real reason was because there was no fence surrounding Moriah. And there's only so much a dude can take before he snaps. Staff was more concerned about me losing my shit and doing a runner (and all the paperwork that ensued) than anything else.

* * *

AUGUST BROUGHT on an unexpected turn of events. Out of the blue one day I received a letter from #2. At first, I wasn't going to read it. We hadn't spoken in well over a year and a half, and the last time we did, it wasn't very cordial. But curiosity got the best of me.

Her letter was surprisingly sweet. It was more or less an apology letter for all the things that went down between us towards the end, and an update on her and the kids. It was also an invitation to mend the bridge between us with the hopes of being friends again.

I was upset and lonely, so I replied, and got a response almost immediately.

And that's how it went.

#2 and I started communicating and discussing us possibly getting back together.

I know, I know. *"What the fuck, Lawn Mower?!!"* Right?

Well, fuck off. I was in a vulnerable spot. So eat a bag of giant, crusty dick tips.

ON A BRIGHT AND sunny mid-September morning, I got pulled out of work and brought to see my ORC. Again.

The whole way there, all I could think about was *what the fuck did I do now?* And *who the fuck died?*

But this time, I wasn't brought to see my ORC. I was brought to the superintendent's office, and as soon as I walked in, I knew what was up.

I was denied parole.

Superintendent: "Lawn Mower, do you know why you're here today?"

Me: "Sir this inmate has a pretty good idea sir."

Superintendent: "Okay, good."

Then he read the denial aloud.

You're an addict.

You're an asshole.

You wrote a book.

And the DA hates you.

I shit you not.

They didn't come out and say that *exactly,* but they did talk about my "long history of substance abuse" and how "you seem very good at writing, so we suggest you keep a journal..." the irony of which was fucking comical. This book started out as a journaling project, then blossomed into this abortion. Also, they were telling me to continue doing the same exact thing that not only landed my lily-white ass in prison, but was now also keeping said white ass in prison.

I almost laughed out loud when he read me that part.

Almost.

Once he was finished reading my denial, I was asked:

Superintendent: "Knowing that you were denied parole, do you want to finish the program, or do you want to sign out and go to general population in a regular prison?"

This was actually a tough question to answer. I still had two months of Shock to finish, and then I would still have to go to prison after that to finish my time. So, everything that I had gone through here was for nothing. It was completely unfair. I had put up with so much bullshit, and I hadn't cracked. I did my best in that fucking program and watched complete assholes do fuck all, and they were still going to go home.

It wasn't fucking fair.

But I decided that I wasn't going to let it all be for nothing, and for once in my life, I was not going to quit because shit got tough.

Me: "Sir this inmate wants to finish his program sir."

Superintendent: "Good. Your shit's being packed and you'll be headed to Lakeview within the hour. You're dismissed."

Wait. What?!?!

Lakeview?!?!?!!?!?!?!?!?!!?!?

That's not what we had just discussed. Not to mention that I had witnessed several people get denied parole then stay at Moriah and finish their program. Yet here I was, being dragged out of the superintendent's office and tossed into a holding cell so I could wait for a bus to Lakeview.

In the four months I had been at Moriah, not one single person that got denied parole had to go to Lakeview. But I'm Lawn Mower, and apparently, I'm special. See my point about how the Old Guy likes to fuck with me?

* * *

THE SUPERINTENDENT WAS damn near on the money. It took about an hour for the bus to arrive. For that hour, I was locked in a cell called "the motivation room," which is Moriah's version of the box. It's a room with a toilet, bed, and sink.

While I waited for my ride, I had time to reflect on just how fucked-up the entire situation was for me.

I was at the *only* minimum-security facility in the state.

There are no fences surrounding Moriah.

There are no guard towers at Moriah.

We literally went running through mountain trails every morning with little to no supervision.

We worked in state parks and out in the community.

We were at Shock because New York State considered us to be *excellent candidates for release on parole.*

And yet, there I sat, being denied said parole, riding on a prison transport bus.

Mind you that I did so well on parole last time that they *let me off parole a year and a half early.*

And technically, no matter what happened, it worked for their benefit anyways. If I completed parole successfully, with no issues, then they would get a gold star in their successful statistic box: it would show that the program worked. If I failed miserably and violated my parole, then I would become a recidivism statistic and they would be able to show that they needed more funding for programs.

It was a win-fucking-win.

But no.

I'm a drug addict (in the process of completing the most difficult, disciplined, and intensive inpatient drug program offered in New York State), I'm an asshole (okay, you've got me there), I wrote a book (so much for freedom of expression or trying to help yourself/others), and L**** hates me (opinions, assholes).

Nothing I had learned or accomplished in Shock mattered. And that just goes to show you how fucked-up DOCCS truly is. Especially because once I was officially done with Shock, there was absolutely nothing for me to do but sit and rot in prison, while the taxpayers wasted their money keeping me incarcerated.

* * *

AFTER MORIAH GAVE me the boot, I was sent to Ulster Correctional where I had to sit and wait for my transfer to Lakeview. I was at Ulster for about thirty days and during that period, I foolishly latched onto #2 big-time. Stupid I know, but as you can imagine, it was a tough time for me, so fuck off. I was also very nervous about going to Lakeview. I had heard countless horror stories about the place, and honestly wet my pants a little every time I thought about the fact that I was on my way there.

One guy at Moriah put it this way:

Guy: "Moriah is a joke and Lakeview is *Shock*. If you graduate from Moriah, good for you. If you graduate from Lakeview, you fucking earned that shit."

Which didn't help lift my spirits any. I felt like having to go to Lakeview was karma for all the shit I talked about the poor fuckers who were sent there when I got sent to Moriah.

And now I was one of those poor fuckers.

Who said God doesn't have a sense of humor?

* * *

I ARRIVED at Lakeview around 11:00 p.m. on a Tuesday night.

After about forty-five minutes of getting screamed at and tossed around like a rag doll, I was brought to a dorm. Out of the six people I arrived with, I was the only one who didn't go straight to the reception dorm.

FUCK.

This meant that I was going straight to a platoon, and right back into the program bullshit at 5:30 a.m. No warm-up. No easing into it. No lube. No nothing. Just straight raping.

Swell.

When I arrived at my dorm, I had a chance to speak to the DI working the desk. I explained my situation, and told him that I didn't have any of my stuff yet. He told me not to worry, that I wouldn't have to do any PT or program stuff in the morning until I got my stuff. Which helped alleviate some of my anxiety, but not all of it. I went to my bed and attempted to get some sleep and prepare for the day ahead of me.

5:30 a.m. brought with it one of the longest days of my life.

The lights came on and everyone jumped out of bed screaming:

"AHHHHIIIHHHHHIIIIHHHHHHH!!!"

Then I heard:

DI: "Who the fuck are you?"

I knew it was too much to hope that he wasn't talking to me, so I answered.

Me: "Sir the new guy sir."

DI: "The new guy? No one told me about a fucking new guy. What the fuck is your name, inmate?"

Me: "Sir Lawn Mower sir."

DI: "Lawn Mower? That's a stupid fucking name. What platoon did you come from?"

Me: "Sir the Polar Bears sir."

DI: "This is a fucking joke, right? I'm being punked here? There aren't any fucking Polar Bears at Lakeview."

Me: "Sir this inmate came from Moriah sir."

DI: "Moriah, eh? How'd you fuck that up?"

Me: "Sir got hit at the board sir."

DI: "No shit. Well, you've already made us late, Moriah. Everyone, get ready for PT. This includes you, Moriah."

He must have seen the look on my face.

DI: "What Moriah, didn't you do PT at Moriah?"

Me: "Sir this inmate doesn't have anything to PT in sir."

DI: "Tough shit. PT in your greens and boots then. You've got eight minutes, go!"

Eight minutes??!!!

Eight fucking minutes?!

We had fifteen in Moriah!!

I already hated Lakeview.

And it only got worse from there.

Once everyone was dressed and ready, the DI pulled me to the side to introduce me to "Big Mac." Big Mac was a seventy-pound log that I had to carry with me at all times. When we left the dorm, I had to carry Big Mac on my shoulder while running around the platoon in an "orbit." What exactly this accomplished, I still have no idea. But I had to do it for two fucking weeks straight. I still have scars on my shoulders from that goddamn log.

* * *

At PT I stuck out like Rebel Wilson at a Bulimia Anonymous meeting, considering that I was the only one in greens. To add insult to injury, like giving a condom to a rape victim after the fact, Lakeview's PT program is completely different from the shit I was used to, and at every turn I was doing something wrong, thus gaining the wrong type of attention from the DIs.

I was basically wearing a sign that said "PLEASE FUCK WITH ME."

And that's exactly what they did.

Six DIs literally dragged me away to a wet, grassy area where some other poor schmuck was rolling around like a log. I found it comical until they told me to roll around in the wet grass like said schmuck until I was soaking wet from head to toe. Then I got to do somersaults in the same wet, grassy area until PT was over with.

Then we had to run.

And run we did.

Now, because I had Big Mac on my shoulder, I quickly fell to the back of the platoon. So to show "platoon unity" (some sort of deranged "no man left behind" bullshit) every time I fell behind, the DI made the platoon stop and do burpees until I caught up. And every time they jumped in the air, they had to yell *thank you, Moriah!*

This didn't sit well with my new platoon.

I can run with the best of them. I average three to six miles a day. But with a big-ass seventy-pound log on my shoulder, speed wasn't my friend that day. We ran about four miles that morning. I puked once, and my new platoon did close to 800 burpees.

By 7:30 a.m., I'd been slapped multiple times, I could barely lift my arms, I was soaking wet from head to toe in the only set of clothes that I had, I had puked, I was bleeding, and everyone in my new platoon wanted to kill me.

Talk about a good start, right?

Then my day got even better.

After the platoon got to shower– except for me because I didn't have a change of clothing– the DI had the platoon bring the PT deck to our dorm, where they set it in the front yard. It was a ten-foot by ten-foot platform that stood about four feet off the ground.

For the rest of the day I had to sit under that deck., When anyone walked by our dorm, I had to crawl out on my hands and knees, charging at them and barking like a fucking dog, because my new platoon was called the Bulldogs.

The first hour or so was humiliating. After eight hours, the guard dog routine fell into a category of its own.

I cried myself to sleep that night.

* * *

THE FOLLOWING day wasn't much better.

Nor was the day after that.

I quickly discovered that the differences between Lakeview and Moriah were like the difference between rape and consensual sex. One was just a bit gentler about it.

I had a very difficult time adjusting to Lakeview, which wasn't much of a surprise. When you do things one way twenty-four hours a day for four months straight, it's hard to do things differently at the flip of a switch; yet somehow, I pulled through it.

I graduated in mid-December, about a month after I would have in Moriah. #2 definitely helped me keep it together while I was there. Her letters and bi-weekly phone calls gave me something to look forward to, which was huge. Especially in there.

After I graduated, it took me a couple of months to get out of Lakeview. I spent a lot of that time writing and talking with #2. I spoke with her almost daily on the phone. Then, just before Christmas, she fell off the face of the earth.

After several days of not being able to reach her, I had The Sister do some Facebook stalking for me.

The Sister: "Shit."

Me: "That good?"

The Sister: "Ugh. Why can I never have good news to give you?"

Me: "Just tell me."

The Sister: "She's engaged."

Me: "Come again?"

The Sister: "To Joke. It's all over Facebook dude. I'm sorry man. What do you want me to do?"

Me: "Nothing."

The Sister: "You sure?"

Me: "Positive."

A couple of days later, I got an e-mail from #2 telling me more or less to eat a bag of dicks. She ended the e-mail with "I know you're going to be upset about this, but you'll get over it. Lol. Hopefully we can still be friends."

What the fuck is it with women and this "still be friends" bullshit?

The same shit she did to Joke while he was in prison, she did to me while I was in prison.

That's karma in a nutshell.

* * *

I SAT in Lakeview for two months waiting to be transferred. It was a crapshoot as to where in the state I would end up. All I could do was hope and pray that I didn't wind up somewhere *really* shitty.

Finally, my day came, and I couldn't believe where I was being sent.

Of all the prisons in New York State, they were sending me back to Marcy. My home away from home.

I never thought it was possible to be happy about being sent to a prison, yet on that day, I was happier than a Catholic priest supervising altar boy tryouts.

* * *

I THINK it's a pretty fair statement to say that when you're actually *excited* about going to prison, then you've probably made some questionable life choices.

There are a lot of really shitty prisons to go to in New York State. There are also a few decent ones as well (as far as prisons go), and while I haven't been to all of them, I was comfortable with the one I was going to.

Was I happy about being sent to Marcy?

Absolutely.

I was close to home, and unless things had drastically changed, I understood how things worked there. Plus, since I tend to make an impression wherever I go, I was most likely to be a superstar there.

My superstar status was confirmed before I even made it into the facility.

When a transport bus pulls into a facility, it has to go through what's known as the "truck trap." This is the fenced-in area you see in movies where there's someone looking underneath vehicles with a mirror.

Once the outer vehicle check is complete, a CO will get on the bus to count all the convicts.

When the CO from Marcy got on the bus, I had to smile, because I knew him well. Joey Bag of Doughnuts. When Joey saw me, he smiled and said:

Joey Bag of Doughnuts: "Lawn Mower! Welcome home, sweetheart."

And I replied:

Me: "Joey Bag of Doughnuts! How the hell are you, you fat bitch?!"

This pretty much set the tone for my return to Marcy.

* * *

I GOT to Marcy late Friday afternoon.

First thing Monday morning, I was called to work at the maintenance department. The CO working my dorm that day couldn't believe it.

CO: "Dude, didn't you just get here on Friday?"

Me: "Yeah."

CO: "Yet somehow, you've already got a job. I've got guys who've been sitting in this dorm for three weeks and they don't have a work program yet. You think you're special or something?"

Oh, you've no idea.

Apparently my arrival at Marcy was anticipated, and there were several civilians and COs waiting for me just so they could bust my balls about coming back to prison. Which I expected, and deserved, so I couldn't be mad.

My superstar status was confirmed even further when less than a week later, I was moved back into the "honor dorm." This was a big deal because generally one has to be in Marcy for a minimum of ninety days before they can even be put on the list for honor dorm. Yet there I was, a week into my stay, back in the best dorm in the facility.

Lawn Mower

About a month into my stay in Marcy, I received some news that brought me a ton of smug self-satisfaction.

Beavis was in jail.

Normally I wouldn't wish jail on anyone, but Beavis was the exception to the rule.

Why is that?

Well, I'm glad you asked, dear reader.

The simplest answer is spite.

A blind three-year-old could tell you that Beavis had a serious drug problem. Comparable to that of, say, Ozzy Osborne in the 80s/90s. Yet, no one in the family talked about it. Worse yet, when they *did* talk about it, I was always the deflection.

Them: "Well at least Beavis hasn't been in trouble like Lawn Mower has."

Them: "At least Beavis isn't a thief like Lawn Mower is."

Them: "At least Beavis isn't a failure like Lawn Mower is."

You get the idea...

And it's been this way for years. I've always been the point of comparison for "how bad" someone has become. Fuck all of my accomplishments, only my failures are noted with my family.

Knowing this has irked me for years. Add to that some of the things I've mentioned in previous sections of this book, and it's not hard to understand why.

One could argue that perhaps it's a bit of jealousy or resentment of some kind, based upon Beavis being considered "better" than me by most of my family.

And to those posing said argument, I have three simple words for you:

Suck.

My.

Dick.

Now where was I? Oh right– Beavis in jail.

I was so bemused by the situation that I almost wrote Beavis a "ha ha stupid" letter and sent it to him in jail. But a good friend convinced me not to. My friend gave me some bullshit about "being the bigger person" and "no need to add salt to the wound." I wasn't a big fan of this tack, but I value this friend and his opinion, so I followed his advice.

What made the situation even more comical for me was the fact that he was in jail for a felony charge. He was also facing a violation of probation, which meant that there was a high probability that Beavis was headed to prison. In Florida.

Two weeks after his arrest, I heard that Beavis was *begging* his parents to bail him out of jail. Apparently, he couldn't 'handle how horrible' it was. Suffering real consequences for his actions wasn't something that Beavis was accustomed to. Guess he didn't like it too much. Plus, he had to detox, cold turkey, while in jail.

The poor, poor, baby.

When his parents suggested treatment, he *adamantly* refused. He told them something along the lines of:

Beavis: "I don't need treatment! I don't have a problem like *Lawn Mower* does."

This is the same fucker who got kicked out of a hospital after *double knee surgery* because he was caught taking his own prescription pain killers while on a morphine drip.

And *I'm* the bad one.

Then all of a sudden, Beavis changed his tune and decided that he would go to rehab. And of course, his parents were all but ready to bail him out of jail, even though he didn't have a bed waiting for him, he merely agreed to go into treatment.

I told The Sister that this was a *very* bad idea and that she needed to talk to Beavis' parents before they bailed him out, or something bad would happen. I predicted that he wouldn't go to treatment and would OD within a week.

A few days later I talked to The Sister and she informed me that Beavis had just gotten out of the hospital. He left jail, didn't go to treatment, went out on a binge, and ODed. He had to be Narcaned and brought to the hospital.

After about an hour or two, he was released and went right back at it.

Later on that week I called The Sister and found out that Beavis was in the ICU.

Apparently, Beavis was out partying with some people and overdosed (again). This time, however, no one called for help or had Narcan. Whoever he was with got scared, drove Beavis to the emergency room, then tossed his body out of a moving vehicle and into a literal gutter. Beavis also had a heart attack and wasn't getting enough oxygen. By the time someone found him and got him inside, it was already too late. His brain was swollen and he had to be put on full life support.

My heart sank. Despite my feelings for him and our differences, Beavis was still family. Growing up we were as thick as thieves, and even though we had grown far apart, I wouldn't wish this on him.

Being in jail was one thing.

This was a different animal altogether.

As soon as his parents got the news they headed down to Florida. Once they arrived, they learned that Beavis was one hundred percent brain-dead. They made plans to pull the plug the following day.

That night I sat and thought a lot about Beavis, our time growing up together, and all the fun we had as kids. I also had a few good laughs at our more epic shenanigans, some of which I'm sure are still within the statute of limitations. And even though I would have punched the motherfucker in the face if we had ever been in the same room together, I still didn't want him *gone*.

While reminiscing about the good times I had with Beavis and listening to music on my jail tablet, the song "Wonderwall" by Oasis came on. For some unknown fucking reason Beavis really liked Oasis, so I sat there listening to the song on repeat for a good while. I guess you could say the song sort of spoke to me.

The following day I was at work and just happened to glance at the clock at 2:04 p.m. when the dude sitting next to me started singing Wonderwall.

This was the type of dude you'd see at a GWAR concert, *not* someone who would even know who Oasis is, let alone be singing their lyrics.

Cold chills are a fucking understatement.

Me: "Why the fuck are you singing that song?"

Guy: "Dude, I don't fucking know. It just popped into my head and I can't get it the fuck out."

Me: "Do you even know who sings it?"

Guy: "Madonna? Puff Daddy? How the fuck should I know?"

* * *

AFTER WORK I called The Sister to get an update.

The Sister: "Beavis is gone."

Me: "Let me guess, 2:04 p.m., right?"

The Sister: "How in the actual fuck could you possibly know that?"

Me: "Well...."

And I told her the story.

Fucked-up, right?

* * *

BEAVIS' death crushed me.

It had more of an impact on me than I could have ever imagined. It's sad to say, but it affected me more than even my mother's death did. Which I still don't fully understand.

I've known many people that I've been close to who have passed from an OD, or another form of drug related death. And as sad as it is to admit, those deaths never really affected me. Yet here was someone that I hadn't spoken to in many, many years, who I wasn't close to anymore, and who I wouldn't piss on if he was on fire. Yet his loss pains me to this day, and will sting for a long time to come.

Beavis' death affected me on a whole new level. The pain I felt at his loss was akin to what I felt at seeing my reflection in #3. It was life-altering. It was raw. It was like a steroid injection into my soul.

The day that Beavis died, I knew, with complete and utter certainty, that the life that I had once lived was one hundred percent behind me and that I was moving on.

I thought that I hated Beavis. For fuck's sake, I wrote *in this book* that I hated him. Had he lived, I could have easily gone decades without speaking to him and had no qualms about it. I had zero interest in being a part of his life in any form, and could have honestly cared less what he did with himself.

Now, I'd do anything just to hear his voice again.

And that really fucking sucks.

I'll forever be grateful to the friend who talked me out of writing that letter to Beavis while he was in jail.

Thank you, my friend. You know who you are.

Beavis' death fucked me up. More so than I'm even willing to admit. And instead of letting it bring me down (something easily done in prison), I used it as a source of strength and inspiration. I even used it as a focal point in my written statement to the parole board. I wanted to ensure they would read the whole thing, so my opening statement was an attention-getter:

"I know this isn't going to get read, but I'm going to write it regardless."

After I arrived at Marcy, my only focus was getting to my board, and going home. During my last few weeks at Shock, I was told time and time again that I had "nothing to worry about," and that "everyone who completes Shock and gets denied parole goes home at their next board."

I knew this to be a bunch of bullshit because I had personally witnessed several "Shock rejects" like myself get denied parole at Shock, go to a new facility, and then get denied parole again. Granted, watching Smiley go home from Shock gave me a bit of hope; still, I was concerned about what the future held for me.

Let me tell you about Smiley...

For those of you who feel that I'm prejudiced against the parole board because I've had a negative experience dealing with them, you're fucking wrong. And to prove my point, I'm going to give you something to think about.

I was at Lakeview with a dude named Smiley who I had met years before in county jail.

Smiley's a decent enough dude, but an epic fuck-up like me. He's also not someone that I'd leave alone around the silverware or good china (had I any), if you catch my drift.

Smiley was on his third or fourth prison bid, the lines were a little blurry on that, sort of like with me. Either way, he was at Shock, with a split bid.

And like me, he got denied parole.

Smiley was denied parole for several reasons: 1. He was a drug addict. 2. He had no respect for people's property or the law. Proof of this was his sixty-seven– that's not a typo– page rap sheet. *Sixty-seven fucking pages*. That's three times longer than mine. 3. The parole board felt that "if released at this time there is reasonable probability that [he] would not live and remain at liberty without again violating the law and that release at this time would be incompatible with the welfare of society."

Pretty much the same shit they said to me.

Now, the theory behind denying someone parole is simple: said person needs to spend more time in prison. Perhaps there's another program or two that they could take to assist in their "rehabilitation" (eye roll). If there isn't another program then they can sit in jail and think about their actions, while making deep and lasting life changes (another eye roll). I could continue for quite a long time on how utterly ridiculous that sentence is, but I won't. Just know I could though.

Smiley not only had a shorter sentence to serve, he had also completed more time on his sentence than me.

So two months after Smiley graduated Shock and was denied parole, he had another parole board to go to. Now during said two months, do you have any idea what Smiley did to "better himself"?

Absolutely nothing. Because there was nothing for him to fucking do. No programs, no work, no school, no nothing. He simply sat around with his thumbs in his ass and read books all day.

And guess what?

They let him fucking go!

Apparently that two months was all it took for Smiley to be rehabilitated, or changed, or what the fuck ever it was that the parole board wanted him to be.

Please don't get me wrong: I was happy for the guy (even after I found out that within two weeks of being home, he was already getting high and selling drugs). But am I the only one who's wondering *what the fuck?* Like what was the fucking point? In total, he spent a little less than ninety extra days in prison.

Am I the only one who finds this not only absurd, but pointless? What fucking difference did those two months between boards make?

If you can make any sense of this shit then I envy your genius, because for the fucking life of me, I can't. Maybe after a year or something, but after two fucking months? This only further proves how truly absurd and ass-backward the parole board is.

Oh!

And let's not forget CB.

CB was denied parole after completing Shock. Why? His charge: DWI with bodily injury.

A month later, he had another parole board where he was denied parole again (for pretty much the same reason, just worded differently).

Three weeks later, he had *another* parole board where he was granted parole and ended up going home on the ***exact same fucking day*** he would have had they said yes at his previous board.

I don't know how much it costs to hold a parole board, but with all the time and preparation it takes, it cannot be cheap.

Shit like this happens every fucking day in DOCCS.

* * *

I SPENT my days working and my nights/weekends watching soccer and getting ready for my board. The closer the day got, the more anxious I became. The board is highly unpredictable, and from the shenanigans I'd witnessed, especially with people who were told "you're definitely going home from your next board," I knew that it was a crapshoot.

And then the day came....

By the time I was finally summoned to the visiting room, there were already several people there. DOCCS had gotten ridiculous with their COVID precautions, so they were only allowing eight people in the waiting room at a time. We were practicing *extreme* social distancing with about twelve feet of space between each dude waiting.

The guy who I was sitting "next to" was rocking back and forth and kept on checking his watch, like he had somewhere to be other than at his parole board.

The parole board was moving at the normal pace, which was "who the fuck knows." One guy went in and walked out less than five minutes later. Another went in and spent almost an hour with them. There's no knowing how much time the board is going to spend with you. It all depends on you, your crime, and your history.

About a quarter after one, the watch-checking guy got up and went to speak to the CO at the desk. I couldn't make out what they were saying, but I knew it had to be good when I heard the CO say:

CO: "You're fucking kidding me, right? Go sit the fuck down."

I wasn't sure what the dude wanted, but I admit that I was curious. Par for the course in prison, I didn't have to wait long to find out.

About five minutes later, a guy walked into the room to see the board, then walked back out almost immediately. The CO asked him what was up, and he told him that the board said they were going to take a break for a few minutes. The guy next to me took that as his cue to go back up and talk to the CO.

Again, I couldn't hear the conversation, but after a couple of minutes of bickering I heard the CO say this:

CO: "Fine, just fucking go. But I'm telling you now, I have no idea when they're going to call for you, and if they call for you and you're not here, I'm going to walk my black ass in there and tell them that you felt that getting your commissary was more important than speaking to them."

The dude nodded his head and walked out the door.

I couldn't fucking believe it!

One would think that going home (or the possibility of going home) was more important than some ramen noodles, but apparently this guy felt differently.

As fate would have it, shortly after he walked out the door, the board resumed. The board finished up with the guy they were supposed to see before their break, and then they called for their next victim.

Guess who it was?

Commissary Guy.

True to his word, the CO got up, walked his black ass into the room, and explained to the board– with the door open so all could hear– that the dude felt getting his commissary was more important than waiting for the parole board. He *also* explained to them that the facility's policy is that if someone is unavailable to get their commissary due to a medical trip, parole board, etc., they would be able to get their commissary on the following day, without a problem.

Usually, COs are lying sacks of shit, but on this, he was telling the truth.

The CO also explained to the board that he informed the guy of this, and the guy didn't seem to care. Then he walked back to his desk with a very smug smile on his face. I have to admit, I had a smirk on mine too. Shit like that amuses me for some reason.

The smirk was immediately removed from my face when they called for the next person: me.

I THINK it's fair to say that I've already covered all the stresses and anxieties that come along with going to the parole board. I'm still a firm believer that parole boards should be abolished entirely and that only determinate sentences should exist. Except in the case of "life" sentences. Then and *only* then should someone have to appear before a parole board in order to determine if they should be released back into society.

I could write a series of books on how seriously fucked-up parole boards are, how there is *zero* accountability for the commissioners, and how rampant the corruption truly is. And maybe someday I shall.

But not today.

Today, I'm going to tell you about parole board number two. Even though technically I'm discussing number three. But since I didn't actually get to go to the "real" number two, I am calling *this* one number two.

Not confusing at all, right?

Over the course of the month leading up to my board, I asked everyone I could find that had previously been in front of the board what kind of questions they were asked (whether they had made their board or not). Each and every person had a different fucking answer.

Guy #1: "They asked me what justice looked like to me."

Guy #2: "They asked me if I felt that justice had been served."

Guy #3: "They asked me about my disciplinary record and why it was so bad."

Guy #4: "They asked me about the difference in doing concrete in New York as opposed to doing it in Florida."

Guy #5: "They asked me about all seventeen of my children, and when their birthdays were."

Guy #6: "They asked me about my cats."

How the fuck they knew that Guy #6 had cats or how the fuck it was even relevant is still beyond me. The point I'm attempting to make here is that you could ask a hundred different people what they discussed at their parole board and you'd get a hundred different answers. So, I really had no idea what to expect when I walked into mine.

What made me even *more* nervous was that the commissioner running point on my parole board was *cracking fucking jokes*, which threw me right off.

His first joke actually left me speechless.

Commissioner: "So, I see here that you've submitted a relapse prevention/transitional plan– which we'll cover later– and also a personal statement."

Me: "Yes sir."

Commissioner: "And the first sentence in your personal statement reads: 'I know this isn't going to get read, but I'm going to write it regardless.'"

Uh-oh.

Me: "Yes it does."

Commissioner: "Well, I want you to know that I actually did read it. In its entirety. So, there..."

And then, like a five-year-old child, he stuck his tongue out at me.

HIS FUCKING TONGUE!!

I can't make this shit up.

So, needless to say, I was a tad flabbergasted. Especially since the last sentence of my statement said something to the effect of "if you have actually taken the time to read this, then I thank you. But if you merely skimmed through it, then you have wasted both of our time." When I was writing my personal statement, I wanted it to stand out and get noticed. Now that I had gotten the attention I had sought, I was starting to regret that decision.

I was also flabbergasted because this guy was a fucking parole commissioner, conducting an interview that would literally determine the course of the rest of my life, and he was doing something that I *would do*. As in, acting like a child.

This worried me.

His next joke– which wasn't necessarily a *joke* but perhaps just more of a dick thing to say– didn't startle me, it just pissed me off.

Commissioner: "So, you're a heroin addict, correct?"

Me: "Recovering."

Commissioner: "Of course, *recovering* heroin addict."

Me: "Yes."

Commissioner: "And how long have you been clean?"

Me: "Seven hundred and seventy-seven days."

Commissioner: "Congratulations. What was your longest period of sobriety?"

Me: "Five years."

Commissioner: "Five years? And how did you manage that?

Me: "Well, four years of it was spent in prison."

Commissioner: "I see. Well, I don't know how else to ask this, but... what, you just couldn't find drugs in prison?

You're an addict. You could find crack in a cornfield if you wanted. Right?"

Did he really just fucking say "crack in a cornfield"?

I wasn't quite sure how to respond to that, but he definitely pissed me off. He was giving me shit, so I decided to give it right back to him.

Me: "Well, I've never tried looking for crack in a cornfield, but maybe I'll take that up as a hobby when I get home. Thanks for the idea."

Which earned a couple of snickers from the ORCs in the room with me.

And then he hit me with...

Commissioner: "Mr. Lawn Mower, do you believe that you're ready to be released?"

Aw, fuck.

All that flashed through my mind was that first parole board scene from *The Shawshank Redemption*, when they asked Red if he believed that he was rehabilitated, and he went on a blubbering rant stating that he was absolutely rehabilitated and how he was a changed man.

And then:

REJECTED

That question– which naturally had to fucking follow me being a dick to the guy– caused me long, sleepless nights, coupled with heartburn and indigestion while I was waiting for my results. I took that question as a sign that a giant ***fuck you*** was headed my way.

And of course, he had to finish our meeting with this...

Commissioner: "Okay Lawn Mower, you've given us a lot to think about. We also have a letter here from the District Attorney..."

He picked it up and started skimming through it for show.

Commissioner: "That we also have to take into consideration here. Is there anything that you would like to add?"

There was in fact a question that I had prepared for this specific moment. Which was...

Me: "In reviewing my record and after speaking with me today, do you believe that there is something I could have done or should have done which would have better prepared me for release?"

This was a very well thought-out and pointed question designed to paint the commissioner into a corner, and his answer might have given me some grounds for an appeal if denied.

But I didn't ask it.

I figured that I was already fucked, and that L**** had fucked me again, so what difference would it make? I merely thanked him for his time and left.

The commissioner was a dick. He acted like a fucking child, and clearly didn't take my board seriously. I was a dick. I gave him smart-ass answers. And then there was L**** and his bullshit.

I knew I was fucked, again.

I walked out of that room with a heavy weight on my shoulders and a tightness in my chest. I didn't like how anything went during my board, and I had a horrible feeling in the pit of my stomach.

As I was walking out, I happened to notice that Commissary Guy was back and that he had his commissary with him, looking a little deflated. He must have found out that they called for him while he was gone; I could hear him talking to another convict.

Commissary Guy: "For real? He really said that to them?"

Guess he thought the CO was bullshitting him.

Oh, and would you like to know what was so important for him to get at commissary?

Five racks of cookies. $4.35 worth of cookies. *That's* what was more important than waiting for the board.

Unreal...

* * *

THE NEXT FEW days *dragged* by. I went to my board on a Tuesday, and I had to wait until 4:00 p.m. on Monday to get my results. I don't know why they do it that way. The second you walk out that door they know what they're doing with you. Shit, they know what they're going to do with you *before* you walk through the door.

All I could do was play my conversation with them over and over and over again in my head. Each time, the pit in my stomach got deeper and deeper, and I felt like I was going to puke.

When mail call came on Monday, I was a fucking wreck.

When the CO handed me the letter, it felt like a lead weight in my hand. Again.

I opened the envelope and noticed that there were *several* pieces of paper in it, which isn't a good sign. That's an indication that you were denied and the extra paperwork is your appeal papers. I flipped to the page in the back and it read:

"As you may have noticed, you were granted parole..."

Wait. WHAT?!

Why no, I *hadn't* noticed that.

I immediately flipped to the first page and started reading it over, and yes, I was granted parole!

I WAS GOING HOME!!!!

* * *

A COUPLE of weeks after I got my results, I was in the yard and saw Commissary Guy. He actually came right up to me and started talking. Mind you, other than seeing him at the board, I had no idea who the dude was.

Lawn Mower

Commissary Guy: "Hey man, how's it going?"

Me: "Fine, you?"

Commissary Guy: "You know, same shit."

Me: "Mhmm."

Commissary Guy: "Did you get your results?"

Me: "Yeah, you?"

Commissary Guy: "Yeah. I got hit."

Me: "Shit man, sorry to hear it."

Commissary Guy: "Yeah. What about you?"

Me: (*knowing better*) "I got hit too."

Commissary Guy: "Damn son. These people fucked-up."

Me: "Word. Yo, you seriously left to get your commissary?"

Commissary Guy: "Hell yeah nigga. I needed dem cookies."

Me: "That's all you got was cookies?!"

Commissary Guy: "Yup. I owed dems shits."

Me: "You do know that you could have gone to get your commissary the next day, right?"

Commissary Guy: "I do now...."

In the immortal words of Forrest Gump: "*Stupid is as stupid does.*"

And that's all I've gotta say about that.

* * *

THE NEXT FOUR months went by in a blur. I stayed busy with work, working out, and soccer.

I had all my ducks in a row, I had a plan, and I had something new this time around. I still have trouble verbalizing what exactly *it* is, but I think determination is the best fit. Everything that had transpired, especially with #3, had changed me. And I definitely wasn't the same person I had been before this all started.

When my release day finally arrived, I knew, without a doubt, that I wasn't *ever* going back.

* * *

RIGHT ABOUT HERE IS THE part where I'm supposed to talk about my life at home, how different my life is today, how far I've come, and all that other bullshit. While I'm not above tooting my own horn in the slightest, I'm not going to talk about any of that (I'll leave that for a new book when I'm broke and need money).

What I will say is this...

I've put enough heroin in my body to kill countless men.

I've used dirty puddle water and smoked cigarette filters I found on the ground to inject some very questionable substances into my body.

And, surprisingly, I'm in damn good health.

Along this journey, I've lost a lot of people close to me because of drugs and addiction.

Yet, *I'm* still alive and kicking.

So, I pose two questions:

1. How the fuck am I still here?

2. Why the fuck am I still here?

I'm painfully aware that I may never be able to answer these questions until this life is over, and that's okay. Clearly, I'm still here for a reason, and whatever that reason is, I plan on spending my days in search of it.

I don't know what tomorrow will bring, or tomorrow's tomorrow, and I don't really give a fuck. What I do know is that all the bullshit that I've been through made me who I am today, and while I don't *like* the shit that's happened to me, I like *me* today. I'm okay with who I am, and I am looking forward to where I'm headed.

Wherever that may be.

And while I don't know what the future holds, I do know two things for certain:

1. Heroin and prison will never be a part of my life *ever* again. I simply cannot go back to that life. That chapter has ended for me, and I've moved on to the next one. If I ever use again, I'll die. I'm not ready for that. I've still got a lot of people that I need to piss off before I go.

2. If you don't like anything I had to say in here, I'll *always* have one of these for you to eat:

* * *

I'VE GONE BACK and forth about adding this small section here, and after some contemplation, I felt that it was necessary to add:

I had been home close to a year when I received a painful phone call one night.

#3 had died.

She was found dead, in a bathroom, at some random dude's house, with a needle in her arm.

The disease of addiction had struck again and taken another life.

Hearing that news was a complete shock to me. I had spoken to her a few days prior, and everything had seemed fine. We had been speaking sporadically since I'd been home, and she had shown no indication of using. She kept the ruse up well; I didn't pick up on any hints that she was still using. Granted, you can't tell much from a simple phone conversation, but still, I feel that I should have noticed something.

It had been about three years since I had introduced her to the needle. And I thought she was clean.

Clearly, I was wrong.

Even though I had no part in her life, and hadn't been a part of her life for a few years by that point, I still felt responsible.

I still *feel* responsible.

To this day, I still carry quite a bit of guilt over her death, and likely will for a long time to come.

This is how I know, without a doubt in my mind, that I will never go back to heroin.

I simply fucking can't.

It has taken too much from me.

And with that, I want to dedicate this book not only to the memory of my mother, but to the memories of #3 and Beavis as well.

None of you will *ever* be forgotten.

Not by me anyway.

The End. For now.....

About the Author

Lawn Mower is the pen name for None Of Your Damn Business. Lawn Mower hails from the nightmarish frozen abyss of upstate New York, spent some time in the limp dick of America (also known as Florida), and now enjoys spending his time at Chuck-E-Cheese's and drinking ice water. If you enjoyed reading EPIC FAIL, please leave a review. If you did not enjoy reading EPIC FAIL, go jump off a bridge. Lawn Mower is a private individual and does not participate in social media or webpages, but if you'd like to contact Lawn Mower, you can send an email to Lawn.-mower.epicfail@gmail.com

Made in United States
Troutdale, OR
09/13/2024

22777590R00286